Integration in Counselling and Psychotherapy

Developing a personal approach

Phil Lapworth, Charlotte Sills
and Sue Fish

D0322341

ISBN 0-7619-6712-5 (hbk)
ISBN 0-7619-6713-3 (pbk)
© Phil Lapworth, Charlotte Sills and Sue Fish 2001
First published 2001
Reprinted 2002, 2004, 2005

Apart from any fair dealing for the purposes of research or private study,
or criticism or review, as permitted under the Copyright, Designs and
Patents Act, 1988, this publication may be reproduced, stored or
transmitted in any form or by any means, only with the prior permission
in writing of the publishers, or in the case of reprographic reproduction,
in accordance with the terms of licences issued by the Copyright
Licensing Agency. Inquiries concerning reproduction outside those
terms should be sent to the publishers.

 SAGE Publications Ltd
1 Oliver's Yard, 55 City Road
London EC1Y 1SP

SAGE Publications Inc
2455 Teller Road
Thousand Oaks, California 91320

SAGE Publications India Pvt Ltd
B-42 Panchsheel Enclave
PO Box 4109
New Delhi 110 017

British Library Cataloguing in Publication Data
A catalogue record for this book is available from the British Library

Typeset by Keystroke, Jacaranda Lodge, Wolverhampton
Printed and bound in Great Britain by Athenaeum Press Ltd.,
Gateshead, Tyne & Wear.

Contents

This book is dedicated in loving memory of our dear
friend and colleague Sue Fish (1946–2001)

List of figures and table

Figures

Table

Acknowledgements

We would like to thank the trainers, supervisors and psychotherapists who have instructed and inspired us over the years towards our own psychological integrations, some of whom are David Boadella, Petrūska Clarkson, Hans Cohn, Lois Johnson, Claudius Kokott, Irv and Miriam Polster, John Rowan and Nicholas Spicer.

Thanks are also due to our 'peer nourishment' group: Michael Carroll, Bill Critchley, Jenifer Elton Wilson, Dave Gowling, Val Magner, Jenny McKewn and the late and much missed Fran Lacey. These people have been a source of support, encouragement and expertise and have provided rich discussion and learning over the years.

A special thank you to our expert reader Jenifer Elton Wilson who is always so generously willing to share her breadth and depth of knowledge and experience, to Keith Tudor for contributing his excellent chapter on change, time, place and community and to Laurie Lapworth for patiently and meticulously producing the diagrams for us.

We are endebted to Alison Poyner, Senior Commissioning Editor, for her interest, support and advice through each stage of the production of this book and to all the others at Sage from whom we have received similar encouragement. Their efficiency and availability have enabled this process to run smoothly and enjoyably.

Our Multidimensional Framework for Integration (Chapters 5 and 6) is original in the form in which it stands. However, it is in itself an integration, a compilation which owes its existence and development to the work of other integrationists who, in turn, have built upon the work of previous theorists (such is the nature of integration, as we discuss in Chapter 1). In particular, we would like to acknowledge Petrūska Clarkson, Jenifer Elton Wilson, Richard Erskine, Maria Gilbert and Arnold Lazarus for their valuable perspectives on working with troubled people and upon whose contributions to the field of integration our framework is based.

We are grateful for permission from Taylor and Francis Publishers to reproduce the modality profile and table of techniques and ingredients (in Chapter 8) from Arnold Lazarus' 'Multimodal Therapy' in *The Handbook of Eclectic Psychotherapy*, published in 1986 by Brunner/Mazel.

Charlotte and Sue would like to acknowledge and warmly appreciate Phil for taking on the lion's share of everything in his role as lead author.

Last, but by no means least, we wish to thank our clients, trainees and supervisees for all we have learnt from and with them in our mutual endeavour for integration in all its meanings.

Preface

At the turn of the millennium, increasingly the divisions between the different approaches to counselling and psychotherapy are being examined and questioned less competitively and more in a spirit of co-operation and exploration. Research has failed to demonstrate that, in general, any one approach, whether behavioural, psychodynamic or humanistic, can be regarded as more effective than another (Lambert et al., 1986) and practitioners have become more willing both to acknowledge the limitations of their own singular approach and to meet the needs of their clients by exploring the possibilities of other approaches outside their own. This trend has led to an increase in the emergence of integrative approaches.

This openness is refreshing and exciting, but it also has potential problems. On the one hand, there is a danger that integrative psychotherapy may develop into its own 'school' (or 'schools') with equally rigid boundaries and the concomitant lack of communication with other approaches that has been seen in the past. On the other hand, given the plethora of approaches to counselling and psychotherapy that already exist, there is a danger of being over-inclusive and thus overwhelmed by theories and practices which may or may not be easily or usefully integrated. It is our belief that integration needs to remain open, exploratory and creative while at the same time being contained and theoretically consistent if it is to withstand the test of time.

There are, and will continue to be, many integrative approaches to counselling and psychotherapy and any one integrative approach cannot answer the diversity and complexity of being human and dealing with human suffering, problems, change and growth, whether as a therapist or a client. We believe also that integration is inevitably a personal affair and, as such, likely to be more effective than the rigid adherence to a template into which practitioners struggle to 'fit' themselves (or their clients). Any individual practitioner's life experience, professional training, temperament, personal style and theoretical range and understanding will be unique to him or herself – so too their clients.

This is not to suggest that there are not already in existence some useful, specific integrative models and approaches which may be adopted to positive effect. We acknowledge some of these existing integrations in the Recent Developments section of the first chapter. However, it is not our intention to present these models in any great depth within this book. They are better served by their own exponents in the books dedicated specifically to them.

Our aim is to discuss and demonstrate the creation and development of over-arching frameworks for integration which, we believe, are necessary to the feasibility of theoretical and pragmatic integration. Our intention is not for practitioners to adhere to the ones presented here, but to create and develop their own personal frameworks and procedures for integration according to their own beliefs and theoretical background as well as their stage of experience and personal style.

In our experience as trainers and supervisors of students of integrative approaches from a variety of courses, we have found that there is often a lack of understanding of 'how to' integrate and a common complaint is the lack of literature addressing this issue. We hope this book will provide some assistance. However, we hope that we also address the needs of more experienced practitioners and supervisors for theory and discussion into which their own creativity, theoretical acumen and experience may be brought.

Throughout this book we use the term 'integration' to describe the bringing together of parts into a whole in the service of our work. We have noticed in the literature the many and various attempts at definitions concerning, in particular, eclecticism and integration. At the same time, we notice that books and articles whose titles specify 'integration' sometimes contain the same material as those whose titles specify 'eclectic' psychotherapy, often whole chapters, perhaps with minor changes, lifted from one to the other! In this book, we prefer to employ the word integration as an umbrella term which includes eclecticism, pluralism, trans-theoreticalism, and so on. As will be seen, we refer to different strategies for integration which distinguish one level of integration from another. We provide Framework Strategies for theoretical level integration, Procedural Strategies for technical level integration and refer to Generic Elements which we see as commonly integrated within and across various approaches (integrative or singular) when working with clients. We believe that whatever the level of integration there is a quest for making whole. Even at the technical level (which some would prefer to call eclectic) some consideration of this wholeness is taken into account when choosing an intervention. This technical level is, therefore, as equally deserving of the term integration as considerations at the theoretical level.

As this book is aimed at both counsellors and psychotherapists, for the most part, we refer fully to both except where repetition becomes too cumbersome, in which case we use the terms therapists or practitioners to include both counsellors and psychotherapists.

The book is divided into four sections. Part I concerns the theory of integration starting with a brief history of its development from Freud to the present day (including short descriptions of some recent integrative models), the identification of generic elements of counselling and psychotherapy which we believe should inform an integrative therapeutic approach and, concluding this first part, two suggestions of how to integrate using the Framework Strategy for Integration and the Procedural Strategy for Integration.

Part II presents an exercise in integration. In these three chapters, the authors explore and develop their own theory of human beings to assist them in developing their own multidimensional integrative framework, which is then illustrated by a client example.

Part III presents five other examples of framework and procedural strategies for integration as illustrations of the development of personal integrative approaches. Part IV considers the requirements of integrative practitioners in terms of training and further development.

Integration in such an essentially fragmented field as psychotherapy is no easy task. Our experience in preparing, researching and writing this book has confirmed for us the difficulty of such a project. Where we have widened our conceptual scope we have sometimes lost the depth of more intense exploration and where we have narrowed our view we have sacrificed the excitement of divergent paths. Perhaps this is the nature of integration and the flowing between convergence and divergence a necessary part of the process. Our hope is that we have provided some practical guidance, as well as useful points for discussion, which will assist counsellors and psychotherapists in grappling with their own personal approach to integration, not only finding integrations within those approaches which share the same parental school but across the at one time rigid and heavily defended boundaries of behavioural, psychodynamic and humanistic/existential schools.

Part I
INTEGRATION: CONTEXT AND CONCEPTS

1

A Brief History of Integration and Some Recent Developments

If we were writing a complete history of integration, we would need to devote not just one chapter but several volumes to the subject, for the history of integration is the history of psychotherapy itself. We might well begin with Freud, who within his own developing psychoanalytic frame attempted to integrate influences from his medical and psychiatric studies, from academic psychology, from his collaborative work with Joseph Breuer as well as from his neuropathological lectureship under Professor Charcot, whose work using hypnosis suggested the power of the unconscious, the phenomena of attachment between patient and doctor and a link between sexuality and neurosis. We would then go on to describe the works of the next generation who broke away, diverged, incorporated, yet always in some ways integrated concepts from and into the structure of psychoanalysis. By volume ten, we would still not have done justice to the many and various 'alternatives' that have developed from those early beginnings, merging, converging, competing or reforming neo-Freudian and non-Freudian strands and developments as they proliferated into the hundreds of approaches that now exist. Needless to say, therefore, this developmental integration over the century will only be covered generally here, our purpose being to show that integration is not a new phenomenon and to explore, in its historical context, the more recent thrust of integration which seems to be of a different order to that of the past.

Within the general development of psychology, psychotherapy and counselling, there have been, and still are, distinct and separate models of counselling and psychotherapy. These models are based on different theoretical and philosophical foundations which are supported and furthered by the respective training organizations and professional associations to which they belong. These different models can be divided into three distinct, though often overlapping, schools of theoretical approach which have informed the practice of counselling and psychotherapy.

The first, already referred to, is the psychodynamic (or psychoanalytic) school with its roots in the theory and methodology of Freud, characterized by the unconscious conflict brought about by instinctual drives and repression. The second is the behavioural school with its roots in the experiments of Pavlov and Skinner and characterized by conditioned learning. The third is the humanistic/existential school with its roots in the works of such pioneers as Moreno, Maslow, Rogers, Perls, Berne, May, Boss and Binswanger and characterized by a belief in self-actualization and choice.

These three schools, though claiming distinction from each other, have spawned a proliferation of approaches to counselling and psychotherapy not only within their own school of thought but across the three schools. These various approaches, though seemingly unique, can often be traced back to early beginnings in one or more of the three schools. Perls, in his Gestalt therapy, developed across schools by integrating Gestalt psychology, Freudian psychoanalytic theory, the theories of the 'interpersonal psychoanalysts' such as Fromm, Adler and Rank and 'radical analysts' such as Reich, as well as existential philosophy, Zen Buddhism, phenomenology, field theory and psychodramatic techniques as developed earlier by Moreno (see Sills et al., 1995). Transactional analysis, although basically an object relations theory, which integrates elements of cognitive behavioural theory and social psychology is considered humanistic because of its philosophy and value system (see Lapworth et al., 1993). Self-psychology (Kohut, 1971) originally integrated elements of drive theory and object relations while centralizing the importance of empathic understanding (traditionally associated with person-centred practice) in the healing of a damaged self. Intersubjectivity theory (Atwood and Stolorow, 1984) has developed from a psychoanalytic root yet its methodology centralizes the relationship's co-creativity of experience more usually associated with Gestalt, person-centred or constructivist approaches.

From psychoanalysis there have been many offshoots. Some examples of these are Jung's analytic psychology, ego psychology, object relations theory and, most recently, self-psychology. The behavioural school has led to cognitive behaviour therapy, constructivist theories, assertion trainings and neuro linguistic programming (NLP). Within the humanistic school, the offshoots have been so plentiful that it is sometimes difficult to keep track just of the names, let alone the theoretical slant being offered. Among the more established humanistic or existential approaches such as psychodrama, person-centred counselling, existential psychotherapy, Gestalt and transactional analysis, there have been developments presented under names such as focusing, reclaiming your inner child, rebirthing, primal integration, and others.

Many psychotherapy and counselling books specialize in some specific approach and many of the general counselling and therapy textbooks have sections or chapters devoted to individual theoreticians and approaches. The reader of these books, therefore, may come to the decision that all counsellors and psychotherapists are to be classified as purists. However, research indicates that many counsellors and psychotherapists use and have studied a variety of approaches besides their 'basic' training and do not define themselves as purists at all. Increasing numbers are identifying themselves as integrative. For example, out of 2,334 practitioners listed in the British Association for Counselling's (BAC) *Counselling and Psychotherapy Resources Directory 1996*, 499 (21 per cent) identify their theoretical orientation as integrative. This is the third most common entry after psychodynamic (930) and person-centred (560).

In the light of the natural evolutionary development of ideas and approaches within the world of counselling and psychotherapy from its very beginnings a century ago, the question arises as to what is the difference between this integration and the movement towards integration that has been happening over the last twenty years. We suggest that the difference is in the intention of the integration. Whereas it was often the intention of past developments and integrations to invent something new, an innovative package to use as a complete model of counselling and psychotherapy, this is not necessarily the case with modern integrative developments. Rather, the integrative challenge of today is to discover overarching frameworks within which compatible or complementary, tried and tested aspects of various theories and approaches can be integrated. This involves taking a meta-perspective of the field of therapy, taking stock of commonalities within theories and approaches (and the concomitant differences) as well as utilizing practical techniques from the wealth of such operations offered by the many and different approaches. It is more of a bridge-building exercise between and within the three schools than the building of a new orthodoxy. Integrative counselling and psychotherapy seek, therefore, to build philosophical, theoretical and technical networks between compatible, workable and useful aspects of the various schools.

By and large, up to the 1960s, counselling and psychotherapy were restricted to the wealthy or the insane – often both. In the social and cultural revolution of the 1960s in the West, therapy and counselling not only matched the zeal and innovation of that time but were an essential part of it. However, though more accepted as legitimate means to personal growth, and in that sense normalized, counselling and psychotherapy were still considered unusual by the wider population. The enormous expansion in the technology of international and interpersonal communication in the 1980s has meant an egalitarianism of information, understanding and knowledge such that counselling and psychotherapy can be offered to and participated in by a much wider and diverse clientele. During this time, the term counselling reached a wide audience in Britain and other countries through 'phone-in' counselling programmes on television, national and local radio as well as programmes presenting counselling and psychotherapy with celebrities or exploring various approaches. Indeed, radio and TV soaps were often to include the need for therapy for many of their life-battered characters. Comedy sitcoms have been attempted which revolve around therapy and therapy practitioners. The result is that the public has not only been informed of the existence of counselling and psychotherapy, but also educated in its terminology, methodology and variety of approaches.

Increasing numbers of people are turning to therapy, therapeutic workshops or groups to address the stress they experience in their modern-day lives. Many companies and organizations now incorporate counselling services in their employee care packages. The therapeutic population is slowly becoming more representative of the general population found in our richly diverse and multicultural society.

Theories and approaches based upon white, middle-class, often male, Western ideologies and values no longer suffice to answer the needs of this population with its diversity of internal and external values, social complexity, differing family patterns and spiritual and cultural beliefs, as well as limitations of time or finance. To answer this need, models with broader scope are required. Developing an integrative or integrating attitude within counselling and psychotherapy may be part of the answer.

This development towards integration is not confined to the world of counselling and psychotherapy but is also evident in educational approaches, political and social reorganization, economic theory and practice, industrial theory, anthropology, psychiatry, pharmacology and medicine. It is evident that while such a trend for integration exists within these individual areas, there is also room for integration across them. For example, psychotherapy and counselling may need to take note of and make room for aspects of social and political change and incorporate new knowledge and discoveries in the world of anthropology and medical science. In other words, integration is essential to an holistic view of human existence.

However, as is often the case where boundaries are being changed, there are some who do not agree with the developments that have taken place within counselling and psychotherapy and would argue strongly against any further developments of an integrative nature. Three major debates have emerged. First, some purist practitioners argue against eclectic or integrative psychotherapy or counselling approaches. Second, a debate continues between eclectic and integrative counsellors and psychotherapists. The third debate arises between the proponents of different versions of integrative approaches.

Some practitioners identifying themselves with a specific or purist approach consider that any attempt to combine different approaches results in confusion and inauthenticity of some kind or another because each specific training is based on different underlying philosophical assumptions. They hold that, even if there is an overlap of a few of these assumptions, to lift a part of any whole would result in a distortion of not only that part but of any other whole into which it is intruded/included. Further, they argue that integration leads to an undisciplined spirit of translation which loses the subtleties and nuances of the individual approach.

Among the more purist writers who led the early argument against eclecticism and integrative approaches were Szasz (1974) and Eysenck (1970). Eysenck argues that the only scientific and sufficiently consistent approach is that of behaviour therapy and that any integrative or eclectic therapy is a confusion of models. He criticizes eclectics for their lack of acceptable rationale and shortage of empirical evidence for their approach. Without mincing his words, he describes eclecticism as 'a mishmash of theories, a hugger-mugger of procedures, a gallimaufry of therapies and a charivaria of activities having no proper rationale, and incapable of being tested or evaluated' (1970: 140–6). From another perspective, the radical critic of psychoanalysis, Szasz, protests against integration, saying that combinations of theories and practices result in inauthenticity:

> The psychotherapist who claims to practice in a flexible manner, tailoring his therapy to the needs of his patients, does so by assuming a variety of roles. With one patient he is

a magician who hypnotises; with another, a sympathetic friend who reassures; with a third, a physician who dispenses tranquillisers; with a fourth, a classical analyst who interprets; and so on . . . The eclectic psychotherapist is, more often than not, a role player; he wears a variety of psychotherapeutic mantles, but owns none and is usually truly comfortable in none. Instead of being skilled in a multiplicity of therapeutic techniques, he suffers from what we may consider, after Erikson, 'a diffusion of professional identity'. In sum, the therapist who tries to be all things to all people may be nothing to himself; he is not 'at one' with any particular method of psychotherapy. If he engages in intensive psychotherapy, his patient is likely to discover this. (Szasz 1974: 41)

Against this purist attitude, integrationists and eclectics suggest that the similarities between approaches are so fundamental that the using of ideas from different approaches will enrich an approach rather than confuse it. Though a confirmed eclectic rather than an integrationist, Lazarus (in Norcross, 1986) writing of his multimodal therapy, gives an argument which is in direct opposition to Szasz by stating that there is no one way to approach people's problems and that individuality and flexibility are the key to good practice. He says: 'If a number of clinicians, unfamiliar with me or my therapeutic orientation, were to observe me with different clients, their views and conclusions about my methods and school identification would differ considerably.' He goes on to suggest that one observer might see a Gestalt therapist, another a behaviourist, another a Rogerian, yet another a psycho-analytic therapist, and so on. He maintains that technical eclecticism (see procedural integration strategy in Chapter 3 and Lazarus' multimodal therapy in Chapter 8) 'draws on all and any effective technique without necessarily subscribing to the theories or systems that gave rise to them.' (p.82) His emphasis is upon flexibility of style and specificity of intervention designed to fit each client's individual and idiosyncratic needs and expectancies, rather than attempting to fit the client into one particular approach or methodology.

The second debate between those using eclectic methods and those using an integrating framework involves, among other things, the belief that integrative approaches require greater academic and theoretical discipline than that required by any form of eclecticism. In the 1960s the term eclectic was more popular than it is today. An eclectic approach to therapy is perceived as one that involves a practitioner assessing the needs of his client and choosing from a range of approaches the intervention which seems best to suit the situation, as described above in terms of Lazarus' multimodal approach. Integration, however, involves a therapist bringing together disparate theories and techniques and modelling/moulding them into a new theory. In this second debate the integrationists argue that their form of transformation results in a more authentic and consolidated approach than that of an eclectic random selection.

Some theorists argue for distinction between eclecticism and integration; others argue that integration is only one form of eclecticism and yet others that the situation is the reverse. It is our view, however, that this debate is often one of semantics. For this reason, we have chosen to stay out of the argument between the two 'sides' by presenting two strategies which, we believe, deal with each respectively. We have called these the 'Framework Strategy' and the the 'Procedural Strategy'. We continue to use the term 'integration' because it appears to be the term of choice among practitioners today but more so because it describes a wholeness of approach which best matches our own philosophical attitude to counselling and psychotherapy.

The third debate concerns the different types of integrative approaches. Here again, we find the debate not only fruitless and unnecessary, but continuing the 'mine's better than yours' competition that has somewhat undermined the credibility of counselling and psychotherapy in the past. These claims are unfounded within both 'purist' and integrative approaches.

Research findings (for example, Luborsky et al., 1975) suggest no evidence that one psychotherapeutic approach is more effective than another. What is important in terms of effectiveness has little to do with the chosen approach and much to do with the relationship between therapist and client. It is also interesting to note that these studies have found greater commonalities between experienced practitioners from differing schools than between senior practitioners and trainees within the same school. Such findings suggest that there are certain important therapeutic elements which are common to most psychotherapeutic approaches rather than particular approaches to counselling and psychotherapy which are more effective than others. These generic elements will be discussed in the next chapter.

It is our hope that these particular debates will fade and that between and within various schools of thought co-operative discussion and sharing of ideas may lead to clearer understanding and discovery for what is, after all, our common task as practitioners, that of the improvement of the service we offer to our clients – be it in terms of healing, change, insight or actualization.

In just such a quest, in 1983 the Society for the Exploration of Psychotherapy Integration (SEPI) was formed. Its aim was to bring together practitioners representing diverse approaches who shared a common interest in investigating ways in which various forms of psychotherapy could be integrated. Some of these practitioners are professionals who clearly identify themselves with a particular theoretical framework but openly acknowledge that other schools have something to offer. Some are people interested in finding commonalities among therapies and some would like to find a way to integrate existing approaches. Many members hope eventually to find integrative approaches based on research findings or are interested in developing clearer guidelines that are more consistent with their clinical experience (Goldfried and Newman in Norcross, 1986: 55). Though there is much healthy debate within this society, it is refreshing that there is a willingness to self-evaluate, to investigate other approaches and to search for methods of integration across approaches and a greater openness to co-operation, mutual exploration and shared endeavour.

In the late 1980s, the United Kingdom Council for Psychotherapy (UKCP) was set up to unite the psychotherapy profession and provide some regulation for the public benefit with its move towards statutory regulation and its first register of psychotherapists in 1993. Its eight sections represent the whole range of approaches to psychotherapy. As most integration of approaches was taking place within the humanistic realm at the time of the UKCP's inauguration, a section was designated as Humanistic and Integrative Psychotherapy. Given that integration is increasingly occurring within and between several other sections, perhaps it is time for this to be reflected in the designation of a separate and distinct integrative section. The description given in the Humanistic and Integrative Psychotherapy section flag statement concerning the integrative aspects of this group could probably stand as a convincing flag statement for a discreet integrative section:

> This section includes different psychotherapies which approach the individual as a whole person including body, feelings, mind and spirit. Members welcome interdisciplinary dialogue and an exploration of different psychological processes with particular emphasis on integration within the section . . . Integrative Psychotherapy can be distinguished from eclecticism by its determination to show there are significant connections between different therapies which may be unrecognised by their exclusive proponents. While remaining respectful to each approach, integrative psychotherapy draws from many sources in the belief that no one approach has all the truth. The therapeutic relationship is the vehicle for experience, growth and change. It aims to hold together the dual forces of disintegration and integration, as presented by the psychologically distressed and disabled. The integrative therapeutic experience leads towards a greater toleration of life's experiences and an increase of creativity and service. (UKCP, 1999: xiv)

It is in this same spirit that we have written this book. We hope to provide guidelines and templates that will help practitioners and students to develop their own integrative approaches to working with clients rather than impose one prescriptive theory or methodology. It is our belief that there is not one but many integrative and integrating approaches to counselling and psychotherapy and these will depend upon the several variables which need to be taken into consideration. Such variables will include the experience and training of the practitioners, their professional and personal style of relating and creating, their life experience and the 'stories' (sometimes called theories) they have evolved to make meaning of their lives and the lives of others. Their work setting may have some influence on the type, frequency and duration of the therapy and their choice of client population will also affect the development of their approach. These same variables will equally apply to their clients. Such respect for individuality, difference and idiosyncratic preference, when held alongside the appreciation of commonalities, the similarity of needs and the shared experience of being human gives hope, at the beginning of this new millennium, for the lessening of segregation and the development of integration in our field.

Recent Developments

As we have said in the Introduction, it is our aim in this book to discuss and demonstrate the use of frameworks and procedures for integration in order to encourage practitioners to develop their own personal, integrative models. However, it seems appropriate in this history section to briefly mention some of the integrative models that have been developed in recent years to give an idea of the exciting diversity of integrative approaches. These are necessarily much abbreviated descriptions and cannot do justice either to the theory or practice of these models. We would urge readers to refer to the original sources for more comprehensive descriptions and discussions.

Cognitive-analytic therapy (CAT)

The CAT model was originated and developed by Anthony Ryle and described in *'Cognitive-analytic Therapy: Active Participation in Change: A New Integration in Brief Psychotherapy'* (1990). It is an example of an approach which started as an integration of theories and methods and then solidified into a recognized model with its own name, training courses, and so on.

CAT has been applied largely within the British National Health Service where conditions require time-limited work. Usually clients are offered 16 sessions, though sometimes eight or twelve sessions have proved to be helpful. It incorporates essential elements of personal construct and cognitive theories such as identifying and challenging distorted meanings and inferences and the ensuing emotions, challenging negative self-evaluations and catastrophic fantasies, helping the choice of appropriate plans and evaluating their consequences, as well as behavioural techniques such as graded exposure, modelling and practice of new skills. In addition, psychoanalytic theory is incorporated, in particular, the main 'ego defences' of denial, repression, dissociation, reaction formation and symptom formation.

Ryle based his integrative theory on what he terms the 'Procedural Sequence Model' concerned with intentional, aim-directed activity. This theory draws upon both psychoanalytic theory, especially object relations theory, and the developmental psychology of Vygotsky (Wertsch, 1985). Learning and the development and growth of human personality are seen as taking place through the process of internalization. The early, unique, interpersonal experiences of childhood (particularly with parents and other adults) become transformed into intrapsychic experiences through which we acquire 'a second voice' in an internal conversation. The external dialogue becomes an internal dialogue with the possibility of life-enhancing or life-restricting 'conversations'. Ryle sees psychotherapy as analogous to the early adult–child learning process and the therapeutic relationship as the arena in which the learning process may be utilized to acquire new attitudes and skills, recognizing and modifying the ways in which a client may avoid or distort this relationship through transference.

Ryle (1990) identifies three main ways in which people fail to modify ineffective procedures:

1 *Traps*: these are circular self-reinforcing processes where a negative belief leads to action which has consequences serving to confirm the original negative belief.
2 *Dilemmas*: possible means are considered but only as narrow, polarized alternatives. One pole tends to be repeated through fear of the consequences of the perceived only alternative polarity.
3 *Snags*: here appropriate aims are abandoned due to the prediction of negative external consequences (e.g. disapproval) or internal consequences (e.g. guilt).

These tendencies are taken into account when reformulating the Target Problem Procedures of the client.

In the practice of CAT, *reformulation* is the essential feature. This represents the description of the client's difficulties focusing upon the procedures in need of change and upon how the client is actively responsible for maintaining these procedures. This is usually completed within the first four sessions with clients vitally playing an active part in the process working towards an accurate and fully understood description which is recorded in writing. Much of this will be based upon the client's clinical history and their behaviour in relation to the therapist in the early sessions. However, supplementary devices such as the Psychotherapy File may be used. Here clients identify with descriptions they see as applying to themselves and can use the file to rate various aspects of their moods, feelings, thoughts, behaviours and patterns. All this is discussed and elaborated upon and finally written down. The first part is in the form of a letter in the first person. Both therapist and client have a copy of this. As Ryle says, 'The emotional impact of this letter is often profound; as patients feel that their experience has been understood and validated they often become silent or may cry and this moment often cements the working alliance' (in Dryden, 1992a). The second part of the reformulation lists current target problems (TPs) and target problem procedures (TPPs) by which the client is actively maintaining their difficulties by means of traps, dilemmas and snags.

The effects of this rigorous reformulation process are threefold. First, the active involvement of clients enhances a sense of ability and efficacy and engenders an active and co-operative role in the psychotherapy. Second, activities ranging from unstructured talking to specific homework tasks tend to reveal how a client's particular difficulties are provoked by and manifested in the therapeutic situation (such transference and countertransferential issues being anticipated by the earlier exploration of problematic personal procedures). Third and crucially, reformulation requires considerable thought and sensitivity on the part of the therapist. Ryle states: 'The fact that the results are written down is daunting but the fact that what is written down is discussed and modified with the patient means that, once completed, the reformulation provides a firm shared basis upon which the rest of the therapeutic work can be built' (in Dryden, 1992a).

Change often occurs during the reformulation process itself. Once completed, the task is for the client to recognize and begin to modify these problematic procedures and loops. Diaries are kept to record repetitions of 'target procedures' which are discussed and explored within the sessions, with additional reference to how they may be being enacted within the therapeutic relationship. This is a process of bringing into awareness what previously has been performed automatically. This awareness is heightened by sessional rating by the client of how far they have been controlled by their TPPs or employed alternative modes.

The end of the therapy is marked by an exchange of 'goodbye letters', acknowledging the pain of loss as well as the gains to be taken away, which serves to continue the therapy and aids in internalization of the therapist for the period between termination and follow-up (usually three months later). Ryle points out that no therapy can make up for the damage or deficits of childhood, but it can provide a 'pilot guide and a tool kit'. The therapist is internalized, not as the 'all-powerful carer of the needy child within the patient' but as a caring and coping 'bearer of understanding' and 'initiator of change'.

Integrative psychodynamic therapy

We have chosen this next model of integration because it demonstrates a marked similarity with the CAT approach while differing in its overall style. It too is an integration of psychodynamic and behavioural approaches and some of the components will be seen to be almost identical (for example, Ryle's 'traps' and Wachtel's 'vicious cycles') while presenting differing emphasis. It is this 'similar yet different' aspect of models of integration that we find both exciting and reassuring. Here we present the bare outline of this integrative psychodynamic therapy to give the flavour of its integration and recommend the interested reader to explore the model further in the original sources as referenced.

Integrative psychodynamic therapy, developed by Paul Wachtel (Wachtel and Wachtel, 1986; Wachtel, 1987; Wachtel and McKinney, 1992), is a synthesis of key facets of psychodynamic, behavioural and family systems theory and has its theoretical base in cyclical psychodynamics. This theory reflects both the cyclical nature of causal processes in human interactions and experiences and the unconscious motives, fantasies and conflicts we maintain in our everyday lives. In Wachtel's words:

> The events that have a causal impact on our behaviour are very frequently themselves a *function of* our behaviour as well . . . By choosing to be in certain situations and not others, by selectively perceiving the nature of those situations and thereby altering their psychological impact, and by influencing the behaviour of others as a result of our own way of interacting, we are likely to create for ourselves the same situation again and again. (Wachtel in Norcross and Goldfried, 1992: 344–5)

From this perspective Wachtel saw that active intervention methods from the behavioural school (and others) could enhance the change potential of more dynamic approaches and be logically and consistently employed within a modified psychodynamic context whereby transference reactions are conceptualized as 'the individual's idiosyncratic way of construing and reacting to experiences, rooted in past experiences, but always influenced as well by what is really going on'. In this way, emphasis is as much on understanding reactions to current situations (including the impact of the relationship with the therapist and the therapist's responses) as on past influences that might explain why such reactions may arise.

Cyclical psychodynamics endeavours to develop a theoretical structure which is coherent and clinically practical by selecting those aspects of 'competing perspectives' which can be integrated. It is influenced, as the name suggests, by psychodynamic theory with its emphasis on unconscious processes, inner conflict and understanding the relationship between therapist and client, yet places primary emphasis not on past events but upon the vicious cycles (in particular 'self-fulfilling prophecies') persisting in the present and set in motion by those past events. The cultural and social context, the how, where and when of the client's neurotic patterns are addressed by behavioural and family systems perspectives. Thus, 'cyclical dynamics integrates the exploration of warded-off experiences and inclinations with direct and active efforts at promoting change'. Both internal and external realities, defining and redefining each other, are crucial to this integrative approach.

Integrative encounter

Our third example is a very different model of integrative therapy based on the encounter group and described by Rowan (in Dryden, 1992a). Its philosophy is humanistic – a belief in the healing power of the corrective enactment and in the self-actualizing tendency of the human being given circumstances that release the natural energy. As with the two previous models cited, it links past, present and future. It has the emphasis on the present.

Rowan identifies what he calls 'three legs' of an integrative psychotherapy. The first leg is 'regressive' by which he means exploring past events either to resolve traumatic experiences or to discover the origins of present problems. He cites psychoanalytic approaches and body therapies as addressing these areas in particular. The methods he describes for accessing and resolving past issues are largely those found in classical Gestalt therapy, psychodrama and redecision therapy. The second leg is 'existential'. This word is used to indicate an emphasis on the 'here and now' and the therapeutic value of the real encounter with other members of the therapy group. This benefit includes raising of awareness, experimentation and feedback from other participants. Rowan suggests that cognitive-behavioural therapy, neuro linguistic programming and the humanistic/ existential approaches are valuable in this area. The third leg is 'transpersonal'. Although Rowan is careful to draw a distinction between the archetypal and the transpersonal, he also points to the link between them. He refers to the 'higher unconscious' of Assagioli (1975) but also includes in the transpersonal such phenomena as intuition and the imaginal world. He describes the spontaneous emergence in groups, facilitated, for example, by enactment and experiment, of mythic rituals and moments of mystical experience which, while temporary, open up 'a sense of spiritual possibilities'.

Rowan sees work in these three areas as taking place through allowing 'action and feelings' to be expressed and explored in a therapeutic way. He describes the process of an encounter group as follows: 'The group produces an issue of some kind through one or more of its members, and the leader finds a way of dramatising that issue so it can be worked through for the benefit of the individuals who raise the issue, and the group as a whole' (in Dryden, 1992a: 224).

Rowan cites Schutz (1973, 1989) and Mintz (1972, 1983) as being two of those at the heart of the encounter movement and he also traces the evolution of 'integrative encounter' in line with the changing expectations of groups and group leadership styles over the last quarter century. The directive Perlsian type intervention has become viewed as overly authoritative and there has been an expectation upon group leaders to facilitate a more self-directed experience. Rowan, while understanding the reservations about the old style of leadership, is also clear that something has been lost in the changes. He advocates an integrative encounter group that incorporates the energy-releasing methods and techniques made famous in the 1960s and 1970s with a spirit of equality and sensitivity.

These are but three examples of the many integrative models that have been recently developed following a century of more evolutionary integration. The reader interested in explanations of several other integrative models is recommended to read *Integrative and Eclectic Counselling and Psychotherapy* (Palmer and Woolfe, 1999).

Though an in-depth exploration of the development of integration from Freud to the present day would make for interesting and lengthy reading, such an endeavour lies outside the remit of our book. However, we hope, in this chapter, to have highlighted some of the more prominent aspects of the evolution of integrative counselling and psychotherapy and made clear the distinctive thrust of the modern integrative movement towards a more individual and personal approach to integration.

2

Generic Elements of Counselling and Psychotherapy

Individual clients will give their testimonies as to the efficacy of counselling and psychotherapy, some with glowing reports of dramatic changes in their lives, some with acknowledgement of 'feeling better', others with stories of staying stuck through and beyond therapy and, sadly, others who experience a worsening of their problems. Most would probably settle somewhere in the middle of this range, claiming neither miracles nor disasters but being appreciative of the outcome they have gained. Is it therapy per se that produces this wide range of results or is it the person delivering it or, further, is it the person receiving the therapy who may bring a quality that another may not which affects the outcome?

The problem in assessing the effectiveness of counselling or psychotherapy is that the personal, qualitative views of clients do not match the demands of Western society for observable and scientific evidence. Therapy deals with people. People are individuals. Individuals making changes in their lives do not always provide the comparable statistical evidence that science demands. The variables in people – the internal, historical, current, biological, hereditary, temperamental, cultural, and so on – make such comparisons extremely difficult. The innate physiological, developmental thrust for survival, life and actualization means that all human beings are changing at all their different levels, all the time. Our need of contact and co-operation with other human beings makes us socially interactive which will also bring about (sometimes force) changes to ourselves and others.

In recent years, different and less quantitative ways of measuring how professionals assist in the 'change process' have become more prevalent. There are now several qualitative research studies which suggest that people can derive benefits from the alliance between therapist and client. It seems that research methodology has needed to change creatively in order to measure the creative change of counselling and psychotherapy. Examples of such types of research can be found in Reason and Rowan's (1981) *Human Inquiry: A Source book of New Paradigm Research*; Rice and Greenberg's (1984) *Patterns of Change*; Mahrer's (1988) *'Research and clinical applications of "good moments" in psychotherapy'*; Safran and Greenberg's (1991) *Emotion, Psychotherapy and Change*; Talley et al. (1994) *Psychotherapy Research and Practice: Bridging the Gap*; McLeod's (1999) *Practitioner Research in Counselling*.

Research findings suggest that therapy, for some people, with some practitioners, works in helping people make changes in their lives. But what are the generic factors in counselling and psychotherapy of whatever approach which facilitate change?

Many practitioners and theorists have postulated the elements which they consider contribute to the effectiveness of counselling and psychotherapy.

Marmor (1982) cites factors from an analytic perspective (though it is interesting to note the relational and behavioural aspects which point to an integration across schools):

> (1) A basic matrix of good patient–therapist relationship resting on both real and fantasied qualities that each brings to their work together . . . (2) Release of emotional tension . . . (3) Cognitive learning or the acquisition of insight . . . (4) Operant conditioning, by means of subtle and often non-verbal cues of approval or disapproval, as well as by corrective emotional experiences in the relationship with the analyst. (5) Suggestion and persuasion, usually implicit, occasionally explicit. (6) Unconscious identification with the analyst, both conceptually and behaviourally. (7) Repeated reality testing and working through. (Marmor, 1982: 66)

Yalom (1975) drew up a list of curative factors in group psychotherapy from an existential standpoint:

> (1) Instillation of hope. (2) Universality. (3) Imparting of information. (4) Altruism. (5) The corrective recapitulation of the primary family group. (6) Development of socialising techniques. (7) Imitative behaviour. (8) Interpersonal learning. (9) Group cohesiveness. (10) Catharsis. (11) Existential factors. (Yalom 1975: 3–4)

Garfield points out that 'because the different forms of psychotherapy are derived from different theoretical orientations and use different terms and concepts, the various forms of psychotherapy appear more different than may actually be the case. Consequently, some common variables or processes are viewed as different even when they are essentially similar' (in Norcross and Goldfried, 1992). He describes several common factors present in most forms of psychotherapy which he believes are prerequisites for potential progress in psychotherapy:

- The relationship in psychotherapy.
- Emotional release or catharsis.
- Explanation, rationale and interpretation.
- Reinforcement.
- Desensitization.
- Facing or confronting a problem.
- Information and skills training.
- Time.

Our own list of generic elements

Influenced by the research findings, our reading and by our experience as practitioners and as clients in individual psychotherapy of several differing approaches, we have compiled a list of what we consider to be the necessary elements of a therapeutic engagement. Naturally, they reflect our own bias and the reader may disagree with some elements. However, we believe that, in the main, they are common to most practices and can inform any integrative therapeutic approach. We list them below before discussing them in more detail:

- The therapeutic alliance.
- 'Double listening'.
- Being acknowledged and accepted as you are.
- Receiving empathy.
- Gaining insight.
- Being in the presence of another who has no personal investment in how one should or could change.
- The creation of a relationship which may have been lacking in the past.
- The therapist as model.
- Normalizing the client's experience.
- Challenging and confronting.
- Time structuring for self-reflection.
- Consistency and continuity.
- The opportunity to practise skills.
- Managing the parallel process.
- Humour.
- The matching of therapist and client.

The therapeutic alliance

Research indicates that the therapeutic alliance (or working alliance) between therapist and client has significant influence on the outcome of the psychotherapy. The alliance is seen as 'a positive emotional bond and a sense of mutual collaboration' (Wolfe and Goldfried, 1988) which is established between the therapist and client. Other researchers (Butler and Strupp, 1986; Horvath and Greenberg, 1994; Stiles et al., 1986; Strupp and Hadley, 1979) support the view that, over and above techniques, a 'good human relationship' is central to the efficacy of psychotherapy. Bordin (1979) identifies three important components of the working alliance: an agreement on *goals*, concordance regarding *tasks* with which the partnership will engage and the personal *bonds* developed between therapist and client which affirm their common commitment and understanding of the activity.

'Double listening'

In therapy, clients have the experience of being listened to and of listening to themselves in the presence of another for whom they have no responsibility whatsoever. This absence of distraction caused by a need to attend to the desires of the other is what distinguishes the experience from that of talking with a friend or colleague where attention is inevitably drawn to their experience or to the need for fairness in attention and sharing.

As a client, problems are caught up in the complexity of inner thought, feeling and sensation. The avenue opened up between client and therapist by the art of intelligent, attentive, active listening provides the client with a pathway along which to propel their stream of consciousness. While converting rambling thought or disturbing feelings into more simple spoken language, the client is given time and perspective to be able to really hear their dilemma, and have it heard, in a more manageable form.

> William, on discussing his envy at a colleague's promotion sighs, 'I'm absolutely green with envy at his luck.'
> The therapist responds by simply reflecting back, 'Green with envy' and emulates his sigh. William continues, 'Yes, I am just so green. Funny that, I'm probably too green to get the job really. I don't have his experience.'

Being acknowledged and accepted as you are

The therapist helps to create a relationship between herself and her client in which the client's individuality is respected and valued irrespective of the behaviours which the client may present or report on. The therapist may not agree with or approve of some of the client's actions or even their beliefs, but will nonetheless retain the genuine attitude of meeting the client with complete acceptance.

Childhood is controlled by judgements and conditions laid down by parents, family, church and society. Therapy works when, at last, the client has a relationship in which, for the most part, these conditions do not exist. The client can take permission to experiment with stating their views on life without the need to continue crouching behind the various successful defences which they created in childhood to allay their fears and to prevent fantasized annihilation.

Clients often come to the therapy situation believing that because they have problems they are per se 'bad'. They are not at all accepting of their 'human frailties', but often critical, cruel and overly demanding of themselves. The therapist by his non-judgemental acceptance of his clients, redresses this balance and offers greater safety to his client to start exploring the problems from a more open perspective. Through his own personal work, the therapist will hopefully have grown to be able to hold greater acceptance of his own 'humanity'.

Without acceptance perceived by the client there is the high possibility that the client's childhood experiences will be simply replicated by adapting in an attempt to please the therapist. The therapist's non-judgemental and accepting position provides a container in which it is safe enough to explore the transference and other dynamics.

> Philip says, 'I've been afraid to tell you this because I'm afraid you'll never want to see me again.'
> The therapist responds, 'You sound as if you're carrying something very heavy for you.'
> 'Yes,' replies Philip. 'I'm dreading that you will be very shocked.'
> 'You might be imagining that I am unable to hold on to all that I respect in you once you tell me this,' says the therapist.
> Philip replies, 'Yes, it's awful.'
> The therapist suggests that Philip select two objects in the room, one to represent this unspeakable thing, the other to represent the man she knows and respects unconditionally. He gives them to her to hold for a while.

Receiving empathy

The *Oxford English Dictionary* defines empathy as 'the power of identifying oneself mentally with (and so fully comprehending) a person or object of contemplation'. We would expand this definition to include demonstrating to the other that one's comprehension of their position is multi-levelled such that their thoughts, feelings, sensations and behaviours associated with the situation are integrated within this understanding. The empathic therapist shows her client that his/her experiences are really seen and understood.

We believe, along with Rogers and Kohut and, more recently, Stern, Bozarth and Erskine, that with our basic human need to be loved and to be put first in at least one other's relational orbit, being accepted and being the primary focus of our therapist's attention is in itself healing. It is this quality of attunement (Stern, 1985) which makes possible the bearing of the unbearable and the management of the unmanageable.

Being empathic requires the therapist to suspend their own frame of reference in order to step into the client's. It is an 'as if' experience whereby the therapist experiences what it is like to be sitting opposite herself in the self of the client, absorbing herself in the other's phenomenological reality while retaining enough of herself to therapeutically process and respond to that reality. This involves simultaneous attunement and objectivity.

In order for the therapist to feel empathic she must be coming from a position of goodwill towards the self of the client. Where this is lacking, empathy is unlikely. To promote effective change, the client needs tangibly to experience this benevolent goodwill from the therapist. But how is empathy shown? We have explored our own experience as practitioners and clients and think that an important channel of empathy is eye contact. Perhaps this is a reflection of the empathic mirroring through the eyes between baby and mother or primary caretaker. For this same reason, non-verbal responses are also felt as deeply empathic. Sometimes an attunement at the feeling level which is then translated into words can feel enormously empathic.

> Adele describes an horrific incident in her childhood where her mother viciously beat her with a stick for some minor misdemeanour.
>
> Adele: 'Do you know, besides the pain, one of the worst moments for me was seeing our neighbour look through the window and then just hurry away.'
>
> The therapist shakes her head to show she feels the depth of Adele's distress, 'You were totally abandoned to your mother's madness.'
>
> Adele cries deeply.

Gaining insight

No matter how warmly the client feels met and understood, she will not necessarily be able to take charge of her own life without insight: 'the capacity of understanding hidden truths etc., especially of character or situations' (*Oxford Encyclopaedic*

English Dictionary, OUP, 1991). In the process of therapy the client will be facilitated towards gaining insights into their situation and experience. There are many levels of insight but often even simple insights have been missed by the client because of their distress and anxiety. Other insights may involve perspectives on the unconscious or on intrapsychic dynamics.

Gaining insight and understandings of our situations, pleasant and unpleasant, may occur through several means. Many of these insights will emerge in the very act of being listened to and listening to oneself without any further intervention from the therapist. Simply providing the space or the one-way focus allows the client to identify patterns, underlying dynamics and habitual tendencies. The therapist may assist in the process of gaining insight by giving the client information through the techniques of – specification, interpretation, explanation, illustration, and so on. Gaining insight empowers the client through widening the perspective of a situation or experience such that their choices are expanded and they have certain truths available to them.

Rosemary presents at her therapy session with anxiety about the possibility that she has contracted a venereal disease. As she yet again expresses her fears and fantasies, she hears herself caught in a cycle of negativity and worry. She brightens and tells her therapist, 'This worrying is unhelpful. I could sit here forever and never get to know the facts.'

The therapist nods empathically and adds, 'Or then deal with the facts.'

Later in the session the counsellor asks Rosemary how she could have her health situation verified. She states that she needs to have herself checked out but then becomes concerned about confidentiality. The counsellor helps Rosemary to see that she is again caught into giving energy to worrying rather than exploring possible solutions.

Being in the presence of another who has no personal investment in how one should or could change

Bion (1959) urged that with our clients we should be without memory and without desire in order to genuinely meet our clients and their experience. Similarly, Winnicott advises that 'cure' is not something the therapist does to the patient but rather that cure 'at its root means care'. He maintains that the therapist must have 'the capacity . . . to contain the conflicts of the patient, that is to say to contain them and to wait for their resolution in the patient instead of anxiously looking round for a cure' (1971: 2). While the therapist has an intrinsic belief in the healing process of psychotherapy, it is vital that she has no personal agenda about the changes that could be made, otherwise she may find ways of pushing or controlling the client to move in a certain direction. She may feel impelled to make her client feel better rather than inspired towards health. This may at times be very difficult for the therapist. It can be very unsettling to sit and witness another's distress without instantly intervening to alleviate the pain. However, one of the major ways in which pain is relieved is through its sheer expression and any intervention to prevent it may merely repress and exacerbate the client's distress in the long term. Equally, intervening with solutions or comfort, though tempting, may be disempowering of the client's own potential for growth and change.

This is not to say that the therapist does not have a professional investment in assisting the client to change. It means that within the crucible of benevolent goodwill and the suspension of personal investment, the therapist brings to bear her knowledge, skills and experience for the service of the client. A sense of treatment direction, for example, is an important component of the therapy situation, but it necessitates the bracketing off of any countertransferential issues the therapist may have concerning the taking of that direction. Treatment direction is a guide for both therapist and client. It is not a blueprint the client must follow. If the therapist is heavily invested in the success of a particular direction or intervention, the outcome will most likely be counterproductive.

David arrives at his weekly therapy session and immediately launches into his problems. 'I've had the most terrible nightmares this week and I've hardly slept at all. It's been such a bad time. I'm so angry. Mary and I had a row about the kids and my boss at work was really critical of my performance. The kids being ill hasn't helped and when my mother said she was coming down for the week-end . . . !'

The therapist makes a gesture with her hands to show the large number of issues in the air.

David acknowledges her gesture, 'Yes, there's just so damn much – please help me. Where on earth shall I start?'

'There is such a lot happening,' replies the therapist.

'It all feels out of control,' says David. 'I'm angry at feeling this way.'

'It sounds like your anger is uppermost right now,' the therapist observes.

'Yes, I think my nightmares have been angry . . .'

Creation of a relationship which may have been lacking in the past

In the movement and development towards adulthood, people live through a variety of experiences of different relationships, with many positive and negative aspects to them. Where these were insufficient for the task of growing up and embracing adulthood with responsibility, reality and spontaneity, therapy may offer the opportunity to address and redress these deficits.

Often for the client, being in a relationship with a person who listens non-judgementally helps to resolve unsatisfactory aspects of relationships from the past. The seemingly simple experience of being met in the here and now by another who is able to attend to past, present and future relationship concerns with acceptance and empathy can facilitate the healing of hurts and confusions that may still be manifesting in the present. This is the reparative relationship described among others by Kohut (1971, 1984), Schiff et al. (1975) and Schiff and Day (1970).

For one of our clients it was therapeutically healing simply that the therapist was sitting ready and waiting for her when she arrived for her sessions. Her experience when younger was that of a 'latch-key' child who would have to let herself in to her empty home after school and wait for her parents to come home later. She rarely experienced being welcomed or acknowledged by her parents who were too full of their days' events to give her attention even when they did arrive home. She told the therapist how important and reparative her new experience was in seeing herself as worthy of being acknowledged and greeted on arrival.

The therapist as model

Effective therapists have for the most part spent time and energy in not only their training, but also in exploring themselves within their personal therapy. It is to be hoped that this process of self-development will lead to a person becoming congruent (not hiding behind a front or adaptation) so that what the client perceives in their therapist is a person whose inner experience or state of being is matched by her outward manner. Where such congruence in openness and communication is not present, the client is likely to feel uneasy with the therapist. The building of trust, so essential for the therapeutic relationship to be effective, will be lacking. Part of congruence is the therapist's own faith in the process of counselling or psychotherapy which will be communicated to the client through their attitude during times of struggle, stuckness, pain and despair as well as times of well-being and progress within the work together. Congruence is not, of course, the same as unreserved communication. A therapist may choose to disclose none of her thoughts and feelings yet still convey congruence.

We do not mean that counsellors and psychotherapists are supposed to be perfect examples of what it is to be human. They too are dealing with the vicissitudes of life. They get ill. They have problems. They have bad days and good days. They make mistakes. While it is necessary for therapists to bracket off their own concerns so that they do not intrude into the therapeutic work, honest and genuine recognition and ownership of aspects of the therapists' experiences, especially their counter-transference when influenced by outside factors, is a vital part of congruence within the relationship. Mistakes acknowledged by the therapist often prove to be turning points within the therapy when explored honestly and openly as part of the ongoing therapeutic relationship. Such honesty models the ability to be in the here and now in the presence of the client without agitation over the client's or their own concerns within or outside the consulting room.

Roddy, the client, is holding back his tears as he tells the therapist of the death of his father when he was a child. The therapist experiences a sudden feeling of powerlessness which momentarily diverts his attention from the client. He imagines this is what the client is feeling as he tells his story but is also aware that this sense of powerlessness is part of his own past experience.

The client, somewhat angrily, says. 'Are you listening to me! Perhaps, you don't understand what it was like for me to watch my father dying.'

The therapist says, 'I'm sorry, Roddy. I was hearing what you were saying but, you're right, I was not giving you my complete attention just then. I was reminded of my own father's death and I felt the powerlessness I experienced then.'

Roddy, now freely crying, says, 'So you do know what it was like for me.'

Normalizing the client's experience

Often when people come into therapy they are immersed in self-definitions. They perceive themselves as 'wrong' or 'bad' or negatively unique in some aspects. This grandiosity flies in the face of self-acceptance and holds them back from the liberation they seek. While respecting the client's feelings and self-perception, the therapist finds ways of helping the client to see himself more tolerantly and to accept that to be human is to be fallible. It is a balance of acknowledging the client's own uniqueness within the universal experience of being human. This does not mean to say that attention, credence and empathy are not given to the very personal aspects of the situation that the client may be experiencing but at the same time a widening of perspective expands the possibility of change. As noted earlier, Yalom (1975) sites this aspect of universality of problems as one of his twelve 'curative factors'.

Feelings too may require normalizing for the client. In our culture, sometimes people feel 'bad' or 'guilty' simply for having a feeling. They see themselves as having some weakness that should be expunged. An aspect of supportive therapy is the normalizing of human feelings and the natural, physiological expression that they require in everyone.

Sometimes, the normalizing of an emotion may be instrumental in transforming that emotion within the client. For example, an anxious client was helped to see that the experience of anxiety might have another perspective when his therapist quoted Kierkegaard's assertion that 'anxiety is the giddiness of freedom' (1980). For the client this held a sense of shared humanity and of the transformation of anxiety into the excitement of uncertainty.

Challenging and confronting

Once there is a real working relationship between the therapist and client, the therapist can creatively challenge and confront the client without fear of damaging that therapeutic alliance. Confrontation has many manifestations. It can mean drawing attention to those aspects of the client's behaviour, thinking or feeling which may be self-restricting or even damaging. These confrontations or challenges need to be experienced as beneficial interventions into the process rather than an attack upon the person.

> Wendy, while exploring with her therapist her ability to be over-controlled, laughs as she recounts how the previous evening she was even controlled enough to drive home while well over the legally permitted alcohol limit. The therapist points out that driving home drunk lacks protective control both of herself as well as of others. The client argues for a while that she had been perfectly safe but soon recognizes that the therapist is also expressing concern for her safety and future well-being. Through acceptance of the confrontation she makes the connection between her own potentially destructive behaviour and that of her alcoholic father at whose hands she suffered.

Another definition of confrontation (Berne, 1966) states that it involves pointing out inconsistencies between different client statements. For example, the therapist could comment, 'You say you are evil, yet you are also worrying about harming your friends in your contact with them. Would a really evil person care about something like that?'

We like Egan's (1990) suggestion that confrontation can be seen as an invitation to become aware. This is an acknowledgement that any new awareness constitutes a challenge to a person's frame of reference. Thus, a simple reflection such as, 'Your colour changed as you said that' or 'I'm struck by your use of the word "horrific"' can invite awareness of a person's half-conscious feelings or assumptions. Or a question 'Have you asked your boyfriend what his Hindu culture teaches about your Jewishness?' can open up avenues of exploration.

Even in psychotherapy styles in which the therapist remains mostly silent, we believe that clients become aware of the minutest movements and breathing patterns of their therapist and can feel confronted within that context too.

Time structuring for self-reflection

For many people whose lives are busy and structured into activities of one kind and another like work, family, classes, chores, and so on, the weekly counselling sessions provide a rare time and space for self-reflection. While there may be the need to work on the issue of finding more time for themselves, it is clear that for many clients this is their first real experience of valuing the importance of giving time to themselves.

> Many clients make remarks like 'This is the only time I have to sit down and be with myself in the whole week' or 'I was so relieved it was Wednesday. I saved things up during the week for this island of time which is mine.'

Consistency and continuity

In a longer counselling or psychotherapy relationship, it is not just the session of an hour or 50 minutes, it is the weekly consistency and continuity of relationship, space and time which clients value and use effectively. Within the 50 minutes, the therapist holds in mind the life experience of the client and is able to weave threads of continuity through their past, present and future. For example, the client may be presenting a current issue within the session and while he does this, the therapist holds in her awareness relevant elements of his past and also his future concerns and interests. She may feel that drawing attention to these other related aspects of the client's life would help the client get a more integrated perspective of his current situation.

> Jack talks about giving up his job and working his way through Africa. His therapist, at some later point, asks him to consider how he has given up his job on previous occasions, with exciting prospects in mind, and has each time ended up disillusioned. She invites him to explore his current thinking in the light of these past experiences to find ways of making a decision from which a more positive outcome is likely.

Another aspect of consistency in therapy is the consistency of the environment. Therapy usually takes place each time in the same space and, where possible, in a space where the surroundings remain approximately the same week after week and where privacy is assured. This means that the client's attention is not distracted, for instance, by stimulus from the environment but their energy can be used to examine their own world rather than that of some changing panoply. It is also an important part of the safe container (see Chapter 11) which allows a person to explore the unknown parts of self.

This also applies to the therapist's overall approach to her work. Her style of work will become familiar to the client such that the client can work within a sufficiently predictable relationship which is safe enough to make exploration and take risks. We expand further on this sense of safety later. Some forms of therapy are far more predictable than others. Although structure is important for safe containment, it is also important not to sacrifice flexibility and creativity in its formation. A balance must be found between an excessive rigidity of structure and the chaos of total freedom – the area of 'bounded instability' (Critchley, 1997) which contains the possibility of change.

In relation to consistency, practitioners need to give consideration to such issues as giving advance notice of breaks, arranging locums if appropriate, and so on.

The opportunity to practise skills

Effective therapy ensures that the client learns to bridge their learning within the therapy room into their everyday lives. The therapist can make interventions which assist in the process of their clients' learning to generalize their specific insights. Some practitioners, especially those who work with groups, encourage active role-play practice in the sessions. In any case, through the articulation of different options, a client introduces herself to new possibilities. Some forms of therapy actively encourage this process with 'homework' assignments or contracts, while others support it through their ongoing attention to the 'reporting back' that clients often do prior to concentrating on a specific area of work or interest.

> Joe contracts to telephone at least two people in the course of the following week as part of his work on wanting to increase his social skills. After 'reporting back' his success in this task and receiving confirmation and encouragement from his therapist, the next step is discussed and it is agreed that he will invite these people round for a meal.

Managing the parallel process

Parallel process refers to the tendency of the client to repeat and reconstruct in their relationship with the therapist the very dynamics of the problems which they are bringing to the therapy. It is part of the counsellor's responsibility to diagnose, understand and creatively work through the ways in which the client is attempting, albeit unconsciously, to evoke this parallel situation.

> Lucy usually arrives late for her sessions. She spends several minutes at the beginning of each session apologizing and listing the many reasons for her lateness and leaves expressing dissatisfaction that she hasn't dealt with what she was wanting to work on in her therapy. How the therapist chooses to respond to this situation will vary according to his/her chosen approach. One therapist may share her observation that Lucy seems to be re-enacting with her how there was never enough time in Lucy's family of origin for the youngest child – namely, Lucy. With that insight Lucy may see how she is depriving herself and repeating that childhood experience. Another therapist would work within the transference either at an early stage exploring Lucy's anxious apologies or later on when an empathic response to her angry dissatisfaction leads to the expression of her deep pain and rage.

Humour

Having access to humour is a vital part of being human. We need it to express our joy and excitement as well as to acknowledge and come to terms with the absurdity of life. Handled with care, humour can be a vehicle for insight, an affirmation of the working alliance, a true moment of meeting in the person-to-person relationship or a gentle means of confrontation. Handled clumsily, it can be humiliating, shaming, reinforcing of negative beliefs (as in 'gallows' laughter), confusing or patronizing. The important difference between these ways of handling humour is in the mutuality of the experience. Even when used as a gentle confrontation, the humour must be shared as an illumination and not at the expense of the client.

Not only are humour and laughter emotionally freeing and relationally bonding, they also have the effect of sharpening the mind to think more flexibly and with more complexity. A study by Isen et al. (1991) demonstrated the enhanced and more creative problem-solving skills of a group previously shown a humorous video as compared with those who had watched a maths film or had been exercising.

This is not to suggest that therapists become stage comedians with their clients or introduce jokes into the sessions in order to 'cheer them up' from their depression. In many instances, humour would obviously be inappropriate and avoiding of serious concerns. This said, however, humour has a place in psychotherapy when the intent is clearly of therapeutic value and insight for the client and part of a secure and developed working alliance.

> A client who suffered from endometriosis thought of herself as 'making a fuss' if she mentioned it. When talking of a situation with her friend, Demitrios, she inadvertently refers to him as 'Endometrios'. Catching the therapist's smile, she realizes what she has said and bursts into laughter. 'I don't suppose he'd be flattered to be called that! But I suppose it's a sign that I do want to talk about it.'

The matching of therapist and client

Even when all the above qualities and conditions are present, there still arises the question of why sometimes the therapy does not work for a particular client with a particular therapist. This may not be anything to do with the competence of the therapist or the particular problems of the client. Sometimes the chemistry between two people, in this case client and therapist, jars to such an extent that it interferes with the therapy process. Hopefully, this mismatch will be discovered in early sessions so that the client may be referred on with no ill-feeling from either party. Whereas people have no choice about the temperamental matching of themselves and their parents, for a healing therapeutic experience this is not only possible but might be essential.

There has been little research in the area of matching beyond gender and race. Garfield (1986) considers compatibility in terms of background, class, education and values. A review by Beutler et al. (1986) of research findings on variables affecting the process and outcomes of counselling and psychotherapy point to the beneficial significance of cultural similarity and attitudinal difference. However, matching according to personality proves more difficult to assess. Garfield writes:

> Rather than a strict matching process, what actually occurs is a selection or acceptance process. Ideally, therapists should select patients for therapy whom they feel they can help. This should be the only criterion . . . therapists should try to be as honest and forthright as possible in their appraisal of the patient and should not let other considerations, such as economic factors, pride, and egotism, influence their judgement . . . if the therapist experiences feelings of anxiety, fear, hostility or heightened sexual arousal toward the client, a referral elsewhere should be made. (Garfield, 1986: 142)

For the person in the more vulnerable, often distressed and sometimes uninformed position of being the client, such considerations are more difficult. However, it is good practice in the initial interview to make it clear that any assessment is mutual and that the decision to work together needs to be made by both client and therapist. Many directories, leaflets and booklets aimed at helping people to find a therapist suggest they 'shop around' for the therapist with whom they feel most likely to work well. For some, this will be the therapist with whom they feel most comfortable. For others, it will be the one by whom they feel most challenged. For others, compatibility of age (older, younger, the same), personality or even regional accent may be the important factors. Whatever they are, more effective therapy is likely to take place if the client is an active and informed participant in the selection process.

Generic elements and their emphasis

Differing approaches may emphasize different aspects of this list. It is likely that a psychodynamic therapist would place more emphasis on the gaining of insight than on some of the other elements mentioned. A person-centred therapist might place empathy at the top of their list while a behaviour therapist might choose to emphasize modelling and the practising of skills. However, though there may be different emphasis given by differing approaches, we believe many of these elements are common to all approaches.

It is this commonality of elements in the process of counselling and psychotherapy which gives rise to the feasibility of integration across and between the different schools. Of course, the content, conceptualization and theoretical construction of the therapies may vary, but these identifiable, common (perhaps, essential) elements allow for co-operation, understanding and discussion between schools and lead to the possibility of integration not only in terms of these elements but in terms of the variety of theories from which they have evolved.

3

How to Integrate

In this chapter, we suggest strategies for two different levels of integration. In Parts II and III we present some examples which use these strategic principles to create frameworks or procedures for integration. Practitioners may choose to use them as they stand, in modified form or totally reworked for their own personal and particular blend of integration. We believe that developing a personal model of integration requires a choice of integrative strategies which lead to the adoption of frameworks or procedures from which a personal integrative model will be evolved. We start with the strategies.

Different proponents of integration offer different strategies for the integration of counselling and psychotherapy. In *The Integration of Psychotherapies* Mahrer (1989) considers six different strategies for integration.

The first of Mahrer's strategies involves *developing new theories of psychotherapy that organize and incorporate other existing theories*. Examples of this would be Goulding and Goulding's (1979) redecision therapy which integrates transactional analysis (TA) with Gestalt theory or, as described in the previous chapter, Ryle's (1990) cognitive analytic therapy in its integration of aspects of psychodynamic theory with a more cognitive approach.

The second strategy for integration involves, through dialogue, observation of live work, or through tapes and videos, increased sharing of methodologies between counsellors and psychotherapists. This then would result in practitioners *gaining fresh practical operations and a wider repertoire of procedures* without changing their basic theoretical belief structure. An example here would be that of a psychodynamic practitioner who, in exploring a client's conflicting ego and id impulses, might use a two chair technique borrowed from Gestalt practice. A reverse example would be a Gestalt practitioner employing a more psychodynamic approach of encouraging a client to free associate.

The third of Mahrer's strategies for the integration of therapeutic practice involves examining the languages and vocabularies of all approaches in order to *develop a more or less common vocabulary across the board of schools of therapy and counselling*. This seems a daunting task, but an example of similar concepts that have different terminology but which, under this strategy, might be found a common term could be 'games' theory from TA, a 'fixed gestalt' from Gestalt and 'repetition compulsion' from psychodynamic theory. Although it is unlikely that consensus between schools could be found to the extent that one single common vocabulary be developed (it is similar to the aspiration, yet failure, in the invention of the proposed universal language of Esperanto), certainly communication between schools can be enhanced by the identification and integration of more minor terms.

The fourth strategy for integration means the *invention of a single, umbrella psychotherapy* which subsumes and integrates preferably all others. This would result in there being only one therapy, probably called the Universal Psychotherapy or even the Truth! Apart from the unlikely development of there being one ultimate truth about the nature of human beings and therefore one supreme truth of psychotherapy, it is obvious that because of loyalty, the diversity of human nature and beliefs and the historical and cultural influences involved, this proposal is impossible.

In the fifth strategy, integration develops from *finding commonalities* between therapies and then *combining* in some form those therapies which have these aspects in common. On looking at our example of the third of Mahrer's strategies, because there is a commonality of particular concepts (albeit described in differing terminology) within TA, Gestalt and psychodynamic theory, these three schools could find a way of being combined in this aspect of commonality. In some cases, this development will occur through inter-school communication and learning, but because concepts tend to interweave, often inextricably, with others within the wider theoretical model and do not concur across the schools, this is not comprehensively feasible.

The sixth and final of Mahrer's strategies suggests that, using research findings, a body of the most effective interventions and treatments across the full range of all approaches may be compiled. Once a complete diagnosis has been made, the practitioner consults this 'solutions manual' and treatment plans accordingly. An example here would be of a practitioner starting work with a client who manifests obsessive behaviours. He would consult the 'solutions manual' and proceed accordingly. Unfortunately for practitioners but fortunately for human beings, people are not complete replicas of each other. They are diverse, unique, complicated and profound. This strategy would mostly fail because it treats the problem rather than the person. Obsessive behaviours in one person might have a completely different aetiology, purpose or manifestation from those of another and need widely differing approaches in order to alleviate the obsessive distress and behaviour.

Having worked our way through these six strategies in order to describe and discuss the various ways in which integration can be looked at, we believe, like Mahrer, that there are only two from this list which are most workable and desirable, and which clarify for us the concept of integrative psychotherapy and counselling. They are the first two strategies suggested by Mahrer which we have adapted and expanded upon. In order to identify them easily and distinguish between them we have named them the '*Framework Strategy*' and the '*Procedural Strategy*'.

The framework strategy

In the 'framework strategy' there is the integration and combination of existing theories and techniques and the development of substantively new counselling and psychotherapy theories from *modified theories* of human beings which serve as integrating frameworks for those approaches which share the same 'parental theory of human beings' (Mahrer, 1989). Thus, the overarching theory of how human beings develop, relate, experience, change, function or 'misfunction', adapt or maladapt, and so on, becomes the framework into which we can integrate our psychotherapeutic theory relating to these considerations. Without a theory of human beings, there can be no theory of psychotherapy. What is suggested here is that the inherent theories of human beings found within one particular approach to psychotherapy may be enhanced by the possibility that further aspects of theories of human beings inherent in other approaches could be embraced without inevitable contradiction. These aspects then widen our theory of human beings as well as our resultant therapeutic perspective. Inclusion rather than exclusion becomes more prevalent.

A 'parental' or overarching theory of human beings could, for example, maintain that people have choice, freedom, responsibility and the potential for self-actualization. From all of these beliefs, existential/humanistic approaches to counselling and psychotherapy will evolve and revolve around.

Another overarching theory may be that human beings are the product of their conditioning and can be programmed to behave in certain ways. From this behavioural parental belief system, approaches which emphasize developing new behaviour through, for example, a regime of planned goals and rewards for specific pieces of behaviour may evolve.

A third overarching theory may hypothesize that people are driven by internal, often unconscious, forces which may be in conflict, and that behaviour is largely the result of how a person manages or finds a compromise for those inner conflicts. This would be aligned with psychodynamic theories.

These three 'parental' theories of human beings have given rise to the three major schools of psychotherapy mentioned in the history chapter, i.e. the humanistic/existential, the behavioural and the psychodynamic. The framework strategy maintains that any theories of psychotherapy or counselling that hold one of these parental theories of human beings to be true can in many respects be integrated one with the other. Thus, on a theoretical level, holding a belief in choice, freedom, responsibility and self-actualizing potential, various aspects of transactional analysis, Gestalt, focusing or person-centred approaches can be discussed integratively and combined into a wider and/or different development of psychotherapeutic theory and influence how we conceptualize our work with clients. The same is true of those approaches under the other two overarching theories.

But it is also true that there are approaches to counselling and psychotherapy, some of which we have already mentioned, which cross from one of the three theoretical schools to another, or even include all three. Are they breaking the rules of integration that we are putting forward here? We think not. If examined closely, it can be seen that these integrative approaches are working under modified, overarching theories of human beings. They are not restricted by theories making an either/or distinction along the above lines but are rather more inclusive in their belief structure to allow for integration across the schools. Transactional analysis, although usually classified under the humanistic umbrella, is in itself an example of integration across the schools. Its theory certainly includes humanistic philosophy in its emphasis on people being born OK and aspiring to self-fulfilment, but it also embraces behavioural theory in its 'stroke theory' (Berne, 1972) whereby people adapt their behaviour in response to others, as well as psychodynamic/object relations theory in its assertion that people internalize significant others (objects and part objects). Thus, the overarching theory of TA is inclusive of beliefs that human beings are self-actualizing *and* open to conditioning *and* introject from the environment in the process of development. With these particular overarching beliefs in human beings, there is no contradiction in the theories of TA. Indeed, the very inclusivity of its beliefs is what makes for the compatibility (and flexibility) of the various theoretical aspects of transactional analysis and allows for ease of communication with other approaches from whichever school.

Here is an absurd example simply to make the point. If our overarching theory of human beings purports the notions that people are programmed by alien creatures from another planet, that they energize themselves by ultraviolet light and that they need laughter more than anything else in order to develop psychological equilibrium, so our psychotherapy (if it would still be called that) theory would evolve to include concepts of how and why alien creatures are programming people, whether this is a good thing or a bad thing and, if the former, how to enhance it, and, if the latter, how to resist such programming. It would also have a theory of the metabolization of ultraviolet into human energy and draw upon this theory in its practice (outdoor therapy in sunny climates, lamp therapy in Britain?) and so with a theory of laughter, how and why it works to provide psychological equilibrium and how it may be used in therapeutic practice to this end. (This is not so far-fetched. We have already referred to research on the effects of laughter in Chapter 2.) Thus our psychotherapy theory evolves, integrating as it might from any other existing schools which hold similar theories of human beings.

It will be noted in earlier examples, as well as in this absurd one, that alongside the development of a theory of psychotherapy from an overarching theory of human beings, practical interventions are concomitantly evolved. In other words, a technical integration automatically follows from a theoretical integration. If we believe that human beings hold internal 'conversations' and our psychotherapy theory conceptualizes these, for example, as on the one hand, the voice of a restrictive parent and, on the other, the voice of a younger part of the self and that the conversation is a replay of childhood interactions now internalized (to which several different approaches would subscribe), then it would follow that a practical intervention into this dynamic might be to invite the client to talk aloud with these two 'voices', to externalize the conversations, in order to bring about some change in the intrapsychic impasse.

However, there may be an argument for using such a 'voice dialogue' technique which is not rooted in our framework strategy of theoretical integration. We may not hold with the notion that people internalize early relationships, and yet still efficaciously use such a technique with our clients, for example, to resolve a current dilemma. This brings us to the second level of integration.

The procedural strategy

This second strategy involves the integration of 'concretely specific operating procedures' (Mahrer, 1989: 75), in other words, what therapists actually do and say with clients in order to attain some change, reinforcement or response. This may include how the roles of therapist and client are described, how a client is invited to focus her attention, how the expression of emotions is encouraged, whether and how a change in behaviour is suggested, how the therapist–client relationship is used, and so on. Thus, at this level of integration, a specific working procedure from another counselling or psychotherapeutic approach may be borrowed. This could be any other approach, even one which does not fit the therapist's theory of human beings, as these operating procedures are independent of any particular theory of counselling or psychotherapy and its overarching theory of human beings. For example, a psychodynamic therapist may choose to use a relaxation technique drawn from behaviour therapy without necessarily any reference to the overarching theory maintained by behaviourism. Equally, a person-centred therapist may choose on a particular occasion to assist a client in dream analysis. She may borrow from a Freudian approach using the procedure of free association or interpret the symbolism in more Jungian terminology or she may draw on the Gestalt technique of inviting her client to be, in turn, the various aspects of the dream and speak as those aspects, without necessarily adopting the theory of these three approaches.

These procedural strategies, or operating procedures, are different from therapeutic stratagems which are components of a theory of psychotherapy. As Mahrer points out: 'Just about everything the therapist does can be included in some larger therapeutic stratagem. At that level, we can describe what the therapist is doing now as relaxation training, and, later, the therapist is doing cognitive problem solving' (1989: 76). We can describe this as the therapeutic stratagem which belongs to a therapist's integrative framework. However, the procedural strategy refers to what is going on at the most basic level of interaction between therapist and client and involves the implication of a sense of direction in what the client is to do or say next. As in the above example of dream analysis which is the therapeutic stratagem, the procedural strategy is dependent on the therapist's knowledge of what to do – free association, interpretation of symbols, 'being' the dream. The direction for the client is dependent upon instruction from the therapist. Thus procedural strategies are what the therapist carries out within the sessions.

Of course, the therapist will have some therapeutic strategy in mind when employing a procedural strategy. Hopefully, she will not be applying operating procedures just for the sake of it. However, her therapeutic strategy will inevitably be determined by her framework strategy for theoretical integration while her procedural strategy need not have any origin within, or connection to, her theoretical base. It can be borrowed from any approach.

Let us suppose that the therapist subscribes to the theory that human beings, when adults, continue to be influenced by experiences which happened in childhood and has evolved a psychotherapeutic theory which maintains that childhood experiences are still 'stored' within the adult person. She may integrate theoretical concepts from various approaches in support of her overarching theory. From this integrative base she may evolve a therapeutic strategy which calls for the re-experiencing and working through of these childhood experiences in therapy in order to prevent, or at least lessen, their influence in the present. Up to this point, she is working within her integrative framework strategy. What she now does within the session in order to facilitate the client in re-experiencing childhood experiences, her procedural strategy, is not necessarily confined to any of the approaches which inform her integrative theory. She may invite the client to 'journey back' through guided fantasy; she may 'set up a childhood scene' with cushions to represent the influential members of the family and suggest the client imagines himself at 5 years old back in the scene, she may simply say 'Tell me about what happened' or 'Let yourself express your anger with your father'; or invite the client to draw the incident(s). She may point out that the client is expressing anger towards her, the therapist, that may be more usefully seen as belonging to mother or may allow, even encourage, the client's anger to be expressed towards her without interpreting the transference phenomenon. In a group, she may direct a psychodramatic reconstruction of the family, or 'sculpt' the family, or provide a totally different experience within the group to counterbalance the client's original experience. The possibilities are many.

These procedural strategies are inevitably dependent on the practitioner's training and experience and can be increased ad infinitum. Mahrer (1989) emphasizes the importance of seeing other practitioners at work and studying tape or video transcripts in order to widen our repertoire of such procedures. Therapists tend, certainly in the course of training, to have experience of personal therapy with therapists from the approaches they are studying and to learn operating procedures that may be more associated with these particular approaches. Experience of personal therapy with therapists of different approaches not only widens theoretical understanding but provides a rich source of procedures which may be usefully employed at this level.

Basically, we believe that the two strategies can be used at the same time. Integration starts with a set of beliefs and assumptions about human beings. This leads to the development of a personal theory or theories which will explain human functioning and suggest a possibility for intervention. These theories will tend to have a bias according to the held assumptions about human beings and perhaps also inevitably according to the therapist's personal experience and proclivities. Out of the theories is developed a set of techniques or operations. Many techniques borrowed from a large variety of other theories may be integratable even if the theories cannot be.

These groups of integrable theories, under their overarching assumption concerning human beings, will tend to have a bias that produces the integrating framework within which a therapeutic model may be developed. For instance, some theories focus on pathology and dysfunction and an integrating framework may be one that provides an explanation for the development of the dysfunction and its maintenance. An example of this is the Comparative Script System (see Chapter 9) which describes human dysfunction in terms of a self-reinforcing pattern by which an original event has meaning made of it by an individual who forms a set of beliefs about himself, others and the world. As a result of his beliefs, he develops patterns of thinking and feeling in response to a similar event and then exhibits behaviour which is likely to bring about a similar outcome to that of the original event. Theories which fit into this framework would be the repetition compulsion, game theory from TA, some aspects of conditioning theory and of cognitive-behavioural theory, and so on. Techniques that can be used with a model developed within this framework could come from a whole variety of approaches: for instance, analytic approaches for the achievement of insight into the original experience; Gestalt techniques for heightening awareness of how present-day thinking and feeling may reinforce past beliefs; behavioural techniques for changing outcome, and so on.

Other theories focus on human beings as potentially self-actualizing. They might use models of healthy functioning such as the Gestalt cycle of experience or Erskine's (1975) model of human functioning. Theories which share this belief in self-actualizing, such as Berne's theory of aspiration, Carl Rogers's theory of the fully functioning human being, the Gestalt theory of awareness, may be usefully integrated at the theoretical level.

Other theories of human beings and their concomitant therapeutic approaches may focus on child developmental stages or on object relations, on theories about how change occurs or on learning theories.

Much research evidence has shown that different therapies produce comparable therapeutic gains (Luborsky et al., 1975; Shapiro and Firth, 1987; Smith and Glass, 1977) and that the strength and supportiveness of the therapeutic alliance is actually a key factor in change (Horvath and Greenberg, 1994; Marmar et al., 1989). Greenson (1965) differentiates between the real relationship and the working alliance, while Gelso and Carter (1985) have identified three aspects to the coun-selling relationship – the working alliance, the person-to-person and the transferential relationship. Clarkson (1995) adds two more strands to the relationship, that of the reparative relationship and the transpersonal.

Using the therapeutic relationship as an integrating framework (see Chapter 7), we can incorporate the work of Bordin, Luborsky, Horvath and Greenberg among others to understand the importance of the working alliance; psychodynamic theories to understand the transferential relationship; theories from Kohut and self-psychology and the cathexis school in transactional analysis to illuminate the reparative relationship; Carl Rogers, Buber and Hycner to understand the person-to-person relationship; and Jung and psychosynthesis for the transpersonal.

Examples of existing models which use the procedural strategy are Beutler's systematic eclectic psychotherapy (Beutler, in Norcross, 1986) and Lazarus's multimodel therapy. We have devoted a later chapter to Lazarus's BASIC ID where Behaviour, Affect, Sensation, Imagery, Cognition, Interpersonal, Drugs/Biology represent the 'fundamental vectors of human personality' (Lazarus, 1981). The client is assessed descriptively in each mode and a treatment plan is formulated which may incorporate techniques from a wide range of approaches. Both of these procedural models emphasize the importance of the systematic selection of techniques or procedures in their work. Lazarus makes it clear that he subscribes mainly to a social and cognitive learning theory and that 'the efficacy of any technique from free association to behaviour shaping will be accounted for in social learning theory terms' (Lazarus in Norcross and Goldfried, 1992: 232). He sees eclecticism (what we are calling here a 'procedural strategy of integration') as neither haphazard nor subjective but resting on the practical application of psycho-logical science. For this reason, we maintain the use of the term 'integration'.

Even at this procedural level, we see integration as the coming together of parts into a whole and suggest that the selection of procedures rests within a conceptualization of wholeness (of the person and the approach) and its concomitant theoretical underpinning. Random interventions which do not take into account the needs of the client (in other words, therapist-centred interventions) or stem from a considered rationale are likely to be counter-therapeutic. This is not to suggest that intuitive or experimental interventions have no place. Many senior practitioners would admit to such occasions. However, in the case of intuition being used, this is grounded within the field of the practitioner's expertise and theoretical understanding and, in the case of experimentation, the experiment is negotiated, worked out and conceptualized with the client within the wholeness of their work together. The intention of the experiment may be exploratory with no specific outcome in mind. Even so, the exploration is in itself the rationale for the experiment. These same practitioners would also be able to contextualize their interventions, however 'spontaneous' they may seem, within specific diagnostic and treatment considerations. We hope this considered selectivity is reflected in Chapter 8 on multimodal therapy.

In this chapter, we have endeavoured to present two levels of integration and to demonstrate that there is no one way of integrating. In effect, there will be as many integrative possibilities as there are therapists. Much will depend upon the therapist as a person, as a professional, their base model training, their wider training and experience, their practice with a variety of clients, the influence of their own experience of being a client and being supervised and their values and beliefs about life and existence.

In the final chapter, we have included some thoughts on the development of the integrative practitioner. We thought it might be useful at this point to consider what qualities characterize an effective, integrating therapist. Whether in training or post-qualification, we believe that an integrating practitioner possesses the following:

1 A willingness to read and study across a range of therapeutic approaches and to keep abreast of current thinking and research in the field of counselling and psychotherapy.
2 An openness to receiving supervision from differently schooled supervisors in addition to having a regular supervisor who can monitor your development and countertransferential issues over time.
3 Similarly, after an initial and in-depth experience as a client with a counsellor or psychotherapist, to explore and experience being a client with practitioners from other orientations.
4 To hold in mind the shared venture of all psychotherapists and counsellors to help people heal rather than take a 'mine is better than yours' attitude, and to maintain a spirit of co-operation rather than competition.
5 To be able to welcome and learn from new experiences with clients so that we are willing to alter our methods rather than fit our clients into our style of work while at the same time keeping a core central theme of understanding of each specific client's needs.

In Part II, we endeavour to illustrate the process of developing a personal, integrative approach starting with identifying our own theory of human beings. However, before we move on to constructing this integrative framework, we invite you to think about this question for yourselves and to consider what aspects of your overarching theory of human beings influence your theory and practice of psychotherapy or counselling. Elton Wilson (1993) offers the following helpful questions which we invite you to think about and answer before you proceed:

1   What do most people search for in their lives?
2   How is 'personality' formed and how can children be helped to develop healthy personalities?
3   How does human unhappiness lead to problematic behaviour?
4   How can the counsellor help the client towards making effective changes?

You will notice, in answering these questions, that you are influenced by your personal experience, by other people who impressed you, by your culture, your religion, by any number of your experiences. We invite you to begin integrating this material in order to provide a synthesis of what is true for you at this point in time.

Part II
AN EXERCISE IN INTEGRATION

4

Developing a Theory of Human Beings

Our intention in this section is to offer an illustration of how an integrative framework may be developed by working through the stages we have outlined as essential in this process. We will start by giving some of our answers to Elton Wilson's questions posed at the end of the previous chapter which will assist us in the first stage of the integrating process, that of articulating our theory of human beings.

What do most people search for?

Our view is that people primarily seek to have their *basic physical needs* met. These include finding adequate sustenance, shelter and safety. Where such basic requirements of existence are lacking, clearly human energy and endeavour are unlikely to be devoted to what might be seen as 'higher things'. It is only when satisfaction of these physical needs is met that an individual can find fulfilment in other areas of their lives. These basic survival needs are inseparable from the innate need to establish a close affectual bond with a primary caretaker who is likely to be the one who supplies the essential nurturing. However, provision of basic physical care alone is not enough. The infant also needs to experience an emotional and physical connection which becomes the basis not only for his capacity to nurture himself but also for his template of loving and being loved. As the infant develops, further physiological appetites emerge. These lead to the seeking of sensory fulfilment in terms of touch, stimulation, sexual satisfaction and physical self-expression.

Human beings are social creatures and as such have basic *social/relationship needs*. We seek to belong to a 'tribe' which can offer us emotional and psychological security in addition to physical safety. We are relational beings who need contact, recognition, acceptance and companionship from others. Furthermore, from the mother–child bond through to later adult relationships we seek closeness, love and intimacy: 'People need other people. Developed and nourished inside a mother for nine months, we are born needing and seeking contact. All through our lives, in one way or another, this need and this search continues' (Lapworth et al., 1993).

Human beings seek temporal and environmental *structure* in their lives. This gives a sense of control in the enormity of time and space. All cultures create annual rituals or celebrations to mark out the passing of time and the hope of times to come. This also applies to smaller and larger time frames. Daily and weekly routines and 'lists' give a sense of security and continuity. Within these needs we also seek to feel fulfilled as regards how we choose to spend our life's time. Work, creativity and play are important aspects of structuring time through which we gain a sense of achievement and purpose.

Environmental structure means the way in which human beings organize their physical surroundings: their homes and gardens, their places of work, their towns and cities and their landscape. All these aspects of structuring the environment answer the human needs for control and order, for security and familiarity, for creativity and a sense of place.

People seek to find ways of feeling good about themselves which can be described as being happy, contented, satisfied and self-fulfilled. These could be viewed as *self-esteem needs*. Coopersmith (1967) says that people develop their base level self-esteem in early childhood according to four factors: significance, competence, virtue and power. Significance refers to how we think we are loved and approved of by those people who are of importance to us. How we perform actions which matter to us will determine our competence concept. In this context of self-esteem, virtue refers to how our actions compare to our aspirations with regards to our chosen moral and ethical standards. Power is part of self-esteem in that it reflects the extent to which we can control our environment and influence our own behaviour and that of others. The higher we rate in all these areas and the nearer we come to fulfilling our potential, the higher our self-esteem.

People seek both stimulation and rest throughout their lives. Each of us has a temperamentally different need quotient in this area. *Stimulus need* is met by the excitement we feel on the physical, sexual, emotional, mental or spiritual levels of our lives in response to events, relationships, challenges and pleasures. Stimulation is also linked to our creativity. We seek rest by withdrawal from social stimulation. Rest may be achieved in sleep, in meditation or even through music. For some people, the soothing effects of rest are achieved through a hobby which engages their attention and distracts them from the demands of a pressurized life. This need for both excitement and peace is reflected in the cycle of creativity and rest which is seen in the healthy child.

All of us at some stage in our lives (having in some ways answered the questions: Who am I? Who are you/they?) seek to address the question – What am I doing here? We need to find *meaning* in our existence. Some people find this meaning in the shared values of community; others seek for a more personal meaning in their lives. One person's meaning may be in their act of parenting. For another it might be in being a stockbroker or gardener. For yet another it might be in their volunteer work in areas of crisis, famine or war. Making sense of our existence is, at some level, a fundamental quest. At some stage, at a more existential level, we need to expand these three questions in order to address them from a standpoint of shared humanity: who are *we*, what are *we* doing here and what do we need to do about it?

Having given some answers to Elton Wilson's question 'What do most people search for?', we, the authors, recognize that it is important to ask ourselves, 'How do human beings experience and attempt to fulfil these needs?' As has become clear in some of our answers, we realize that these needs and their fulfilment (or failure to do so) are revealed in people's thoughts, feelings, bodily affective states and behaviour in relation to themselves, other people and the world. All these, therefore, will need to be considered as part of our integrative framework for psychotherapy.

How is 'personality' formed and how can children be helped to develop healthy personalities?

We believe that infants have from birth and probably from conception their own particular temperaments. Some babies are naturally quiet and 'contented'; they express themselves and draw attention to their needs when they arise but seem flexible and adaptable to their circumstances and are very easily satisfied when their environment meets their needs. They sleep a lot and seem not to be unduly disturbed by changes in their environment. Other babies need less sleep, are more alert to their environment and seem constantly to be seeking stimulation. Yet others are very easily unsettled, express their discomforts vociferously and are more difficult to soothe, and so on. Of course it is impossible to rule out the effects of interuterine and birth experiences on the baby where his/her visceral relationship with the world may already have shaped this temperament. However, these sorts of natural differences seem to occur regardless of perinatal factors and thus, in the context of nature versus nurture, human beings seem to be born with a natural seed of personality. We believe that personality is then shaped by a combination of the child's innate temperament, his natural drives and hungers, and the interplay between himself and the way the environment responds to him. This includes the very early self–other bond of the baby and his primary caretaker – the nature of which is likely to influence a person's sense of self and relationships for the rest of their lives.

Human beings create meaning from their experiences. Depending on early experiences and treatment at the hands of caretakers, human beings make lasting assumptions (somatic, emotional and cognitive) about themselves, others, the world and their role in the world. These assumptions and attitudes lead to patterns of functioning that become habits of the future. Such patterns can be useful and productive or limiting and dysfunctional. The young child, long before she has the full capacity to think for herself, makes a bodily affective relationship with the world, gathers information and draws conclusions which form the foundation of her later patterns of relating to the world. We find Bollas's (1987) term 'the unthought known' a very powerful encapsulation of this early formation of the self.

Few of our 'conclusions' are actually conscious, and the phrase conveys the collections of sensations, affects, imagery and perceptions which make up these early 'decisions' or 'organizing principles' (Stolorow et al., 1994).

There are many ways in which experiences shape personality. An infant who was neglected and abused may well develop a self who expects the world to be a hostile or lonely place. A child who was praised for quiet industry and punished for noisy ebullience may in all likelihood become a quiet, reserved, hardworking adult.

Another dynamic in shaping a child's personality is created by the natural drives and hungers which we have described in answer to Elton Wilson's first question. They include the propensity to grow, to express themselves, to love and be loved, to fight and compete, to explore and create and destroy, to feel and think for themselves, and to manage their lives. If the people in the child's environment respond to her needs and help her to express, understand and manage her feelings, she can grow to adulthood, healthy and capable of interdependence with others rather than being overly dependent or independent. In order to satisfy their basic human hungers for survival, relationship and achievement, people, especially during the vulnerable stages of infancy and childhood, will, through the process of positive and negative reinforcement, be conditioned to conform to the wishes, needs and hungers of those around them.

Human beings, through the entire course of their life's time, will be involved in the challenges that each stage demands of them. If previous stages are distorted or under-resourced, the present stage in which the person is living may be adversely affected. Even in adulthood we continue to be influenced and shaped by our innate temperament, our natural drives and hungers, our environments and our experience at previous stages. Human beings grow, change, develop or adapt in order to survive.

Clearly, our answer to this question has brought into focus our belief in the importance of time including the stages, over time, in a person's life and also the effect of past experience on the present. This means that our integrative framework will need to encompass a temporal dimension.

How does human unhappiness lead to problematic behaviour?

When the environment wittingly or unwittingly encourages a child to give up part of himself in order to adapt to it, some of the child's needs are left unaddressed. Unconsciously, he adopts a personality which will ensure his survival and acceptance in the family (or other setting) and abandons the part of him which seeks fulfilment. Henceforth, he may believe that he is living his life to the full, but he will carry his unresolved needs in the form of some manifestation of unhappiness. This may be depression, anxiety, nameless worry, rigidity, and so forth. Thus the person is left with conflict: part of them, albeit an unconscious part, seeking completion and the other part 'knowing' how life must be – the way it has always been. He then seems doomed to try again and again to resolve the conflict, seeking situations which offer the possibility of resolution but which somehow turn out to be repetitions of the original failure. While in his conscious mind he may believe, for instance, that it is possible to be loved, his unconscious 'unthought known' (Bollas, 1987) could be that he is fundamentally unlovable. Again and again he reaches out to someone unobtainable or unloving so that in the end his need is still unmet. At the same time, he has confirmed his beliefs about the world and kept his experience of life constant. Although this makes him unhappy, it has the effect of providing the reassurance that comes from the familiar.

As we said earlier, some of our natural feelings are neither positive nor creative. They can be envious or destructive. If these are acted upon without the mediation of thought, they can lead to problematic behaviour. Similarly, if children are repeatedly exposed to violent and destructive 'models' (parents, family members, and so on) they are more likely to build their self-esteem on aggressive features than will a peer who has had assertive and co-operative behaviours modelled for him. Again, we emphasize in our answer our tendency to repeat patterns from the past.

How can the counsellor/therapist help the client towards making effective changes?

We have described at some length the generic elements which may facilitate a client's change in Chapter 2. Shmukler (1999) condenses these elements into five main factors that research has indicated as effective in therapeutic change. They can be summarized as follows:

1 The client believes that therapy will help.
2 The establishment of a strong working alliance.
3 The client receives (either directly or indirectly) clear feedback on their view of themselves and the world.
4 There are corrective experiences and the opportunity to experiment with new ways of behaving.
5 There is opportunity for reality testing inside and outside the consulting room.

These factors shape our view of the therapist's role. It is important for the therapist to understand that 'problematic behaviours' are survival behaviours in the client's frame of reference and as such not easily relinquished without safe ones being adopted in their place. This means that the therapist needs to meet her client without pre- or present judgement, but with what Rogers (1957) calls unconditional positive regard.

The therapist can be of help to the client in her search for effective change by being involved without being over-invested. The strength of a therapist's efficacy lies in his ability to be empathically attuned to his client while retaining a degree of neutrality such that they are separate. We have talked about how a person is shaped by their environment from birth and perhaps before, and we have described how this shaping can lead to a person's denial of parts of themselves. A therapist must be willing to meet and understand both the person who is before them and the hidden one who as yet has not been allowed to be integrated or expressed. In acknowledging and valuing the thoughts, feelings and behaviours of his client, the therapist invites the client to respect and value her own thoughts, feelings and behaviours. In helping her voice the unvoiced and in helping her name and understand the 'unthought knowns', the therapist assists the client to integrate all the aspects of herself, to acknowledge her unmet needs and to find ways of living her life more effectively, unrestricted by past experience. In addition, the therapist attempts to provide opportunities for the client to experiment with new ways of being both within and outside the consulting room.

Having answered Elton Wilson's questions, we are now in a position to start to construct a framework which will allow us to integrate theories and techniques in a way which we trust will be therapeutic for a client. Before we do so, however, we are aware that we hold some additional assumptions about human beings which will powerfully influence our approach.

One is that mature human beings, within the existential and to some extent environmental limitations of their lives, are responsible for much of what happens to them. Furthermore, they make choices about how they think and how they live; they choose their responses to dilemmas and they have responsibility towards themselves, others and the world.

Another is that people have the capacity and tendency to actualize themselves and, given the right conditions, will naturally seek to fulfil their potential in the areas described in answer to the first question. Third, and partly arising from the first two, we believe that change is possible. A belief in self-responsibility, in the tendency towards growth and the possibility of change are the hallmarks of the humanistic tradition and we are aware that while we draw upon psychodynamic and cognitive behavioural theories in our work, we do so from a philosophically humanistic standpoint.

In the next chapter, we show the development of our integrative framework based upon the theory of human beings we have outlined so far.

5
Developing an Integrative Framework

In this chapter we endeavour to demonstrate how an integrative framework can grow out of a therapist's identified philosophy and beliefs about human experience. We do this by creating a framework based on the answers we gave to the questions posed in the previous chapter. We start with an overview of this emerging framework that is encapsulated in Figure 5.3 (p. 46) which shows the composite factors we have identified as fundamental to the therapeutic experience. We then describe the different elements of the framework in more detail, including examples of some theories that we find useful in addressing each aspect. In each section, the theoretical discussion is followed by suggestions for procedural strategies.

Overview

At the centre of all experience we place the self. Within this framework, the self is defined as the individual and unique essence of the human being, the consciousness he has of his being and identity. We subscribe to the self psychologists' (Kohut, 1971) view of the self as the part of the personality that is cohesive in space, enduring in time, the centre of initiative and the recipient of impressions.

In answering the first of Elton Wilson's questions, we have identified various needs that a person seeks to satisfy. These needs of the self can be summarized as:

- Physical survival.
- Social/relationship.
- Structure.
- Self-esteem.
- Stimulation/rest.
- Meaning.

These then will be at the core of the framework. It is the fulfilment of these self needs (or aspects of them, depending upon what the client presents) which, through counselling or psychotherapy, the practitioner is seeking to facilitate.

These needs are experienced and expressed through various aspects of the self. These are the different facets of the person's experience such as her thinking, her bodily states, her feelings, and so on which form her patterns of relating to herself and to the world. Each aspect can be the focus of a therapist's work and, indeed, change or growth in any of the aspects will affect the others. However, a human being is more than the sum of its parts: integration must start here. It is therefore important that therapists consider all these areas in their approach to their clients. Consequently, our second step in developing a framework is to use these aspects to identify five areas of the self experience which will structure part of the therapist's assessment, clinical thinking and choice of intervention.

The five interrelating aspects of self experience we have identified are *Physiological, Behavioural, Affective, Cognitive* and what we broadly call *Spiritual*. These five aspects of the person, and the needs which are experienced and expressed via these aspects, can be diagrammed around the self and self needs as in Figure 5.1.

Figure 5.1 **The integrating pentagon**

As will be evident in how we explain the formation of human personality and the causes of problematic behaviour, we have a strong belief in the influence of past experiences on present functioning. Consequently, our framework needs to include some focus on the temporal dimension of experience. In order to represent this dimension, we place the pentagon in a diamond representing the past, the present and the potential future as in Figure 5.2.

In choosing the temporal representation we have borrowed from the work of Elton Wilson (1999). She starts with Menninger's (1958) 'triangle of insight' which describes the connection between past relationships (*back then*) and present relationships both within (*in here*) and outside (*out there*) the therapy room to link past and present. To this she adds the future dimension (*in view*), adding a fourth point to the triangle and integrating such solution-focused ideas as the recognition of ignored strengths in order to increase options and the identification of 'possible futures'. In our diagram, a diamond shape illustrates how the field of work is widest in the present. This represents our belief that – to paraphrase Berne (1966) – we can heal the past in the present in order to assure the future (Figure 5.2).

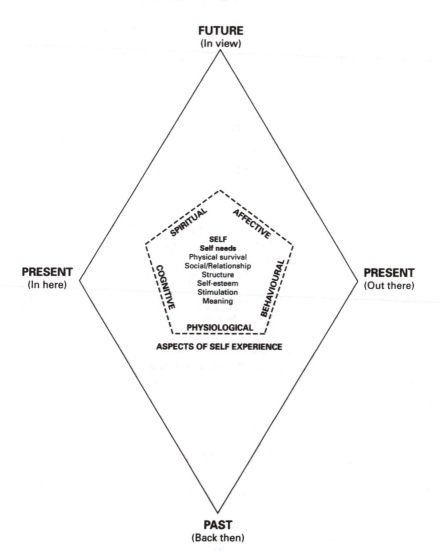

Figure 5.2 **The time frame**

In the area delineated by the temporal frame, we have added the words *Relationship* and *Context*. This underlines two vital elements which affect our approach both to choosing psychotherapy theories and also practice method. We believe that a human being, from his first moments of life, defines himself and is defined in relationship with others, that his identity is reinforced in relationship and that it is in relationship in the present that he can explore, understand or change that identity. We also believe that the context (environmental, social, cultural, racial) within which a person lives and within which the therapy takes place is a fundamental part of the story and any understanding of a person's identity and their options must take place within an awareness of that context (Figure 5.3).

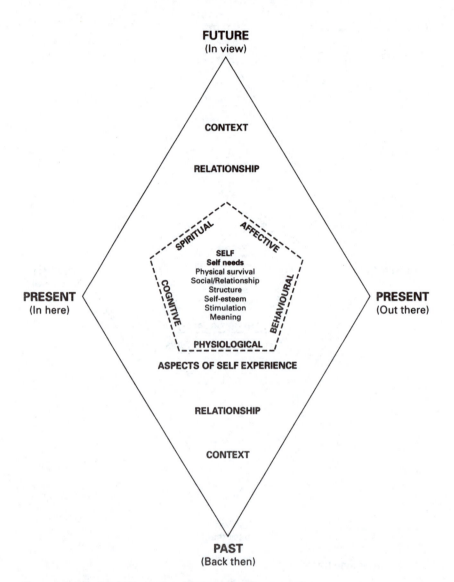

Figure 5.3 **The Multidimensional Integrative Framework**

So far, we have created an integrating framework that contains the elements which we have identified as relevant to the practice of therapy as evolved from our theory of human beings. We refer to this as the *Multidimensional Integrative Framework*. It is a visual map of the complex variables which comprise any person – the individual seeking therapy and the therapist themselves. These variables are inextricably interconnected and any effort to describe them separately results in the loss of the interconnections which are vital to any understanding of the parts as well as the whole. Gradually, over time, the therapist and client construct a complex understanding of the client's world. This 'picture' will be made up of the various pieces of the puzzle which the client has been presenting. Just as the client will have areas of strength and vulnerability, for example, a need to analyse and to avoid emotions, the therapist will also have a certain strength of style and some deficits. A therapist may be skilled at conceptualization and the analysis of negative beliefs but unobservant of physiological phenomena. We would not expect a therapist to be expert in all areas. However, we do believe that it is our responsibility as therapists to pay attention to the client's state in relation to all these facets and their related needs.

Having described an overview of the Multidimensional Integrative Framework, we will now focus more fully on each of its aspects, starting from the centre and working outwards. Part of our task will be to identify theories and procedures which may be useful in assisting us to work therapeutically via the five facets of the self, within relationship and context, addressing past, present and future influences and aspirations to achieve the self needs of our clients.

The Self

At the very centre of our diagram we place the self, seeing it as the essence of the human being and her consciousness of experience, cohesive and continuous in time and space. In order not only to survive but also to flourish, this essential self continuously refers to relevant, previously integrated information from within itself while also being in the process of integrating any new information or experience. This constant, dual process of self-experience and self-reflection enables individual human beings to develop throughout their lives. The purpose of counselling and psychotherapy is to assist clients in reassessing how they experience their past and present lives such that they can resolve internal conflicts, let go of noxious patterns and recognize and incorporate the nourishing.

There are many theories of the self which may assist the work of psychotherapists or counsellors. Freud postulates a sense of wholeness of self when he includes within his definition of self, the ego, id and superego. Likewise, Jung (1971) sees at least one sense of self as being a totality of the ego and the archetypes. Masterson implies wholeness when he writes of 'the sum total of self representations in intimate connection with the sum total of object relations' (1985: 15) and Gestalt theory emphasizes wholeness both of experience and of self, seeing self as both process and enduring identity with 'consistent personality, enduring characteristics, habitual styles of contact, learned self functions and self organisation' (Mckewn, 1997: 76). Thus emerges an implied concept of cohesion when talking of the self. Sometimes, it is the lack of a sense of cohesion, even a sense of disintegration, which brings clients to therapy. They want to experience themselves as whole again – or whole for the first time. In our view, the task of the therapist will be to help such clients by sustained empathic enquiry and introspection (Stolorow et al., 1987), to recognize and reclaim repressed or split off (disowned or disassociated) parts of the self or divided parts of the self as described by Winnicott (1965) as true and false self organization. These may be addressed within any or all of the aspects of the framework which we will later describe.

Self needs

The six self needs of *physical survival, relationship, structure, self-esteem, stimulation/rest* and *meaning* have been described at the beginning of this chapter. Each of these needs will be part of each human developmental stage. It is the task of the therapist to help the client where there has been insufficient fulfilment of these needs at whatever developmental stage. Arguably, the further back in time the deficit, the greater will be the instability of personality structure in the present and the greater the need of the therapist's understanding of the reparative needs of the client.

Many approaches directly address these self needs which to some extent are based upon Maslow's (1976) hierarchy of needs. Our framework provides for a wider perspective upon these central needs in addressing them through the various aspects of self experience, relationship and context within the temporal frame.

The pentagon of aspects of self experience

The five aspects of self experience that we have identified cannot, in fact, be separated. They are constantly interrelated. However, it can be useful to focus upon them individually and to examine the work of relevant theoreticians and practitioners in order to heighten our awareness of how these aspects contribute to the whole experience. In the following pages, we focus upon the five aspects in turn. In each one, we cite just a few of the important contributors in that particular field and explore some of the treatment strategies that may apply.

Physiological aspects of self experience

The human body houses the intellect and affect and also expresses our behaviour. Thus, one of the major indicators of a person's experience is his physical body. Schore (2000) says that the body is the base of the mind. Clinicians need to be as alert to the physical clues their clients offer them as they are to the content of the conversation. This involves, among other things, attention to body structure, movement, posture, smell, and appearance. While, at an intuitive level, this takes place automatically as part of social intercourse, the therapist refines this ability to assist with such things as attunement, diagnosis, treatment planning, monitoring, and so on.

As with each of these facets, differing emphasis will be placed upon them according to the therapist's own experience, training and personal therapy. In this physiological domain, some practitioners find it useful to use the ideas of leading body workers to further inform their work as therapists.

The Austrian psychologist, Wilhelm Reich (1897–1957), as part of his system of character analysis, speaks of muscular armouring or body armour. This gives useful information which can be used in the analysis, diagnosis and treatment of clients. Reich used the term 'muscular armour' to portray the chronic tightness of human muscles caused by the repression of emotions. These can affect any of the muscles of the human body including the voice box and eye muscles. Such muscular armouring leads to what Reich terms 'character armour'. This character armouring prevents the organism from achieving its natural potential and also from remaining vital and available to environmental stimulus. Reich and later his pupil Lowen (1976) divide human physical types into five character structures: the psychopathic, masochistic, oral, schizoid and rigid.

The psychopathic character structure

The physical characteristics of the psychopathic character structure are manifested in two possible ways. In the overbearing type, their power will be observable from the waist upwards so that most of the strength and movement comes from the top half of the body which is disproportionate to that evidenced in the lower half of the body – these individuals will look top-heavy.

The other type of psychopathic character structure, called the seductive or undermining type by Lowen, demonstrates more evenly distributed body mass but a disproportionate amount of energy flows in the pelvic region. Both types have in common the lack of free flow of connective energy between their upper and lower bodies and may have a fairly rigid observable aspect to their jaw and eye areas. The denial of feelings is one of the major symptoms of the psychopathic attitude.

The masochistic character structure

The masochistic attitude is one of external submission and internal superiority. This seemingly contradictory condition creates a tension in the energy flow such that it causes stagnation. The effect of this is a sense of holding back and tucking in manifested in a submissive posture which serves to contain a highly charged internal sense of being. Their bodies are usually thick set and muscular and are seen to have a greater density of body hair than in the other structures. As a result of their intense 'holding in' they have limited aggression and this is often replaced by complaining or pleasing.

The oral character structure

This structure is one of neediness which may be masked by a forced sense of independence. These people can be recognized by their 'wobbliness'. They may seem like young foals with most of their strength observable in their heads and trunks and less in their legs and arms. There is often a childlike appearance in the body structure of these individuals and this delayed maturity gives the impression of a need to lean on or cling to others. They might often present with a sense of inner emptiness and mood swings.

The schizoid character structure

The schizoid character tends to show a narrow and contracted body. He dissociates from his feelings so that his thinking is inadequately, if at all, connected with his feelings or behaviour. He tends to withdraw from external reality and avoids meaningful relationships. His energy is blocked in the central regions of his body by holding muscular tension in the neck, hip, shoulder and pelvic areas.

The rigid character structure

The rigid character will present like a palace guard – straight backed, head held high and a strong sense of purpose, that of protection. The rigid character is afraid of vulnerability and sees this as an admission of weakness. The apparent stubbornness and pride are a defence against being seen as submissive.

In his book *Character Styles*, Johnson (1994) draws upon the work of Reich and Lowen as an important aspect of his characterological-developmental theory which integrates this approach to character analysis with ego psychology, object relations and self psychology theories. He provides valuable insight into the development of such physiological and psychological structures under the pithy and empathically descriptive headings of 'The Hated Child', 'The Abandoned Child', 'The Owned Child', 'The Used Child', 'The Defeated Child', 'The Exploited Child' and 'The Disciplined Child' and includes physiological interventions and exercises in his therapeutic objectives for each character structure as well as those for the other, interrelated, self facets we have defined in our framework.

Physiological armouring seems to indicate very early patterns of psychological and emotional experience. The French obstetrician, Leboyer (1975), after studying the effects of Western birth techniques on infants, thought that the harsh, loud, cold and clinical methods used to bring babies into the world had the immediate effect on them of triggering their defensive reactions – aggression or withdrawal. On their very first day of life, their shock could be measured in the distortion that their muscle structure displayed. He gradually developed the Leboyer birthing method which entailed gentle methods of child birth. In follow-up studies (Rapoport, 1976) of the children born with his method, their body structure had not taken on defensive positions and there was less of a split between the muscles of one side of their bodies compared to the other. This resulted in a degree of ambidextrousness which was far higher than that shown by babies born in a more 'shocking' environment.

Some therapists may address such very early issues with 'rebirthing' techniques, physical holding, even bottle feeding their clients. Other therapists may be equally effective in providing a 'holding environment' within the emotional and psychological containment of the therapeutic relationship. One of our clients who was not held physically nor directly worked with physiologically at all, nevertheless described her therapy in very physical terms. She saw the success of her therapy and her working through of early childhood issues as due to 'being gently held while naked'.

The psychologist Dychtwald, in his book *Bodymind* (1986), lists five components that are influential in the development of the human bodymind: heredity, physical activity and exposure, emotional and psychological activity and exposure, nutrition, and finally environment.

1 The heredity aspect to our unique bodymind constellation involves all that we are given at conception in terms of our genetic make-up.

2   Physical activity includes every action that we have ever experienced. These actions influence our bodymind, some positively and others traumatically.

3   Emotional and psychological activity also affect our bodymind make-up, but are not as easily measurable as the first two components:

> Emotional stimulation of muscles can have the same effect on the body as purely physical activity, except that it is usually more difficult to detect the source of stimulation and the way in which it has been selectively, and often unconsciously, exercised. The body begins to form around the feelings that animate it, and the feelings, in turn, become habituated and trapped within the body tissue itself. The bodymind then, when seen from this perspective is to some extent the continually regenerating product of a lifetime of emotional encounters, psychological activities, and psychosomatic preferences. (Dychtwald, 1986: 22).

If a person has been brought up constantly to show a brave face, his unexpressed sadnesses and fears may well have an adverse affect on his health and body structure.

4   What we are fed, our nutritional history, especially as children, will have an effect on our structures.

5   Our environment comprises the process of all those outside influences upon us during our life's time.

Thus we can see the wide-ranging and interrelating facets that are included at this physiological level and some of the theoretical constructs that may influence our therapeutic focus and approach.

In terms of procedural strategies, as has been suggested, we may not address these physiological manifestations in a physical way but through the avenues of other facets of the self. This will vary from therapist to therapist though physical contact with clients is more likely at the humanistic end of the psychotherapy spectrum than at the psychodynamic end (which may seem a little odd considering Freud's tendency not only to touch his clients but to massage them in order to promote 'free association'). Our own procedural approach is, at times, to draw attention and awareness to breathing patterns and held body postures and to explore the associated feelings and thinking. We may suggest relaxation techniques to assist in 'letting go' of the muscular tension or invite experiment with alternative ways of using the body while sitting or walking. We sometimes have physical contact with our clients in terms of touch and holding. This is based upon our belief that therapy attempts to promote fulfilling human relationships and that sometimes offering touch is a natural human response. The withholding of touch may be retraumatizing to the client and reinforcing of negative beliefs. Indeed, recent research has identified (Schore, 1994) that neural pathways essential to the establishment of effective self-regulatory functions are created in the first 18 months of life and that physical touch is an intrinsic part of this process. The research indicates that a person who has not established these neural pathways early in life may be helped to create them by contact which includes touch.

Our assessment of the usefulness of physical touch needs to be finely gauged by consideration of the client's therapeutic need at any given time. Touch at certain points or stages may be counter-productive, even traumatizing, and prevent the client from fully experiencing, expressing and grieving the lack of physical or emotional holding within the early parent–child dyad. It is likely to be coming from the need of the therapist to 'make things better'. However, we believe that at certain stages of the therapeutic process judicious use of touch, with the agreement of the client, can be therapeutically reparative.

We think it is unfortunate that a climate of fear surrounds the issue of 'to touch or not to touch' our clients, brought about by findings against some practitioners who have abused the ethical boundaries of the therapeutic relationship. However, unless specifically trained in bodywork approaches, we do not consider it ethical, professional practice for therapists to employ hands-on bodywork techniques with their clients as such skills are outside the competency of the practitioner. Therapists may find it useful, therefore, to recommend that their clients consult a qualified body practitioner to help with relaxation, unlocking of body armoury, meeting contact needs, and so on. The therapist can then focus on other aspects of the therapeutic process and not become physically involved with their client in any way that is outside their professional ability and qualification.

Fundamentally, human beings, if fully aware of their physical needs, will find healthy ways of meeting them. Due to hereditary factors, artificial conditioning, deficits in the physical environment and lack of attunement with the other aspects of the self, one's physical health may become disturbed. Some illnesses are the body's adaptation to certain situations, as a way of remaining healthy. An example here is how the body sometimes produces common cold symptoms as a way of clearing the lungs of some of the results of living within a polluted environment. Therapists need to be alert to those physical dimensions of their clients which may indicate an organic problem that needs treatment by a conventional or comple-mentary practitioner in support of the therapy. It is good practice to ask any client bringing a physical symptom to the attention of the therapist to have it checked medically to ensure that there is not an organic origin for that symptom. This is the case even if it seems likely that the symptoms could be psychosomatic and due perhaps to depression or anxiety. Other practitioners such as osteopaths, herbalists, homoeopaths, acupuncturists or masseurs may also usefully complement the therapy.

It is important that the therapist is aware of those aspects of their clients' physical lives which may be supporting their presenting problem. In addition to their training, it is helpful for the therapist to have information available about what constitutes appropriate physical care. This includes some knowledge about nutrition, exercise, side effects of drugs and medication, and so on. For example, it is helpful for the therapist to have some information about the positive effects of exercise on depression. It could be important where a client is complaining of palpitations and panic attacks that the therapist has information about the physiological effects on the human system of large doses of caffeine. Asking a client about their consumption of coffee and tea might prevent the therapist from moving to working solely psychologically with feelings of anxiety and panic which may, in part, be chemically induced. Another example of how nutrition and lifestyle can have a direct effect on behaviour and psychological state is found in the case of children with attention deficit disorder. Besides medication, it is really important that these children avoid consuming foods with high 'E' numbers as these exacerbate their condition.

Behavioural aspects of self-experience

The branch of psychology known as behaviourism resulted from the attempts to make psychology scientific. It was thought that this could be achieved by concentrating on the tangible aspect of existence – that is, behaviour (observable action) – and excluding the intangibles such as emotions and thoughts. According to behaviourists the overall well-being of an individual can be improved (or impaired) by influencing his behaviour.

In his research into learning theory, the Russian physiologist Pavlov (1849–1936) developed the concept of classical conditioning. This concept states that an unconditioned stimulus (for example, hunger) which leads automatically to an unconditioned response (such as salivation), when presented repeatedly with a conditioned stimulus (a bell), causes the conditioned stimulus alone to produce the same conditioned response (the sound of the bell elicits salivation).

Another aspect of the learning theory developed by behaviourists is that of operant conditioning. When faced with a desired goal and an unknown solution to achieving it, random acts are experimented with in an effort to solve the problem. Once the goal is achieved, when faced with the same or a similar situation, the individual will try fewer options and reach the goal sooner until finally he will attempt to repeat the exact action which originally gave him the desired result.

Through the work of such researchers as Pavlov, Skinner, Thorndike, Watson and Rayner, Wolpe, Eysenck, Rachman and others, the behavioural model postulates that all behaviour is determined by habitual learning through classical and operant conditioning. Pathology is diagnosed from discrete behaviours which are seen to be the result of previous faulty learning. In the same way as healthy behaviour can be modified through learning, unhealthy behaviours can be altered through the process of unlearning.

In 1965 (Breger and McGaugh) there emerged a general feeling that behaviour therapy was not separable from a cognitive approach. Lazarus (1971), who first coined the term 'behavioural therapy', conducted follow-up studies on clients who had received purely behavioural approaches to their problems. This research indicated that behavioural techniques were not enough to maintain the changes made by the clients. He devised a framework for working with clients at the procedural level which he called the BASIC ID (see Chapter 8). This adds to the behavioural approach many of the aspects we have included here in the integrating pentagon which, as we have emphasized, we believe are inextricably interconnected.

From this behavioural perspective, we may integrate into our theoretical approach the understanding that many of our clients' behaviours have been learnt in the conditions imposed upon them by their childhood environments, reinforced over time by similar circumstances and maintained in the present by similar, or similarly perceived, experiences. Thus the notion of cognitive perception is incorporated as intrinsic to the reinforcing of learnt behaviours. Helping our clients to gain awareness of 'habitual' behaviours and the reinforcing thoughts (the 'cognitive behaviour') that may be maintaining them is an important first step in changing those behaviours. We find the transactional analysis (TA) concept of 'games' very useful here as it provides such a graphic way of understanding how our inner experience is manifested in actions which elicit reinforcing reactions from the environment.

On the procedural level, we may employ strategies such as experimentation, graded desensitization, flooding and positive reinforcement, to assist our clients in changing those behaviours which are restricting their lives. Assertion and social skills may be taught as part of the therapy. Learning to self-reward through verbal or other means (for example, treats) for changed behaviour may also be part of the therapy. Interventions at this behavioural level might include:

- Suggesting a client loudly repeat a statement he has made.
- Inviting a client to stand in a grounded position and practise speaking to an 'authority figure' with whom she usually feels anxious.
- Physical 'trust exercises' within a therapy group.
- Giving homework tasks entailing some new or different behaviour.

The latter intervention was employed with one of our clients who complained of a disrupted sleep pattern. He was waking every two hours consistently throughout the night and, though he could get back to sleep within ten minutes or so, was understandably tired the following morning. The therapist suggested that he set an alarm clock to wake him every hour and a half, explaining that this would interrupt the habituated pattern. The client reported the following week that after the first time of being awakened by the alarm clock after an hour and a half's sleep on the first night, he had not set the alarm again and had slept right through the night. Whether this was simply and quickly breaking the habituated pattern or more a case of aversion therapy (the client resented being woken by the alarm) is unverifiable. The important thing for the client was that it worked.

Therapists' observations of their clients' behaviours are clearly influential. The client who is repeatedly late for sessions or who procrastinates about completing necessary tasks, who smiles incongruently or who avoids situations that seem to cause anxiety may need to focus on these behaviours as the main thrust of their therapy, or at least to acknowledge them as part of the broader picture of their concerns.

The therapist needs also to be aware of her own behaviour in the consulting room and its effect on the client. Therapist responses, however neutrally intended, need careful monitoring. Showing pleasure at some reported behaviour is likely to reinforce it. Likewise, showing disapproval is likely to extinguish or at least invite the client to conceal that behaviour. The slightest nod, subtle remark or sound may be taken as approval and the merest frown or glance as disapproval. Vigilance in this respect is important, particularly in the early stages of therapy when the client may not yet feel comfortable enough to check out with the therapist the meaning of responses which may be misperceived. It is to be hoped that observational skills will help the therapist to identify the response she may have elicited in her client and allow her to follow this through with further checking and discussion. However, a useful question to hold in mind is: 'How might my client experience *my* behaviour towards him and is this therapeutically facilitative?'

Affective aspects of self experience

At various times throughout the therapy, clients will express their feelings or come to learn to do so. The therapist needs to develop an understanding of the role of emotions in maintaining physical and mental health.

There are many theories and research studies on emotion. One of the first theorists in this field was the English naturalist, Charles Darwin (1809–82). In *The Expression of the Emotions in Man and Animals* (1873), he proposed that emotions are of biological survival value. He observed the biological utility of emotional expression and determined that the emotions are an attribute of all human beings, independent of race, culture, and gender. He found that emotions are innate and can be traced as a constant through the evolution of the species. He delineates eight categories of emotion and their concomitant expression. Each category comprises those emotions which share the use of similar parts of the face in similar ways:

1 Suffering: shown with weeping and sobbing.
2 Low spirits, anxiety, grief, dejection, and despair: shown by a furrowed forehead, drawn-in eyebrows and depression of the corners of the mouth.
3 Joy, high spirits, love, tender feelings, devotion: expressed through laughter, smiling and a softening of the muscles around the eyes.
4 Reflection, meditation, ill-temper, sulkiness, determination: shown with frowning and a set mouth.
5 Hatred and anger: shown by sneering and baring of the teeth.
6 Disdain, contempt, disgust, guilt, pride, helplessness, patience, affirmation, negation: shown by the dropping of the eyelids, sneering and grimacing.
7 Surprise, astonishment, fear and horror: shown by an open mouth, protrusion of the lips, wide eyes and raising of the eyebrows.
8 Self-attention, shame, shyness, modesty: shown by lowering the eyes, blushing and blinking.

Since Darwin's time, research around the evolutionary function of emotions has burgeoned. Compared to Darwin's eight categories of emotions, Izard (1979) recognizes ten fundamental emotions: interest, joy, surprise, distress, anger, disgust, contempt, fear, shame and guilt. He suggests that emotion comprises three interactive and interdependent components: neural activity of the brain and somatic nervous system; striate muscle or facial-postural expression and face–brain feedback; subjective experience. Izard's theory states:

> A new emotion is experienced as follows: an internal or external event is processed by relevant receptors. This results in a change in the gradient of neural stimulation and the

pattern of activity in the limbic system and sensory cortex. Impulses from these areas are directed via the hypothalamus to the basal ganglia, which organises the neural message for the facial expression that is mediated by impulses from the motor cortex. As this specific facial expression is registered, sensory impulses from the face are conducted back to the sensory cortex, and cortical integration of facial expression feedback generates the subjective experience of emotion. The emotion process is initiated by neural activation, that is, a change in the density of neural firing. This neural activation of emotion is brought about either by person-environment interactions in the form of perception, or by intra-individual processes, such as memory, imaging, anticipating, thinking, proprioceptive impulses, and endocrine activity. (Izard, 1979: 116)

As can be seen from this description of emotions, they cannot be separated from or understood apart from their physical and conceptual components. Izard and Buechler (1979) believe that each emotion has a distinctive motivational property. They suggest that anger generates energy and provides a feeling of power and confidence. Distress or sadness motivates the healing of loss and elicits empathic responses. Fear motivates withdrawal from danger and interest motivates learning and skill development.

The works of both Darwin and Izard are used in support of the evolutionary-expressive models constructed to explain human emotions. There are other bodies of theories which take up different approaches to the understanding of emotions. They include physiological theories, cognition-arousal theory, cognitive appraisal models and the social psychological model. Through their research, Greenberg and Safran (1987) have created an integration of these different models:

The central postulates of our synthesis of the literature can be summarized as follows:

1. Emotion, cognition, and behaviour are fused.
2. The cognitive-affective system is adapted to the ecological niche.
3. Emotion has an adaptive function, which is largely interpersonal in nature.
4. Emotional experience involves the synthesis of information from sources both external and internal to the organism.
5. The conscious experience of emotion is the product of a pre-attentive synthesis of subsidiary components.
6. Emotion is a form of tacit knowing.
7. Emotional experience tells us what events mean to us as biological organisms.
8. Emotional experience is integrally linked with personal identity. (Greenberg and Safran, 1987: 166-7)

As we can see from the above, emotions are an essential part of the self-regulation of the human organism. This view is powerfully supported by the work of neuroscientists in the final decade of the century (Schore, 2000; Van der Kolk et al., 1999). However, in order to fit their individual temperaments as well as possible into the families into which they are born, and to attract caretakers to attend to their vital needs, babies and young children may control or deflect their natural feelings or, alternatively, escalate arousal in an unmanageable way. The role of therapy, therefore, in relation to the emotions, is to 'undo' such patterns where appropriate and desirable in order to reattain the natural self-regulation of the organism.

The neuroscientist Panksepp (1998) describes seven genetically ingrained emotional circuits found in the subcortex of the mammalian brain. These are rage, fear, panic/separation, distress, maternal/paternal behaviours, seeking, social bonding and play. While any of the first three, seen as the three emergency circuits, are triggered, the other four are suspended. This has obvious repercussions for diagnosis and treatment considerations in the therapeutic setting. Equally, psycho-therapists need to take cognizance of the research findings suggesting that the right hemisphere of the brain experiences the world with accurate sensory images while the left hemisphere provides interpretations which, however useful, are not necessarily accurate.

Emotional literacy involves becoming aware of emotions and finding ways of expressing them in safe and releasing ways. Much of therapy involves helping clients to define and appreciate their adaptations and defences and to develop and practise new and spontaneous ways of integrating their feelings.

In terms of psychotherapy theory, there is agreement across many approaches of the importance of the expression of emotions; current emotions as well as those held from the past. Freud saw the importance of releasing 'strangulated affects' (Breuer and Freud, 1895), though psychodynamic theory is now more likely to use Freud's terms 'catharsis' to describe the process of freeing repressed emotion by association with the original cause and the elimination by 'abreaction' – the free expression and release of that emotion.

Jung's feeling function would also be applicable here. He states: 'Feeling informs you through its feeling-tones of the *values* of things. Feeling tells you for instance whether a thing is acceptable or agreeable or not. It tells you what a thing is *worth* to you' (1968: 12). He distinguishes between the feeling function and emotion by describing the former as a rational function and the latter as having physiological manifestations. However, he seems to accept that there are degrees of feeling and emotion and that, therefore, these may be descriptions of a continuum. We have noticed that people who seem out of touch with their emotions (certainly with the expression of emotions) also have difficulties knowing what they want. Working initially at the feeling function end of the continuum, in other words, helping people to get in touch with what they value, like, prefer and want, can facilitate movement along the continuum towards the recognition of emotion and its expression.

Another concept we find invaluable in our work with clients concerning feelings comes from transactional analysis theory. This is the concept of racket feelings (Berne, 1966; English, 1971; Lapworth et al., 1993). English suggests that within families of origin certain feelings are allowed or encouraged while others are forbidden or discouraged. If, for example, sadness is not allowed expression in the family but anger is seen as a legitimate feeling to be expressed, the child will substitute anger at those times when sadness would be a more appropriate response. In this way, the original or 'authentic' feeling is repressed in favour of the substitute or 'racket' feeling. This learnt behaviour concerning feelings persists into adult-hood. A person who expresses anger rather than sadness often feels unheard, uncared for and puzzled by others' reactions to her. At times when she is seeking nurturing or closeness, her anger alienates her from others. The task with such a client would be to help identify her racket feeling of anger and facilitate the expression of her repressed feeling of sadness, while acknowledging, understanding and respecting the 'survival strategy' (Elton Wilson, 1996) of the client as a child within her family.

It is interesting to note that recent neurological research (Schore, 1994) supports the long-held theoretical hypothesis that patterns of depression, anxiety and unmanageable feeling states are established in the brain of the infant and can remain into adulthood. In the first 18 months of life, the absence of a caretaker who is appropriately soothing and stimulating prevents the building up of neuro-modulators in the prefrontal cortex of the brain resulting in, for example, either an excess of stress hormones or a shutting off of arousal mechanisms so that primitive responses are repeated again and again while neural pathways which would enable effective reflection on experience are unused. The research suggests that these deficits are reparable in later life and this has important implications for psycho-therapy. The work of Kohut (1971), which describes the infant's need for an idealized and mirroring other and the emergence in therapy of yearnings related to these unmet needs, anticipates this research.

In working with emotions at the procedural level, one of the first tasks of the therapist will be to assess whether the client's difficulties may be a result of a lack of self-regulation caused by the fact that, as a young child, the client was not able to internalize the soothing presence of another person due to either absent or ineffective parenting. If this is the case, the therapist's task may be to enable the client to re-experience the overwhelming affective states of her infancy and, using the therapist as the yearned for, calming other, begin to establish an acceptance of herself and the ability to contain and soothe herself. As we mentioned above, it is sometimes appropriate to work at a non-verbal level in the accomplishment of this task. It is also important to help a client to begin to understand herself and to make sense of her experience, thereby setting up the vital, right-cortical activity. It is often the empathic attunement of the therapist (what Schore, 2000 calls 'right brain meeting') that facilitates the client's expression of emotion and her integration of that emotion. The therapist attends carefully to the client and then uses a process of searching his own feelings and experiences in order to understand and immerse himself in the client's subjective experience.

Often a client's repression or distortion of their feelings and the development of racket feelings stem from a later stage of development, for instance, within the family or at school. Again, the therapist may need to help a client reclaim, accept and understand her hidden feelings in order to enable her to live more rewardingly. In such instances, the therapist will start by empathizing with the client's felt experience and then gently explore underlying feelings. For example, the therapist may simply say, 'You look scared right now' in response to facial and bodily clues of fear, in order to facilitate the client in acknowledging, contacting and expressing their feeling of scare. At times, the therapist may heighten the feeling by asking the client to repeat something louder or to talk directly to the person (imagined in the room) with whom these feelings are felt or to whom they are directed, whether from the past or in the present. The therapist may encourage the direct expression of feelings, whether 'here and now' or transferred from the past, towards herself. Equally, when appropriate, she may disclose her own feelings in facilitation of her client. This may be to model the safe expression of feelings, to explore the transferential relationship or to identify and connect with the 'split-off' feelings of the client communicated by projective identification.

We mentioned the cathartic release of feelings earlier in the section. Feelings may be released more fully if some physiological intervention is made, such as inviting the client to breathe more deeply as they express their sadness, to pound a cushion while expressing their anger, or to allow their body to shake in the expression of their fear. Sometimes, abstinence from any intervention which draws attention to emotional expression is, perhaps paradoxically, the most conducive to the expression of emotion for some clients. For them, feelings are often connected with experiences of shame which may be re-experienced if attention is drawn too closely to their feeling expression. The attuned therapist will remain unobtrusive with such a client until their relationship has developed and deepened to allow for the client's shame to be acknowledged and worked through.

Cognitive aspects of self experience

Cognition is the mental process involved in thinking, perceiving, knowing, believing, imagining, evaluating and assessing. Cognitive therapists view cognitive processes as the mediators between emotion and behaviour. The assumptions which cognitive therapists hold about human beings are:

1. The person is seen as an active agent who interacts with his or her world.
2. This interaction takes place through the interpretations, inferences and evaluations the person makes about his or her environment.
3. The results of these 'cognitive' processes are thought to be accessible to consciousness in the form of thoughts and images, and so the person has the potential to change them. (Moorey in Dryden, 1990: 228)

In order not only to survive but also to thrive, human beings need to possess the ability to access a practical, operational thinking capacity. As we discussed earlier, neurophysiological research is showing that the capacity to manage and make sense of overwhelming emotional states depends on the development of the right frontal cortex of the brain. This process is facilitated by the presence of a calm parent figure who both soothes the infant's emotions and helps him to make sense of them. When this task is achieved successfully, an interplay develops between our bodies, minds and emotions and we will be able accurately to adapt to the challenges of our environment.

During the first seven years of life the child is absorbing and integrating vast quantities of general information about the phenomenon of being human. At the same time he is also learning about being human within his family and culture. Until the age of seven the child's thinking capacity is far more primitive than that of the adults in his world. By the age of approximately 12, a child's thinking capacity is equivalent to that of an adult. Sadly, many decisions about how a person views himself, other people and the world in general are based on his earliest experiences and his more primitive thinking. That primitive thinking is itself based upon the 'organizing principles' developed in the relationships of the precognitive stage of infancy. These are described by Stern (1985) as RIGS (Representation of Interactions that have been Generalized). Unless there is some drastic re-appraisal, for example, in the form of therapy, education, life experience, and so on, people continue to live their lives as grownups with those child-chosen guidelines as their rationale.

A person's beliefs, fantasies and images are included here under this cognitive heading. As stated above, beliefs and thought patterns from earlier years tend to influence how a person thinks, feels and behaves in the here and now. They become the frame of reference which he imposes upon the world and he acts within this frame as if it were an undisputed reality. This restriction on experience is well described by several approaches across the schools: in transactional analysis by 'script beliefs' (Berne, 1972) and the 'racket system' (Erskine and Zalcman, 1979), in psychoanalysis by 'pathogenic beliefs' (Weiss and Sampson, 1986), in cognitive-analytic therapy by 'traps', 'snags' and 'dilemmas' (see Chapter 3), in cognitive-behaviour therapy (Beck and Greenberg, 1974; Beck et al., 1979; Blackburn and Twaddle, 1996) by 'logical errors' and 'negative automatic thoughts' and in rational emotive behaviour therapy (Ellis, 1962/94; Neenan and Dryden, 1996) by 'irrational (self-defeating) beliefs'.

At the procedural level, the therapist may usefully draw upon techniques from the cognitive school. These may include: modifying negative automatic thoughts by challenging the thoughts and underlying assumptions, reality testing (questioning the evidence for such thinking, 'Socratic questioning'), looking for alternatives, re-attributing the cause of or responsibility for an event, distancing and distracting, decatastrophizing and exploring the advantages and disadvantages of particular thoughts or courses of action. For a more detailed description and explanation of these cognitive techniques we would refer to the excellent chapter by Moorey (in Dryden, 1990) to which we have referred earlier.

Within the therapeutic relationship, the client's 'organizing principles' will emerge as a result of careful exploration of his subjective world and the sense he has made of his experiences. It may also emerge in the transferential expectations he has of his therapist. The therapist may then use interpretation in order for the client to gain insight into his transference and thereby open the door to a different way of thinking. In our work, we are in agreement with the Gestalt and inter-subjective perspectives and believe that the therapist co-creates the relationship between therapist and client. In exploring what we believe to be transference, therefore, we would start by trying to empathize with our client's point of view and understand how we have contributed to her experience. Only afterwards would we invite a client to reflect on her meaning making and explore possible links to past relationships.

Making meaning of existence is central to being human. This we have implied by the position we have diagrammatically given to such consideration. It is one of the core self needs of our framework and is explored and finds expression in each aspect of the pentagon as well as in relationship and context within the time frame. It is not, therefore, a purely cognitive endeavour but we have also included it here to suggest the importance of exploring with our clients the philosophical assumptions and values they may hold and which affect their lives and how they live them. The existential psychotherapy writers (for example, Binswanger, 1946; Boss, 1963; Cohn, 1997; Deurzen-Smith, 1988; Frankl, 1964; May, 1950; Yalom, 1980), in particular, have much to inform our work as therapists, as well as in our personal quest, in the area of meaning making.

Spiritual aspects of self experience

So far in our discussion of the development of an integrative framework, the three authors have been in accord. We may each place a varying emphasis on different aspects of the pentagon, on different theories and procedural strategies, but there is no fundamental disagreement. However, in approaching this fifth aspect which we have termed spiritual we found there was a greater range of differing beliefs which led to difficulty in designing a concerted view. We found this interesting and challenging as it led to long discussions between us and our colleagues. Our differences were even more surprising in the light of our discovery that all three of us had very similar experiences of religion and 'spiritual' ideas when we were young.

We asked ourselves if we should include the spiritual aspect or not and, if so, what relevance has it for psychotherapy. What we agreed upon is that occurrences happen in people's lives and during therapy which are unexplainable. They appear to be 'transpersonal' or beyond our present human understanding and should be valued and respected. We also agreed that there is an aspect of the human experience which may be called an existential search for meaning. Some see this as a spiritual path. Either way, it is a vital part of a person's life journey. We decided to include this aspect of the self and offer our different viewpoints in order to acknowledge the existence of this facet which is so difficult to define.

We found the very title of this area challenging and mulled over words like magical, transpersonal, transcendent, mystical, numinous, intuitive, and others. In the end, we chose the term spiritual because it applies to aspects of experience which relate neither to physical nature nor matter and because, among the three of us, there was the majority view that the word spiritual, in general usage, describes that part of human nature which seeks understanding of and unity with some 'other' force.

Phil Lapworth does not have a clear enough perception of a distinct spiritual aspect to the human condition to feel at ease with its inclusion. He writes: the spiritual aspect of existence is one which eludes me – mostly because I have difficulty understanding what this word means as distinct from the other experiences of self. Perhaps it is simply a matter of definition but I find the word 'spiritual' confusing as a description of experience. Life, life-force, life-energy, physis, elan vital, are terms I can more easily adopt to describe human energy, life-fullness, aspiration and endeavour, but for me these are animated or vital principles of the human organism and do not require the term 'spiritual'.

As examples of spiritual experience, people often describe instances such as watching the sun set, hearing birdsong or an orchestral symphony, feeling the presence of another, and so on. To me these are at times wonderful, amazing and beautiful and I may feel joy, wonder, awe, spine-tingling elation in response to such experiences. But why is this spiritual? For me this is my emotional response to perceived beauty or the powerful force of nature or the intimacy human beings can achieve. In therapy, I feel moved and privileged when a client gains a life-altering insight, or laughs spontaneously for the first time, or shows a love for themselves previously hidden beneath self-hate. This I would describe in emotional and relational terms – linked to genuine joy in the potential beauty of life.

Another response is to recount inexplicable events, synchronicity, mysterious happenings, spontaneous healings, telepathic communication, predictive dreams, and so on. Again, I have experienced such happenings, I call them inexplicable. What the respondents seem to be saying is, 'if we don't understand it, it's spiritual'. I find such a 'catch-all' definition unsatisfactory and prefer to stay with the uncertainty of these experiences.

My own atheistic and existential beliefs are part of my quest to make meaning of life. This does not mean that I do not have regard and respect for others' meaning-making beliefs, including those whose beliefs would embrace the use of the word 'spiritual'. Over the years in my work as a psychotherapist, I have worked with clients whose spiritual beliefs have spanned many of the differing world religions. I have worked with people who believe in reincarnation (and therefore in past lives), in soul retrieval, in gods and goddesses, in the dead being able to communicate with the living, in transubstantiation, transmigration and so on. While I do not hold these beliefs myself, I hope, from an integrative stance which holds that there is no one truth, that I am open to accepting and respecting the uniquely personal beliefs of my clients. I agree with the stance of Massey and Dunn (1999) when they write:

> In our work we leave these terms undefined; we listen without preconceptions to the phenomenological descriptions of those who relate their 'spiritual' experiences to us. Encountering others with their full potential necessitates remaining open to others' spiritual experiences. While these experiences may seem to a listener to enhance or inhibit personality and social growth (Maslow, 1964/70) or to serve as a way of accepting unalterable realities such as past guilt, death, or inevitable suffering (Fromm, 1969), we listen to rather than evaluate the meanings of the narrator's experience. (Massey and Dunn, 1999: 115–29)

In my multidimensional integrative framework, therefore, such aspects of human experience would be subsumed under the other four aspects we have described and certainly come within the relational and contextual environment we have emphasized. Thus, much of what follows is not necessarily excluded from the integrative framework. I would simply include it elsewhere.

Charlotte Sills writes: I find it hard to know what I do believe in this respect. I find that my views change. I think that I believe we have within us a spiritual need. I notice that human beings seem to have a natural drive to actualization – in other words, to become the best human beings they can be. I ask why that is and wonder whether the answer lies in the fact that we must become the best we can be in order to transcend the boundaries of the simply human, to touch something 'higher' and connect with something greater than ourselves. While I am aware that the need for this something 'higher' may be a desire to find an idealized parent figure who was absent in childhood, I am also aware of the great number of fine, wise and mature people who attest to the existence of a god or higher force. The question I find difficult is where to find that something 'higher'. The word 'higher' is itself significant. I have been influenced by Christianity which describes a hierarchy in which the Almighty is 'above' the earth, greater than us. In this case, spirituality would have no place in the consulting room and clients should go elsewhere to find spiritual guidance. However, more ancient spiritual traditions locate God in the earth, the plants, the rocks – everywhere. I am also moved by the Zen saying, 'Look within. Thou art Buddha'. If the spirit is everywhere, then it could account for those moments of joy or ecstasy which Lapworth describes. It would also mean that spirituality, and the client's perhaps unconscious search for spiritual direction, have a place in the therapy room. It is interesting that the word psyche which comes at the beginning of the word 'psychotherapy' actually derives from the Greek word meaning spirit. Perhaps psychotherapy is a spiritual search after all.

I link this aspect to the client search for meaning in their lives. Human beings are meaning-making creatures. We try to understand our world and seek to control or manage our environments by making sense of things. However, I constantly see a search which goes further than this. It is the existential question posed by our apparent need to find a meaning outside the obvious, beyond building lives that make sense. I do not see it as my job as a therapist to guide my client. However, I do believe that it is my responsibility to be aware of this need as it emerges, make space for it, avoid putting obstacles in its way and to offer support to the client who follows her path further than I have followed mine.

Sue Fish writes: the spiritual aspect of self involves an aspect of being human which belies measurement or scientific understanding. All societies, both past and present, have involved themselves in patterns of thinking, acting and feeling about the meaning of life on this planet and the meaning of an individual's birth, life, death and the unknown thereafter. This investigation moves from the intuitive to the systemization of faith in the form of religion. Religion and spirituality are therefore fundamentally different. Religion, like any other institution, can either function supportively or destructively in the quest for spiritual identity.

The spiritual aspect of self is presented in very many different ways in the context of the process of therapy. As the spiritual is uniquely individual and relies on faith, belief, rites and rituals for its existence and continuation it is not easily given universal parameters, explanations or guidelines. It may not be as easily supported by rationale as the other aspects of the pentagon.

Often the spiritual 'elders' in a society, besides fulfilling the role of caretakers and therapists of their followers' souls, also offer counselling in general to members of their congregation. While often of benefit, this type of counselling may lack sufficient objectivity as it usually has as one of its cornerstones the edicts and beliefs which underpin the religion concerned. There seem to be four different points at which the transpersonal is raised in the therapeutic process:

1 A client has a spiritual question or quest as their initial reason for seeking counselling or psychotherapy. When a client presents at the initial session stating that he wishes to explore spiritual matters, the therapist needs, as part of her

assessment of the client, to look at whether that goal is a defence against other painful issues or part of their further integration as an actualizing human being. As with any presenting issues, the therapist's responsibility is to ascertain how qualified and suitable they are for the situation. If it seems to the therapist that their lack of information about the client's particular spiritual beliefs might impede any progress, she may choose to refer the client on to someone more suitable. If the therapist assesses that she can be facilitative, as with any other issue, the therapist's challenge then is to develop a working alliance with the client.

2   The transpersonal component often arises nearer the end of the therapeutic journey. As the client's other needs, hungers or drives become satisfied, space may emerge for their contemplation of issues of the soul. The psychiatrist and inventor of transactional analysis, Eric Berne, argued that people have six basic psychological hungers: stimulation, recognition, contact, structure, sexual and incident. There are vast varieties of ways of meeting these hungers and many of them are satisfied within the rituals of religion but I suggest that there is a seventh human hunger which is spiritual. Where counselling or psychotherapy is primarily engaged in the integration of self, the integration of one's spiritual self is part of that process. Spiritual enlightenment does not require any specific learning but stems from, among other things, open-mindedness, compassion, passion, wonder and full awareness.

3   The spiritual manifests within the consulting room when a client has strong religious beliefs and resorts to the benign or hostile elements of their religious framework for emotional and cognitive support or undermining. As stated earlier in this chapter, one of the major forces which influences the construction of our personalities is that of the religions to which we may be exposed at a young age. This may result in people emerging as adults with a belief that edicts of their particular religion are the sole truths. The purpose then of the therapeutic journey would be to allow the client to make his own that which may have been introjected without question.

4   Lastly, the spiritual aspects of the self manifest in a counselling session when the work which the client is doing at that moment seems to be accompanied by some phenomenon which belies the usual scientific explanations. This may involve an inexplicable connection or knowingness between therapist and client or between therapist, client and environment, all of which have a transcendental 'feel' to them.

I would like to underline that although I believe psychotherapy and spiritual work may well overlap, I am trained as a psychotherapist and not as a spiritual guide. Just as I would refer a client to a specialist if I thought they needed in-depth body work, so I would refer a client to a spiritual leader to gain spiritual guidance.

Two quotes to stimulate your thinking on this subject are from Moore and Hillman. Moore (1992) suggests:

> Care of the soul, looking back with special regard to ancient psychologies for insight and guidance, goes beyond the secular mythology of the self and recovers a sense of the sacredness of each individual life. This sacred quality is not just value – all lives are

important. It is the unfathomable mystery that is the very seed and heart of each individual. Shallow therapeutic manipulations aimed at restoring normality or tuning a life according to standards reduces – shrinks – that profound mystery to the pale dimensions of a social common denominator referred to as the adjusted personality. Care of the soul sees another reality altogether. It appreciates the mystery of human suffering and does not offer the illusion of a problem-free life. It sees every fall into ignorance and confusion as an opportunity to discover that the beast residing at the centre of the labyrinth is also an angel. The uniqueness of a person is made up of the insane and the twisted as much as it is of the rational and normal. To approach this paradoxical point of tension where adjustment and abnormality meet is to move closer to the realisation of our mystery-filled, star-born nature. (Moore 1992: 29)

Hillman refers to therapy as soul-making rather than analysis: 'Growth lets the soul do its own thing, like a plant. This organic mystique implies minimal work. Soul-making, too, has a mystique, the mystery of death, which encompasses organic growth and employs its images in the work of soul. *Making* is a term which reflects what the psyche itself does: it makes images' (1979: 95).

Environmental factors: relationship and context

Continuing the explanations of the facets of our framework, outside our integrating pentagon and within the diamond of our past, present and future time frame, we have designated two important environmental factors for attention, namely, relationship and context. If self needs are experienced and expressed through the five aspects of self described by the pentagon, it is within relationship and context that these needs may be addressed. These environmental factors in the past have influenced and shaped a person's development in becoming who and how she is. She may find herself stuck in the present, repeating the influences of the past, creating or choosing some of her relationships and contexts that simply continue her script. However, it is only within present and future relationships and contexts that she may also find restorative influences and constructive meaning. This is the task of psychotherapy.

Relationship

We have diagrammatically placed this relational dimension of our framework so as to indicate how the self, its needs and aspects of experience are inevitably contained within and influenced by relationships in the present and from the past and in aspirations (or fears) for the future. A person's relationships will involve her close family members, the extended family, friends (and enemies), neighbours, work colleagues, mentors and casual acquaintances and, of course, the therapist. Lapworth writes:

> People need other people. Needing people, we are, therefore, born socially and into a system. We are conceived and developed within, as well as born into, a relationship with another human being. Unless test-tubes and incubators become the system and the

social milieu is replaced by computers, there is no escaping this social aspect nor the system which holds it. (Lapworth, 1994: v)

The fulfilment of self needs is only possible through some aspect of relationship with others. Contortions of the self occur when the social environment does not adequately respond to a straightforward presentation of those needs. The self then adjusts and adapts to the inadequate social environment. The client in the consulting room has not only adjusted her intrinsic self as a child but is continuing to do so in her current social systems, which will include the therapeutic relationship. Within the interdependent connection of human beings, some adjustment is inevitable, healthy and desirable. Part of the task of the therapeutic journey is for the client to be able to distinguish these positive and creative adjustments from those which are detrimental.

At times, therapists use some means of constructing a genealogical history or sociogram with which to develop an overall picture of a client's past and current significant relationships and the client's place within them.

Systems theory suggests that where one element of any system changes, the system will adjust in one of three ways: the changing member will be forced to reverse her change; another member or members of the system will significantly and complementarily change; or the changed person will choose to leave that system or is expelled from it. This accounts for some people giving up therapy when the consequences of their changing disturb the equilibrium of their social relationships.

While the client will bring issues or information concerning his wider social network to the therapy, the only relationship the therapist will have direct experience of and influence upon is that between herself and her client. This relationship can be viewed as a fractel of one or some of the client's other major relationships from the past or the present.

Psychotherapy research (Bergin and Lambert, 1978) indicates that whatever theoretical approach is used the therapeutic relationship is the most important factor in determining successful outcome. The therapist must be attuned enough for the client to feel met, understood and accepted, yet different enough to be experienced as offering a way to find new options and ways of being.

In the past hundred years, many theorists have written about their views of what is essential to the therapist's role. Freud advocated a stance of neutrality on the part of the analyst – the 'rule of abstinence' – although it is well known that he did not follow his own rule as he regularly had tea with his patients, lent them money, and so on. Indeed, Freud's followers embraced this rule far more adamantly than did their mentor and the idea that the client could be studied and understood as an individual separate from the therapist (the blank screen) continued well into the second half of the twentieth century. Psychoanalysis, with its emphasis on unconscious drives, concentrated on exploring the unconscious and interpreting the way the patient recreated his early experiences in his attitudes and feelings towards his analyst. Cognitive behaviour therapists chose not to make the transference central to the work, concentrating instead on the client's patterns of thinking, feeling and behaving in the world. They focused on the clients' problems and attitudes as separate from the relationship.

A focus on the relationship between therapist and client began to be foreground in the 1960s and 1970s largely due to the influence of the emerging humanistic tradition. Rogers (1957) described six conditions for successful therapy, three of which (the core conditions) were essential attitudes of the therapist. His impact on the psychotherapeutic world has been enormous. Object relations theory (Bowlby, 1969, 1973, 1980; Fairbairn, 1954; Guntrip, 1971; Winnicott, 1965) brought about a development within psychoanalysis acknowledging the need for people to seek attachment and relationship. Such acknowledgement was given not only to the client's transferential needs but to the therapist's own countertransferential influence and understanding within the two-way therapeutic relationship. Kohut (1971, 1977) and his followers, from a psychoanalytic self psychology perspective, described empathic immersion on the part of the therapist as the essential ingredient in healing disorders of the self. There was increasing acknowledgement of the importance of the interaction between therapist and client in its influence on the client's experience. Various theorists began to analyse the relationship itself and its different facets. We have written about these various facets of the therapeutic relationship in Chapter 7.

Despite this increased focus on the relationship (see Feltham, 1999), many psychotherapy and counselling approaches still place the focus upon the client. However, some schools of therapy have emerged over the past twenty years which attempt to embody the idea of a 'two-person psychology'. Gestalt psychotherapy (Beaumont, 1993) describes the co-creation of the relationship and emphasizes that the self of the individual is not a constant, but emerges as a result of the interaction between the person and his environment. A Gestalt therapist, therefore, is acutely aware that the self of the client evoked in the consulting room will depend not only upon the client's patterns of organizing his world, but also upon what is happening between him and his therapist, the responses of the therapist, and the patterns that the therapist brings with her. The intersubjective perspective (Stolorow et al., 1994) also focuses on the interplay between the 'organizing principles' of both therapist and client.

From their integrative perspective, Erskine and Trautmann believe that a 'major premise of integrative psychotherapy is that the need of relationship constitutes a primary motivating experience of human behaviour, and contact is the means by which the need is met' (1996: 316). They see the therapeutic relationship and the therapist's use of self as essential to the client's process of developing and integrating contact and satisfying their relational needs. These needs are identified as security, validation, affirmation and significance, acceptance by a dependable and protective other person, confirmation of personal experience, self-definition, the need to have an impact on the other person, the need to have the other initiate and the need to express love. The therapist responds to these current needs of the client by providing a contact-oriented therapeutic relationship which is emotionally nurturing, reparative and sustaining and employs the facilitative methods of inquiry, attunement and involvement.

As we, the authors, have been influenced by both the humanistic and the analytic traditions, our view of the relationship and its role in therapy draws on a belief in the importance of transference and the repetition of the past, the importance of the co-creation of relationship both within and outside the therapy room and also the healing power of a therapist who is willing to immerse herself empathically in the subjective experience of her client while attempting to bracket her own frame of reference. We endeavour to balance these three elements in our work.

Using the Multidimensional Integrative Framework diagram as a map, we hold in mind the relationships within our time frame (Elton Wilson, 1999). We consider the present meeting (*in here*) with the client which includes agreements about our therapy work together, the relationship we create as two people in the world and also the relationship which will contain echoes of our client's, and our own, past relationships (*in here* from *back then*). We will also take account of our client's current relationships with others in her life (*out there*) and explore relational patterns which may have evolved from earlier in their lives (*out there* from *back then*). It is our experience that clients bring into the therapy room the dynamic patterns of their relationships in their reports of current difficulties and also as lived out in their relationship with us (*in here* from *out there*). We see our role as being to help the client understand and explore these relationships and the meanings they contain. We explore past events and past relationships, when relevant, in order to understand how the early decisions made by clients, and the sense they made of their relational experiences, may have led them to organize their world according to limited, subjective perceptions and options. As part of their increase in understanding, we invite clients to look towards the future (*in view*). This entails facing the reality of the likely outcome if they continue their present patterns of relationship.

As part of this exploration of relationships, we may invite the client to consider how this sort of situation has ended before, how they are maintaining the situation, what beliefs about self and others are being reinforced and how they might change these beliefs to ensure more satisfying and creative relationships in the future, exploring what they need now in order to establish relationships which enhance both their contact in the world and also their development as an individual.

Sometimes the client may not be able to envisage a different way of relating as a result of the impoverished experiences of her very early life (see neuro-physiological research described earlier in this chapter). In this case, the therapist's task may be to hold in mind a potential future for his client while endeavouring to offer the kind of reparative relationship in the present that will allow for the future formation of nourishing interactions in the wider world.

Context

With regard to the contextual aspect of our framework, we have placed this dimension diagrammatically to show its wider containment of self, self needs, aspects of self experience and relationships with others. The German psychologist Lewin (1951) argued that it is not possible to fully understand any individual without viewing them in the context of their environment. Lewin's field theory states that individuals organize their entire environment in terms of their needs of and the condition of that environment. What is of significance and interest to any observer of the human condition is the interdependence between any individual and their environment.

The therapist is required to take into account a mass of information pertaining to the individual alone. However, the individual cannot be taken out of context. As part of their assessment and treatment, the therapist needs to be aware of their clients' relational, occupational, cultural, social, socioeconomic, sexual, religious, racial, linguistic and geographical context, at this period of time and in the past. She also needs to take account of these same aspects of her own environmental field. What might be the implications in the relationship, for example, if the therapist is white and the client is black; or if the therapist is black and the client is white; or if both therapist and client are black; or both white?

Meeting and understanding her clients in context involves the therapist in an exploration of herself. She needs to own and work through the restrictive perceptions of her own context, to challenge her own racism, sexism, homophobia and heterosexism, ageism, her cultural assumptions and her relational expectations. It is not enough simply to acknowledge that her client is, for example, black or gay or male (or all three) and make assumptions. She needs to attune herself to the phenomenological experience of her unique and individual client of what it means for them to be black, gay or male at this point in time, when they were growing up and in the history of their society. Further, all this needs to be placed within the context of their age, their gender, the political context, the geographical area and the social milieu at home and at work as well as with the therapist in the therapy room. The therapist needs to understand the impact of her culture and her beliefs on the client and be aware that many unconscious attitudes and prejudices – for instance, unconscious institutionalized racism – will be affecting the way she behaves. Her clients will be the best source of feedback in these areas, given the safety and opportunity to voice their experience of her. Additionally, therapists' practice may be enhanced by resourcing themselves through the literature on multicultural therapy, pink therapy, politics in therapy and other contextual aspects (see section on Context in the reading list in Appendix I) as well as widening their horizons through reference books and fiction related to these issues.

In summary, when two people meet in the therapy room, their two frames of reference will overlap to varying degrees. Similarities of culture and background can lead to acceptance, understanding and connection, but can also lead to unhelpful assumptions and blind spots. Differences in culture and background can lead to misunderstandings and prejudices yet, when there is an atmosphere of open enquiry, difference may provide the grit of excited interest and new insight.

In our book *Gestalt Counselling* (Sills et al., 1995) we use the term connectedness to describe the field theoretical perspective (Lewin, 1951). Nothing exists in isolation – everything is connected to something else. A person may judge a speeding driver as thoughtless, drunken or hotheaded but he would have to adjust his perception if he were exposed to additional data informing him that, for instance, the driver was rushing to a critically ill relative or transporting vitally needed supplies.

> To understand human beings, we need first to see the whole situation before attending to the parts. But the environment changes according to circumstances. The individual organizes the totality of the environment according to different situations and different needs, sometimes making one particular aspect 'figure', sometimes another. Importantly

and with exciting implications for the counselling relationship humans constellate the field around them so that they in effect create it. In any meeting a field is co-created. The therapist and client have together a 'betweenness' in which the field is then potentially new every moment. (Sills et al., 1995: 78)

The time frame

Finally, in our explanation of our multidimensional framework diagram, we come to the outer parameters which represent the dimensions of time. We have mentioned several times our belief in the importance of past experience (*back then*) on present life (*in here/out there*). We referred to it in discussing the development of different aspects of self and, particularly, in describing the long-term impact of early relationships on a person's understanding of the world and their way of relating within it. We have mentioned the future (*in view*) only briefly. We believe that the future dimension is an essential focus. Research by, for example, Bordin (1994) points to the important place that goal setting has in determining outcome in psychotherapy. Elton Wilson (1996) highlights the creative use of solution-focused therapy (De Shazer, 1985) in combination with insight regarding past patterns where projecting into the future and anchoring desired states in the present are essential parts of the therapy.

In our work, we use the future dimension in two ways. One way, as described above in the relationship section, is to invite the client to predict the outcome of continuing to live in the way they are doing presently. For example, we may ask the client, 'If you carry on in this way for the next five to ten years where will you be?' One of our clients, a dedicated businessman, was shocked to recognize in his answer that his style of living would almost certainly lead to burn-out or premature death. The other aspect of the future is that of goal setting and creative visualization of the future. Here a client strongly envisages their desired future and imagines it in as much detail as possible using each aspect of the pentagon. For example, when looking at the behavioural aspect of his potential self, one of the things our overworking businessman sees himself doing is spending far more time with his family by cutting down his work load from six days to three, and enjoying other personal interests. Having made his potential future as real as possible in his imagination, he is then helped to identify which aspects of his present lifestyle and patterns of beliefs need to change in order to assure the preferred future. Part of this strategy may include building upon strengths and areas of success which may already exist within his experience.

Different approaches give different emphasis to the three dimensions of this time frame. Psychoanalysis concentrates more on the past dimension. Gestalt psychotherapy dedicates more energy to focusing on the present reality. Solution-focused psychotherapy and almost all cognitive therapies incorporate the future dimension. Each therapist will use their own integration of these three dimensions of time in their psychotherapy. This will depend upon their training, their theoretical perspective and on what their client presents as their major reasons for coming into therapy.

An interesting subsection of diagnosis is noticing how a client distributes their energy in relation to time. Some clients dwell upon the past, others deny its relevance, and yet others have little or no recollection of it. Some clients choose to live in their 'golden' or 'ghastly' future believing that everything will be all right/dreadful when . . .! Others will not take responsibility for any planning for the future while others take total responsibility for past, present and future. Another category of clients includes those who live for today as if it has no connection with yesterday or tomorrow as distinct from the often advocated living in the here and now which respects the role that both past and future play in the present. Some clients and therapists may extend this time frame beyond their lifetime's past and future to include past incarnations and future reincarnations which clearly may have implications for the therapy.

Overview of the Multidimensional Integrative Framework

Now that we have worked our way through the Multidimensional Integrative Framework, we would like to emphasize again the inseparable interconnectedness of these several aspects which for ease of description and theoretical conceptualization we have delineated.

We have described some of the theoretical concepts and ideas which our framework allows us to integrate, that is to say, those theoretical constructs which are cohesive and consistent with our overarching theory of human beings from which the framework is derived. Other practitioners will, of course, not only have their own different theoretical emphasis but will integrate their own theoretical perspectives within the framework according to their own understanding and experience. In practice with clients, as we have stressed, the centrality of a respectful, contactful interpersonal relationship is paramount. Our framework exists in service of the client and the therapeutic relationship, not the reverse. The framework may, however, be helpful as a reflective tool for sorting and ordering our conceptualizations and impressions as well as noting relevant information. While holding an inclusive and flexible overview of the whole framework and its interconnected aspects, we have found it useful first to focus on a particular self need (the focal theme often presented by the client) as described inside the pentagon, then to explore that need in relation to some or all of the five aspects of self experience with reference to the relational, contextual and temporal dimensions. However, just as there is no one integrative psychotherapy, neither is there one integrating framework (as shown by our inclusion of several other frameworks in the next section); nor is there any one way to use the framework we have provided.

We suggest that as therapists we need to be aware of each of those aspects of our clients as described by our framework, and the wholeness of which they are but a part. The self, self needs and aspects of experience set within the frame of relationship, context and time can be used to remind us of this wholeness as well as to give individual focus to the interrelated parts. As we write of these parts under separate headings, we invite the reader, from the start, to begin to see their interrelatedness and to think in terms of an integrated whole. As we write of the physiological, for example, it is important to remain aware of the manifestations in other aspects of the person. When working with clients, even when focusing on one particular aspect, awareness of what this may mean for the whole person will also need to be maintained.

The Multidimensional Integrative Framework as a diagnostic tool

The Multidimensional Integrative Framework may be used quite simply as a means of building up a picture of a client and their presenting problem. For example, a client may start a session complaining of a back pain. At this point in time, neither the therapist nor the client can with any certainty assess which self need this symptom may be expressing. In terms of physical survival, the client may have a tumour on the spine; it could be sign of a strain in his relationship with his partner; he may be over-structuring his time in physical work; he could feel bowed by criticism from his boss. Equally his back pain could be a sign of lack of rest or it could be the beginnings of a chance for him to take time out to reflect upon the meaning of his life. These possibilities may be borne in mind by the therapist and explored more fully over time.

With regard to aspects of self experience at the physiological level, the practitioner may quite appropriately think about whether the client should be receiving some corrective physical treatment and discuss such a possibility. However, the client is not just a back pain and the back pain is not the whole of the client's experience. Using the integrating pentagon as a guide, the therapist may, using reflections, questions and other interventions, explore the client's experience more holistically and begin to create an internal picture (sometimes shared with her client) of the client's situation. This may result in a compilation of information from the client such as the following:

Physiological: 'I have intense pain at the base of my spine, my shoulders are tense and my neck is stiff.'

Behavioural: 'I have to walk very slowly and sit very carefully. I can't lift things at all. I can't even put my children to bed and I can't have sex with my wife.'

Affective: 'I feel really angry that I'm so restricted. I want to scream but I can't because of the pain. I'm also sad because I can't hug my children or put them to bed at the moment. I feel out of contact with them and my wife, you know, like I'm not loving any of them enough.'

Cognitiv . 'It was so stupid of me to lift those paving stones on my own. I knew I really needed help but then I kept telling myself to get the job done without such a fuss. Also I'm confused because some people have said keep still and others say keep moving.'

Spiritual: 'One of my "alternative" friends suggested that perhaps my back is trying to get over to me that I need to slow down and take some time to evaluate my priorities in life. She may be right.'

As the client continues his exploration of his back pain, the therapist may seek to discover what relational and contextual connections he can make:

> *Relationship*: 'Now, of course, I've let the whole family down. I'm doing very little with my children, my wife has to help me a lot and I've had to cancel my mother's visit next weekend! And I think you probably are disappointed in how I'm not taking good enough care of myself.'

> *Context*: 'I was meant to give a presentation at work tomorrow and I don't think I can stand or sit long enough to do it. And, somehow I don't feel like a "real man". The guys in the pub would think I was pathetic if they knew all this.'

Finally, the therapist will incorporate into her growing picture of the client's situation, the relevant temporal information:

> *Time*: 'Come to think of it, I have often hurt myself before important events in my life. I thought I was looking forward to giving this presentation . . .'

In this brief example, each aspect of the framework is clearly related to all the others. By careful listening, observing and reflecting back, the skilled therapist can facilitate the client in expressing his whole experience. This may help both the therapist and the client to a greater understanding of him and his present situation.

Extended diagnostic concepts

Whether we are using the framework or not, the moment a client contacts us, we are involved in some sort of assessment or diagnosis. We may attempt to be as non-judgemental as possible, open to meeting the client with few preconceptions and ready to receive what the client presents to us with acceptance and under-standing – all of which are the requirements of an effective therapist. However, as human beings, we cannot help but make meaning of our experiences, and this applies to therapists too. At the very least, we will have a need to make some sort of sense and order of what the client presents to us, be it their story, their problems, the way they sit, the way they speak or the manner in which they relate to us. What is important is that we do this for the benefit of the client and are aware when our own experiences or prejudices may get in the way of facilitating the client. We believe that assessment and diagnosis are more likely to be beneficial to the client if they are kept within our awareness by a formal approach or framework. To this end our integrative framework can provide us with a diagnostic template to help us to order our knowledge, experience and understanding and to assist in making facilitative interventions.

For example, Ware (1983) developed a conceptual framework concerning the assessment and treatment planning of certain major personality types or adaptations. We find this helpful in conjunction with our framework. He discusses treatment in terms of three of the aspects of self-experience described on our pentagon, that is, the therapist chooses to connect with the client's behavioural, cognitive or affective aspects respectively. Ware suggests that each personality type reacts differently to each of these processes. He describes them in terms of three different doors – *open, target* and *trap*. The open door with any client is the one that is available for immediate rapport and positive contact. The *target door* is the one that is the least available aspect of experience available to the client and is, therefore, the one which will, over time, assist the client to fuller and more satisfying experiences in life. The *trap door* is that aspect of experience usually favoured by the client as a means of defence against other aspects, one which, if approached too soon, may result in avoidance, deeper distress, impasse or failure of the therapy. This does not mean to say that the trap door aspect needs to be always avoided. Once the client has some integration of their particular first two doors or aspects of the pentagon, real change or cure will occur when they can also use their third process effectively. Use of these doors is mainly advisable over time but is also pertinent in terms of a single session. We will briefly look at how the three aspects of the pentagon relate to these three doors. We utilize the six personality styles identified by Ware.

The behavioural aspect

The behavioural aspect of the pentagon is the open door for people who use *passive aggressive* or *antisocial* behaviours to cope with their world. The affective aspect is the target door, while the cognitive aspect is the trap door as it can be used evasively and defensively either in over-intellectualizing or in outwitting others respectively.

The behavioural aspect of the pentagon is also the open door for people who have a *schizoid* adaptation. However, the cognitive aspect is the target door, while the affective aspect is the trap door as over-attention to feelings in the early stages of the work is likely to cause further shutdown on this aspect of the client's experience.

The affective aspect

The affective aspect of the pentagon is the open door for people who exhibit *histrionic* or *hysterical* traits and, therefore, use much of their energy in showing emotion. The cognitive aspect is the target door, while the behavioural aspect is the trap door as, being impulse driven, confrontation of behaviour will illicit fear and defensiveness.

The cognitive aspect

The cognitive aspect of the pentagon is the open door for people who exhibit *paranoid* or *obsessive compulsive* features. The affective aspect is the target door, while the behavioural aspect is the trap door as the person with a paranoid adaptation will easily feel attacked or undermined and the person with an obsessive-compulsive adaptation will tend to increase their obsessional behaviour in response to this focus.

This is necessarily a very brief summary of Ware's concepts concerning personality adaptations and we would suggest further reading of his original article for a more in-depth discussion. However, we include it here to illustrate how the work of others may be usefully incorporated within our multidimensional framework. Equally, concepts such as the defensive manoeuvres or 'interruptions to contact' (the processes of introjection, desensitization, deflection, projection, retroflection, egotism and confluence) described in the Gestalt literature may be incorporated into our framework to assist in assessment, diagnosis and treatment planning. These considerations of defences help us to identify a client's basic self needs and how the meeting of those needs has become distorted or burdensome. Within the therapeutic relationship, the client can experiment with new ways of recognizing and addressing those needs.

Although we find this integration of Ware's doors, Gestalt and other perspectives compatible with the multidimensional framework, the reader has many others from which to choose. Likewise, in the next chapter we will be demonstrating the practical use of our integrating framework from the integration we have personally developed. Our emphasis again is upon the idea of many styles and approaches to integrative psychotherapy based upon personal experiences rather than upon the idea of one definitive integration. The Multidimensional Integrative Framework allows for each practitioner to integrate from their own personal perspective.

6
An Integrative Framework in Practice

In this chapter, we endeavour to illustrate the use of the Multidimensional Integrative Framework in the process and practice of psychotherapy by following some of the stages of work with a male client. In particular, we hope to demonstrate its integrative use as a means of describing and understanding the client and his presenting issues, of formulating (and reformulating) hypotheses and theoretical conceptualizations, of developing a sense of possible treatment direction, and of assisting as a guide to procedural strategies.

We will give particular attention to the employment of the framework in the early stages and throughout the development of the therapy within the first year as it moves from a 'time-focused' contract to a 'time-extended' contract (Elton Wilson, 1996). We will then use the framework to help summarize the issues and foci of the therapy as it continues into a 'time-expanded' contract (Elton Wilson, 1996). While it is impossible, in the printed word, to capture the subtleties, the ebb and flow of two people working together, we hope we provide enough of a sense of the therapeutic process to demonstrate how our integrative framework may be used in the service of that process co-created with and for the client.

Case study: Barry

The first the therapist was to know of Barry was through an employee assistance programme administrator who was attempting to set up some brief therapy for Barry, a 38-year-old computer technician. The therapist agreed that she had a space in her practice but that it was important that Barry instigate the arrangement for an interview. After several weeks, Barry's initial contact with the therapist was by letter, in which he explained that he had been made redundant and as part of the redundancy package his past employer was willing to pay for a maximum of 12 therapy sessions. What was significant about his letter, which was short and to the point, was that he provided his address and e-mail but not a telephone number. The therapist wrote back suggesting that he telephone her in order to arrange an initial meeting. He phoned at one of the given times and they arranged an appointment. During this brief telephone call the therapist noted that he sounded much younger than his age and slightly 'tongue-tied'.

Punctual for his appointment, Barry turned out to be a tall, thin man, with light brown hair cut in a 'short-back-and-sides' style. He had thick glasses which the therapist found somewhat distancing in that they made his eyes seem large and unreal. He wore a white shirt, black tie and blue jeans which were belted tightly at his waist. His shoes were large, black army-style boots. The therapist noted that Barry seemed rather 'tied in' at his waist, neck and ankles.

During this session, Barry was not very forthcoming, requiring the therapist to engage with him through gentle questioning. He would answer her questions hesitantly with little elaboration, simply waiting for the next question. She learnt that he had been working for a computer company for the past ten years and due to the company's 'rationalization' policy, along with several other employees, had been made redundant with the offer of three months' pay and the provision of therapy. The one time he became more talkative was when describing his job which entailed the management and maintenance of the company's computer system. He said that he liked the challenge of analysing intricate circuits: he was really surprised that he had lost his job. He added, 'People in the firm knew they could count on me to fix any machine, no problem.' His tone of confidence was noticeable to the therapist.

However, when describing why he had accepted the offer of therapy, Barry explained, without affect, that he had lost any sense of purpose. His motivation to find another job was low, despite the fact that he needed to earn a living. He had decided to try therapy thinking that it might help him 'get on top of things' again. The therapist commented on his technical skills and his ability to 'get on top of things' in respect of his work and wondered aloud how he might translate this to himself. He replied that he thought that he was missing something, a part, and was not at all certain as to whether this was the part that used to have a job or maybe 'something else that most people have'. At this moment, he seemed to deflect from pursuing this train of thought by taking off his glasses, dropping his head as he cleaned them. The therapist asked, 'Are you hoping that I will help you to find another job or help you explore this other part?' To which he responded, 'Well, in the first place I need to get a job and I don't know about the other.' She agreed to support him in exploring his options concerning future employment and also suggested that he may have a need to explore his experience of losing his job and the sense of purposelessness this had engendered. Agreeing on this focus, they contracted to meet for an initial series of six sessions with a review at the fifth session.

After this initial assessment session, the therapist used the Multidimensional Integrative Framework to begin to build up a picture of Barry from the impressions and information she had gained so far. Her first notes are shown in Figure 6.1.

From this initial gathering of information and impressions, the therapist already tentatively hypothesized that Barry had a schizoid adaptation and that with the guidance of Ware's doors to therapy (Ware, 1983, see Chapter 5), she knew that the way to make a safe connection with Barry would be first through focus on his behaviour. She would need to encourage him to communicate his internal thoughts and that, fundamentally, in the longer term, he would need to own and express his feelings. In the light of what, at this point, was a time-focused contract, she thought the behavioural focus on his re-employment would be the most important in addressing his self needs of physical survival (job and money), social/relationship

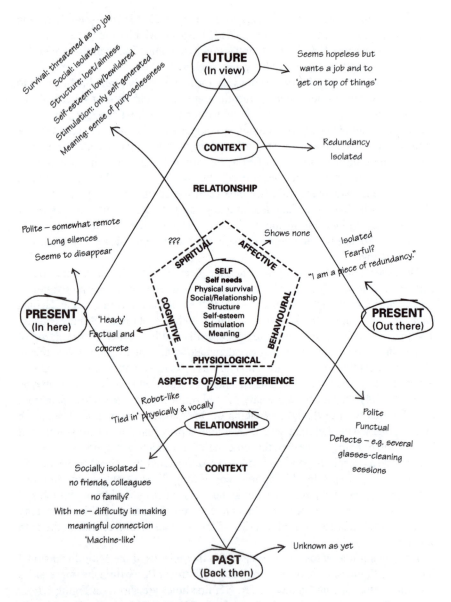

Figure 6.1 **The therapist's initial impressions**

(he seemed to relate to others through his work), structure (so far she had gathered that work was his main means of structuring his time), self-esteem (the pleasure he seemed to derive from being 'counted on'), stimulation (his interest and skills in information technology) and meaning (his sense of usefulness to others and his fascination with understanding things).

Some of the behaviours on which they focused in these first five sessions were, for example, his avoidance of going to job centres, writing to, rather than telephoning prospective employers and spending lengthy periods of time on the internet. Within the sessions, they explored his tendency to stare at the floor rather than make eye contact and his cleaning of his glasses which seemed to be a deflection from expressing any feeling. He introduced his childhood family in the fourth session with the comment that he remembered his mother also cleaned her glasses whenever he wanted her attention. The therapist inquired as to what that experience was like for him but he was unable to form any impression. At the end of this session he said he knew that the next session was to be a review but that he already felt he would end at the sixth session as he saw no point in digging up the past and, in any case, he thought that she was wasting her time trying to help someone as useless as him. 'I'm sure you're much more successful with your other clients.' The therapist asked him to think about how he was assuming a great deal about her thoughts and feelings and also might be pre-empting another imagined 'redundancy' by prematurely disconnecting himself from her support.

During the fifth session, Barry agreed with the therapist that he probably had been wanting to get rid of her before she had a chance of getting rid of him. He realized that he seldom in his life had felt wanted and that his job had been an exception to this. Empathically responding to Barry's disclosure, the therapist shared with him her understanding of how much more his job had been to him than just a source of income, and how great, therefore, his loss. She noted that this resulted in quite a busy spectacle-cleaning frenzy, though for part of that time he maintained eye contact with her for the first time. Later in the session, having reviewed their journey to this point, Barry requested to continue with the therapy for the full 12 sessions. He had been offered interviews for two jobs and was apprehensive at the prospect of being interviewed. He thought his therapist's support might enhance his chances of landing one of the jobs. They contracted for a further seven sessions with an emphasis on preparation for these interviews. The therapist held in mind that although this was a useful continuation of their original agreement of focus, the yet unexplored area was 'the missing part that others seemed to have'. Should Barry proactively make this figural, she would be open to supporting this need. However, again, she considered that the behavioural changes which Barry was undertaking were, perhaps, enough of a focus for this short-term work.

The following few sessions were occupied by Barry wanting to prepare for his job interviews. In exploring this focus, Barry's deep inability to make satisfactory social connections surfaced even more. She invited him to talk about himself to an imaginary panel of interviewers and was struck by Barry's nervousness which was displayed through long, agitated silences and 'tongue-tied' delivery. It came as no surprise to either of them that Barry failed to secure the first job for which he was interviewed. During their discussion, the therapist searched for any fantasies that Barry might be projecting onto the interviewers. He was surprised to uncover that he had thought the main interviewer was not interested in him right from the start of the interview. The therapist reminded him that he had also earlier thought that she herself might not be interested in him. In exploring this further, Barry realized that he was acting in the stressful situation of the interview as though he was in the presence of his mother and/or his elder siblings. At this stage, he began to describe the story of his early childhood making the first tentative links between past and present.

As part of his story, the therapist learned that his parents, Paul and Diana, had in the space of eight years produced four children, two boys and two girls and that, when the youngest of these children had become old enough to go to school, his mother had accidentally become pregnant with a fifth child, Barry. Not only had they not wanted any more children but she had been accepted on a training course to become a drama teacher. Although, they were not churchgoing, their Catholic beliefs prevented them from having a termination. Throughout his childhood, although he did not remember many details of it, he remembered thinking that he was an outsider in the family. His mother had been deeply connected to her third child, who was in fact her namesake. His father had seemed most interested in his second son, David. It had seemed to Barry that the eldest two , Paul and Pauline, and the younger two, Diana and David, had often paired off and played together with no space for him. This lack of belonging was compounded when, shortly before Barry's birth, his father accepted a job which involved long periods of time abroad.

Barry connected with the possibility that he expected people in authority or with some sort of power over him would either reject him (as mother did) or move away from him (as his father and siblings did). During his preparations for the second job interview, the therapist inquired if there was anyone in his life who had shown a real interest in him. He recalled his paternal grandfather, Fred, a clockmaker and repairer, being extremely kind and patient with him. His grandfather had made space in his workshop for Barry in which to play with the spare clock pieces. A shift occurred when, in preparing for the second interview, the therapist suggested that Barry imagine himself as his grandfather in the role of interviewer. Sitting silently for a while, he then, for the first time, smiled saying that he felt quite calm. Imagining himself then in the role of the interviewee with his grandfather asking questions, he retained his calmness and talked about himself much more confidently. This exercise helped Barry remember the benignity and interest his grandfather had had in him and to consider that these qualities could be present in others.

The therapist gradually pieced together a childhood history which very much echoed with the aetiology, as described by Johnson (1994), of the schizoid character style which he graphically names 'The Hated Child'. These children, very early in their existence or even at the discovery of their conception, are usually, either consciously or unconsciously, not wanted. As a consequence, they choose to withdraw or retroflect their efforts at connection with others, almost seeming to prefer to return to the safe, self-containment of the womb. Their being unwanted leads to a primitive decision that they have no right to exist and that the world is a dangerous place.

This conceptualization of Barry's character structure confirmed the therapist's initial hypothesis that she needed to provide, albeit within this brief time, a therapeutic relationship which was potentially holding and safe. The balance must be maintained between closeness and distance. She knew that to push too much or too quickly towards closeness, intimacy or understanding might result in Barry's withdrawal. Indeed, she had been concerned that the behavioural work they had done might have been retraumatizing for him in restimulating experiences of his childhood. However, in evoking the presence of Fred, his grandfather, she had provided a stabilizing influence (as well as her own) which allowed Barry to experiment without feeling that his 'strategy for survival' (Elton Wilson, 1996) was being threatened.

At the eleventh session, Barry reported that he had been successful in his second interview. The work he was offered was only part-time but it paid well and there was the possibility of full-time employment in the future as the company was expanding rapidly. The therapist congratulated him on his success and asked how he felt about it, curious to see how Barry was responding to this positive outcome. She noticed that he seemed indifferent to her congratulation, his voice remained flat and inexpressive and he cleaned his glasses as he reported his news without any sense of pleasure. However, he did slightly smile as he thanked her 'and Fred' for their support.

The therapist reminded him that they had one more session arranged in which they could review their time together and say goodbye if that was his intention. Somewhat to her surprise, he told her that he had already written to the EAP thanking them for their funding and informing them that he would like to continue with his therapist on a private basis. He showed her the reply supporting him in this and said that he would like his final, funded session to be the first of a longer term commitment to therapy. This positive and self-initiated development was immediately discounted by his saying, 'Of course, you may not want to go on with me. You may not think I'm worth it. You probably don't have the space for me to continue anyway,' all of which the therapist decided to ignore in favour of remarking positively on his decision-making and agreeing to continue to work with him. She thought that positive reinforcement at this point was more important than confronting his 'irrational beliefs', especially as ignoring such beliefs was a behaviourally appropriate technique of non-reinforcement.

They agreed to continue their weekly sessions with a time-extended commitment for 12 months and an agreed four sessions notice of finishing. Barry saw his continuing therapy as 'maintenance' for himself in his new job. He was particularly apprehensive about working in a new and strange environment with people he did not know. Additionally, Barry could see that his recent redundancy had affected him on many levels. It had highlighted his isolation and a sense of meaninglessness without social contact and time structure. Above all, it had reinforced a belief that there was something 'wrong' with him, that there was an indefinable 'part' of him missing. They agreed that exploring and discovering what this part of him might be and reclaiming it would be a major focus of their work together.

Using the Multidimensional Integrative Framework as a guide, along with discussion with her supervisor, the therapist began to form a sense of the direction in which her work with Barry might develop. Her theoretical integration included object relations (Fairbairn, 1954; Winnicott, 1958, 1965), intersubjectivity (Stolorow et al., 1987), self psychology (Kohut, 1971, 1984), attachment theory (Ainsworth, 1979; Bowlby, 1969, 1973), Gestalt (Perls et al., 1972) and transactional analysis (Berne, 1972), each of which she found compatible and complementary within our integrative framework and from which she could take guidance as to her procedural strategies. Her notes relating to these first twelve sessions are expanded here from her personal shorthand.

Self and self needs

Barry seems to have a fundamentally restricted sense of self and the vague sense of self he does have seems withdrawn into himself. There is little self energy flowing outwards towards others or into the world. Early lack of response, indeed rejection of the spontaneous and organismic selfhood of Barry, seems to have resulted in a defensive retreat into himself and detachment from others. I hypothesize that his sense of self will grow and flourish through the meeting of his self needs via the other aspects of self experience shown on the pentagon within relationship and context.

Most of Barry's self needs seem only to have been met, and this somewhat inadequately, through his work. I envisage that Barry will need to widen and deepen these relational and contextual aspects of his life if he is to meet his self needs more adequately.

Physiological

Barry seems held in tightly. He moves awkwardly. Being tall, this exacerbates a sense of his being ungrounded, despite the heavy boots, out of touch (literally) with the world. He lacks a body sense of self. His breathing is shallow as if he cannot fully 'take in' or 'give out'. Attention may be needed to both his breathing and his sensations – particularly that of touch – and bodily relaxation, letting go of what is held in.

NB   Does he need such thick-lensed glasses/are they a desensitization to contact with others and the world? He seems to make better eye contact on occasions when he takes them off, though see under Behavioural.

Behavioural

Open door (Ware, 1983): minimal eye contact – encourage maintaining eye contact. Glasses seem very significant – as a block to contact when on, as a deflection from feeling, by fiddling with them, when off. Carefully, devise experimentation with glasses.

Barry's main time structure is withdrawal (his activities are non-social, computer related). Explore alternatives for social pastiming and activities. Perhaps, later, attend social skills training group – assertion, personal effectiveness.

Procrastination/performance anxiety – build on present gains (job) through visualization and decreased perfectionistic expectations.

Affective

Trap door (Ware, 1983): Barry has shown little affect at all except for smiling occasionally and even this has an artificial quality. He talks in a flat, robot-like manner. My hypothesis of Barry's schizoid adaptation, based on Johnson's (1994) work, leads me to believe that in response to his cold, even hostile, early environment Barry would have felt chronic rage and terror – both of which would have been 'frozen' and/or retroflected to avoid both the untenable experience of them and the further hostile retaliation they may have engendered. Barry's withdrawal is a flight response rather than a fight response in conflictual situations which he tries to avoid anyway. He will need to acknowledge and later express these strong emotions in slow systematic stages, learning to manage his anger (which he may fear will be uncontrollable and destructive rage) and fear (which will contain the terror of annihilation of self and other). In other words, his defences need to be made conscious, gradually and carefully/caringly dismantled, so that his rage may be transformed into self-power and assertion, and his terror into appropriate fear and vulnerability. Our relationship (see later) will be vital in its ability to hold this expression. Grief is also likely to emerge as the defences decrease, both mourning the loss of self and the early lack of love. Barry's work is some semblance for him of a sense of self and of being loved (wanted/needed). Losing his job seems to have precipitated him into grief/depression which he experienced in his way as low motivation and an inability to 'get on top of things'. Regaining employment has temporarily allowed him to submerge his grief but will need to be addressed at some point in our work.

Cognitive

Target door (Ware, 1983): Barry's introjected, negative, self thoughts are mostly around his being rejected, useless, unwanted and not belonging, as well as under-lying beliefs that he has no right to exist and that there is something wrong with him. Others are seen as powerful and threatening. The world is seen as a threatening place. These beliefs need identifying, challenging and changing over time within a context of understanding and appreciating their origins in his past. Initially, Barry was reluctant to 'dig around in the past' and had few memories. However, having rediscovered Fred, he seems more open to thinking about his family and his past. Already his denial of his history and its effects upon him is lessening and he appears willing to make cognitive connections (if not yet affective ones) with his childhood.

Needs to develop ways of stopping negative thought patterns and creating positive and nurturing self-talk.

Spiritual

So far, Barry has not talked of any spiritual beliefs. I am aware that people with a schizoid style/adaptation have a tendency to escape or find something 'special' by spiritualizing: 'At least God loves me'. They avoid contact with people in this life in the belief that intimacy will be found in the next. Barry has mentioned that his parents were Catholic but not churchgoing.

Relationship (in time environment)

This is the crux of the matter. *Out there*: Barry has no friends, close colleagues or family. He is socially severely isolated and avoids people, except at work, at all costs.

In here: it is amazing that he has come into therapy at all. It is an enormous risk for him. I feel touched that he is willing to trust me however uncomfortable he still seems to be with me. Our working alliance seems well formed.

Conceptualizing the schizoid relational experience – *Back then*: starts at birth (maybe before) with a failure in attachment and bonding (Bowlby, 1969, 1973). The required 'good enough mothering' (Winnicott, 1958) was lacking, in fact parenting was rejecting and hostile. In Ainsworth's (1979) terminology, Barry shows 'anxious/avoidant attachment' in his avoidance and ignoring of the social existence/proximity of others (except, to a degree, with his work colleagues).

In here: Though he is with me in the room, I sometimes feel he is so out of contact with me, I could easily be the chair I'm sitting on. Any flashes of contact seem almost accidental and Barry quickly deflects from them.

Back then: Barry was unplanned and unwanted. His mother resented his existence. She had parented her four older children to school age which allowed her to apply for teacher's training. Barry's conception and birth disrupted her life-plan. Barry has yet to contact/disclose much of his early experiences in relationship to mother. So far she appears to have been cold, unresponsive and sometimes hostile to him as a child, certainly unavailable to him emotionally. His relationships with his older siblings were distanced by age and interests. His father was absent a great deal through his work abroad – which Barry's mother also resented. (NB *In here*: need to give good notice and sensitively handle my holiday arrangements with Barry.) Barry seems to have created his own inanimate world with mechanical toys and, later, computers which have become a substitute form of relationship via the internet – not even vicarious relationship with people on chat lines, simply in surfing for information.

Out there: Barry seems to project onto others and the world, the harsh and rejecting experiences of his childhood (disinterested, critical interviewers and work colleagues) and to be negative towards himself (I'm useless/worthless). Hypothesis: this interpersonal and intrapsychic manifestation arises from the early internalization of the 'bad object' (Fairbairn, 1954) which is also rendered unconscious in avoidance of pain and discomfort.

In here: transferentially, it is likely that Barry will project onto me his harsh and rejecting mother and distance himself from me by withdrawal from such perceived harshness. Equally, as he has done already, he may retroflect this harshness, seeing himself as useless and worthless and, therefore, unworthy of my attention. In TA terms, his Critical Parent ego state is both projected onto others and activated internally towards his Child ego state within which he compliantly adapts by withdrawal. Countertransferentially, it is important that I do not collude with invitations to be the Critical Parent, to reject him or appear disinterested and that I share my thoughts and feelings as appropriate in order to keep in relationship with him when I am feeling distanced from him or he is withdrawing from me. It is important that I remain aware of the co-created reality of our relationship and genuinely own my part in it.

Barry is held in ambivalence concerning relationship – both desiring contact (as in those early moments/days/weeks of life) and avoiding it (as was necessary in response to the hostile early environment). My task is to help us to develop a safe, 'good enough' therapeutic relationship, a 'holding environment' in which Barry can experience a 'corrective emotional experience' (Alexander and French, 1946) and allow himself to acknowledge and express the rage and terror 'held in' from that pre-symbiotic period without retaliation. I need to hold in mind Barry's ambivalence (desire/avoidance) towards relationship. My supervisor's provision of the image of a tortoise inside its protective shell is helpful. I must gently approach and encourage him out of that shell if I am to make a relationship at all. If I am too close, too soon, too suddenly, Barry will withdraw. Perhaps I need to be prepared for several appearances and withdrawals along the way to helping Barry to develop his capacity for intimacy and healthy dependence with others. *In view*: Be patient but keep moving!

In self psychology terms, it is evident so far that Barry's early needs of mirroring, idealizing and twinship (Kohut, 1971, 1984) were basically unmet, except, perhaps, his twinship needs when working alongside grandfather in his workshop as a child. Barry lacks the 'transmuting internalizations' (Kohut, 1971) necessary for the development of self and self-esteem. In our work together, by my empathic attunement to Barry, my acceptance of him, my communication of my understanding and my sensitive handling of my empathic failures, Barry's archaic needs will have the opportunity to emerge and be accepted so that he can integrate into his adult personality those needs which have been so far split off and unacknowledged. By my acceptance and understanding of those needs, I hope to enable Barry to get more of his self needs met in his life and, in particular, in his relationships with others.

Context

Barry lives 'on the edge' of contact with others and the world. By this I mean, he does not totally isolate himself but he is not actually involved. He lives in a small fourth-floor flat above a shopping precinct – busy and bustling during the day and at weekends, deserted at night. I imagine him at home surfing the internet with the sounds of others – traffic, talking, shouting, laughing – rising from the street below. Equally, his chosen work entails constantly moving from one part of the building to another, from one group of people to another, to look after their computers. There is minimal, actual, sustained contact with others – but some. He seems to have replicated his family context whereby he is 'in the family' but not a part of it. He lives in a world which both values his skills and denigrates them, the 'IT man – always a bit odd/the outsider'. I wonder how he sees himself nearing 40, living alone, with no intimate relationship and no friends. We have not yet broached the subject of his sex life. My fantasy is that he has never had sex with another person.

Time frame: see above, especially under relationship.

Back then: Barry seems more willing and able to make connections with the past. His memories are few at present, but I consider that as he feels safer he will allow his past experiences into his awareness.

In here/Out there/Back then: tentatively, I am gradually introducing the idea that how Barry experiences me in the therapeutic relationship reflects both his current relationships with others and those from the past. He seems to have accepted the connection I made between his perception of criticism/disinterest from interviewers with a similar fantasized response in me and with the origins of that perception being in his actual experience as a child.

In view: just as Barry has, as yet, only a vague concept of his past (from which he has dissociated), he has but a vague concept of his future. In the short term, he wants to keep his newly gained employment and wants my support in this endeavour. When I asked where and how he saw himself in five years' time, he said, 'I hope I'll be working full-time.' I asked how he saw himself, apart from his working life, and he could not answer. When I suggested his future sounded rather lonely, he replied, 'No, there will be friends.' I will hold this as, perhaps, an expression of his true desire for relationship, though at present I wonder if my questions invited an adapted answer, more of a should than a self-generated and formulated want. On the other hand, his 'feeling' that there is something, part of him, missing may indicate that somewhere his organismic need of relationship struggles to be articulated.

The therapeutic process

Barry and his therapist agreed the time-extended contract for one year. The therapist clarified that this would be inclusive of a two-week break at Christmas (only eight sessions away) and Easter and a four-week break over the summer with the agreement of four weeks' notice of finishing should either of them decide to terminate the therapy before the year was out. Barry seemed satisfied with this time scale and they agreed a fee for weekly sessions that he could afford.

Over the next several sessions Barry was preoccupied with his new job. He was mostly intent upon describing the types of computers and programmes he was working with and the therapist tried to meet him at his level of interest despite her lack of enthusiasm for computers. She found it hard to maintain her concentration and felt distanced rather than in contact with him at times. However, she noticed that he was instigating communication with her, was less faltering in his delivery, made occasional eye contact and sat back more comfortably as if more at ease with her. She appreciated his enthusiasm and decided not to intervene into what, for Barry, was a development in communication, but rather to respond as best she could by her quiet attention, her interested gaze and the occasional verbal response or question. She found that if she stayed in touch with his and her own process rather than the content, she felt more in contact with him as a person, despite all the technical jargon that seemed to be a deflection from contact. Getting behind the content assisted her into his world.

> *Therapist*: Barry, I notice you've removed your glasses. Is there something else going on for you as you describe this particular computer problem you've been solving?
> *Barry*: It's a hard one. It's a new programme.
> *Therapist*: The computer problem's a hard one ? It sounds like a challenge.
> *Barry*: It is. But I'll solve it. Definitely.

Therapist: When you take off your glasses, sometimes it's when you are concerned about something. You sound very sure, but still I wonder if you have a concern.

Barry: It's not the programme.

Therapist: It's not the programme? You can solve the programme. It's something else.

Barry: People are different.

Therapist: Mmmm, people are different from programmes. When you said, 'It's a hard one' were you meaning something more to do with people?

Barry: I think so.

Therapist: With the people at work?

Barry: They've been there a long time.

Therapist: And you . . .?

Barry [agitating with his glasses for quite a while]: I'm the new boy.

The therapist was both touched and enthused by this poignant disclosure. For the first time, Barry was not expressing himself through the metaphor of machinery. Inadvertently, through the enthusiasm she felt, she then hurried to maximize on the intimacy of the moment. Seeing the glasses solely as a deflection, she decided to experiment with an intervention.

Therapist: Tell me what that's like, being the new boy. How about putting your glasses down while you tell me ?

Barry put his glasses down. The moment was lost. He could not speak. He sat forward in his chair and his breathing became fast and shallow. The therapist realized that she had rushed him into too much, too soon. She had not only asked him to tell her about what was clearly a disturbing experience for him, she had asked him to do so without what she now saw as the 'comfort' as well as the distraction of his glasses. Rather than continuing her gentle inquiry she had become much more directive. After a while, Barry put on his glasses and sat in silence, noticeably calmer but withdrawn into himself.

In the silence, the therapist berated herself for her clumsy intervention. However, she knew that she could more usefully reflect on her error later, and that she needed to connect with Barry before the end of the session if they were to retrieve some of the gains in contact so far achieved. Though he seemed to have regained his composure through withdrawal into himself, she was concerned that this experience might have been traumatic enough for him to quit therapy.

Therapist: I'm sorry you're having a hard time at work and I'm really sorry if I've given you a hard time here today in asking you to put your glasses down.

Barry remained silent and unmoving, looking at the floor.

Therapist: It's hard for you out there. It's hard for you in here. I guess there's some connection.

Barry [falteringly]: I'm the new boy here too.

Therapist: And I haven't respected that enough today. Maybe you've experienced me as being as difficult as your new colleagues.

Barry: They're always in a hurry. They want things done yesterday.
Therapist: Just like me.

In reflecting on this important and difficult session, the therapist made several observations, connections and reformulations of her hypotheses using the multidimensional framework as a container to explore and record them.

Behavioural/Affective

While Barry's fiddling with his glasses may be a deflection from the full expression of his feelings, for him it is also, perhaps, a vehicle for his feelings, the only way, at present, that he is able to communicate feeling anything at all. The glasses seem to serve the dual role of comforter and communicator.

Relationship

Back then: his mother used to fiddle with her glasses when he wanted/needed her attention. For Barry they may express a form, however meagre, of intimacy; in moments of need this was the only representation of contact.

In here: I need to hold this possibility so that I can better attune to his contact need and acknowledge my understanding of that need – rather than confront the deflective nature of the glasses which may or may not be indicated later. Perhaps my own use of my reading glasses at some appropriate moment may normalize and model how to stay in contact rather than as a deflection. But, clearly, I need to wait for an opportune moment and not rush into this.

In terms of relationship/context (*in here/out there*) I have replicated Barry's experience of being hurried/rushed to do things at work which probably exacerbates his fear of getting things wrong (and his belief that there is something wrong with him), alienating him from his work colleagues and from me.

NB   Transactional analysis theory makes a link between the 'Hurry Up' driver ('Don't Be Long') and the injunction 'Don't Belong'. This is also likely to be his internal experience – being rushed by his internalized mother who wanted him to grow up quickly and be independent, to be as grown-up as his siblings even when a baby so as not to hinder her plans. Countertransferentially, I need to be aware of Barry's induction for me to play this role but I also need to curb my own tendency to hurry things. Remember the tortoise.

In the unconscious co-creation of the drama of that moment – his experience of my empathic failure – we may have stumbled into Barry's internal world. His description of himself as 'the new boy' is his most personal disclosure to date and has wide-reaching ramifications – at work, with me, in the world in general. *Back then*: in his family he was the unwanted new boy, the outsider, the child 'on the edge' of it all (as at school later). I felt moved as he said these words – and warm towards him. Though my intervention turned out to be a challenge, I wonder if my unaware intention was a Rescue (Karpman, 1968) – to treat him as if he was not 'a new boy' – which, in the event, was to treat him (Victim) just as his mother

(Persecutor) had done. NB I need to allow him to be the new boy and let him grow up in his way, in his time.

The continuing therapeutic process

In the ensuing sessions leading up to the Christmas break, they focused on Barry's experience of being the 'new boy' at work, making the links back to his childhood experiences as well as making reference to his being the new boy in therapy. Barry acknowledged that although he had not articulated it in this way before, this was a familiar experience for him. Just as he had always felt to be the new boy in the family, he had always felt he was the new boy even in his previous jobs, however long he was there. They recognized that despite the uncomfortable nature of this 'new boy' role, it also paradoxically served to keep him 'special'. He saw that this may apply to his role with the therapist.

The therapist was careful to stay attuned to Barry's pace and depth. However, she decided it was necessary to bring up the subject of the break over Christmas as Barry seemed to be avoiding acknowledging this contextual reality. In response, he informed her that he would be working right through the break, even on Christmas Day, as the company needed a skeleton staff on duty. He had, not surprisingly, volunteered to work.

Therapist: You've said how that's financially good for you. I wonder if there are other advantages?

Barry: There won't be too many people around.

Therapist: Not too many but some.

Barry: Yes.

Therapist: It sounds like you'll be well occupied over Christmas with some company but not the usual number, and presumably not the usual rush.

Barry: Yes, I won't be so pressured.

Therapist: There'll be less pressure at work. I wonder if that applies to here too? How do you feel about my not being around for two weeks?

Barry [fiddling with glasses]: That's OK.

Therapist: That's OK?

Barry: Well, I'd rather not have a break from coming but you obviously need a holiday.

Therapist: That's true but it sounds like it may not be a relief from pressure for you like at work. I can understand you might see it as an interruption to our work together.

Barry: I do feel that a bit.

Therapist: And if you put a name to what you are feeling?

Barry: I feel disappointed.

This was the first feeling word Barry had used in the four months they had worked together. It was a big step for Barry and the therapist was tempted to remark on it. However, she controlled her enthusiasm and remained silent but attentive. Barry did not look uncomfortable as he spent the last few minutes in the silence.

Following the break, Barry reported that he had been 'fine'. The therapist noted, however, that he was not as forthcoming as he had previously been and that she needed to engage him by gentle questioning much as in the early stages. This advance and retreat was a pattern she came to expect and respect throughout their work together. She felt that he needed her interest in him to be constantly reaffirmed.

Over the next three months, Barry seemed more amenable to interventions that focused on his physiological and behavioural 'aspects of self experience'. The therapist saw these, within the crucial holding of the therapeutic relationship, as likely to allow some melting of his frozen affect, as well as a means of confirming his right to exist (to take up space, to be present, to be felt in the room). At times, she would draw his attention to his breathing, suggesting that he experiment with slowing and deepening his breath. She would also invite him to repeat things louder or slower and to make eye contact as he did so. Barry often found these experiences uncomfortable, but he nonetheless showed a willingness to experiment in his communication with her and did not withdraw into himself. The therapist observed that Barry seemed to be 'softening', was less robot-like and more of a human presence in the room. He was more likely to instigate communication at the start of the sessions. However, this was not the case in a particular session about eight months into their work.

For the first time, Barry arrived late for his session. He sat impassively and stared out of the window. The therapist waited for a while to see if he would make any contact with her. Barry seemed to be ignoring her.

Therapist. I feel there's something you want to say to me. I am here and very willing to hear you.

Barry stayed silent. The therapist did not want to push him and yet she suspected that if she echoed Barry's passivity, he would disappear even more.

Therapist. You may not want to talk at the moment but you seem to be saying something in your silence. Would you be willing to look at me?

Barry removed his glasses, placed them at his side, and looked at her. The therapist maintained eye contact with him despite the coldness she felt to be emanating from him.

Therapist. And if you breathe a little deeper right now?

There was a long pause. Barry breathed slightly more deeply.

Barry [flatly]: I can't come any more.

The therapist waited to see if Barry would expand upon this. He did not.

Therapist. You can't come to therapy any more? I'm really sorry to hear that. What is it that's led you to make such a decision?

[Pause.]

Barry [reaching for his glasses] I don't know.
Therapist. Is there some connection with your being late?
Barry: I couldn't get here on time.
Therapist. That's OK. That happens sometimes. Was there something that prevented you being here on time?

[Long pause.]

Barry: I didn't want to come.

Therapist: You didn't want to come but you did come. It sounds like you made a decision to come despite not wanting to. Perhaps, you wanted to bring something here in the belief it might be useful to do that.

Barry: Yes.

Therapist: Do you know what that something might be?

Barry seems to be deep in thought before eventually speaking.

Barry: There was an incident at work today. There's a new boss in one of the offices. I don't like being shouted at. I went home rather than coming straight here. Then I came here.

Therapist: And you arrived late. Did you wonder if I might shout at you?

Barry: Yes . . . No . . . I got confused.

Therapist: It sounds like it was really disturbing for you that this new boss shouted. Did he shout at you directly?

Barry: She.

Therapist: I'm sorry, she . . . she shouted at you?

Barry: She told me to go away and come back later. I'd only just opened the door.

Therapist: So she hardly saw you?

Barry: No, she didn't see me.

Therapist: Let me see if I've got this right. You were going into an office to check the computers. You opened the door. The new woman, not even seeing you, coldly shouted for you to go away and come back later.

Barry: That's right. I felt dismissed.

Therapist: You felt dismissed. You know, Barry, I felt a bit like that when you arrived today. You didn't seem to see me. I felt ignored. And then you said you couldn't come any more. I wonder if you were wanting to dismiss me?

[Pause.]

Barry: Partly. I was confused.

Therapist: Perhaps, you thought I might dismiss you for being late and you were getting in first like at the beginning of therapy?

Barry: I didn't want you to be dismissive of me. I didn't want you to shout at me.

Therapist: What did you want?

[Long pause.]

Barry: I wanted you to listen. I wanted you to understand.

The therapist, beginning with behavioural and physiological interventions into his silence, had facilitated Barry into relational contact which enabled Barry to disclose his ambivalence to being there (*In here*) and the connection with his work incident (*Out there*). The parallels between *In here* and *Out there* were highlighted in the self-disclosure by the therapist of how she had felt in response to Barry. This sharing of her experience (which she understood to be projective identification) facilitated Barry's first voicing of his want to be heard and understood.

The therapist stayed with Barry's perception of the incident at work. She was aware that there may have been several explanations for how the new boss behaved. She may have been otherwise engaged, anxious in her new position, needing to raise her voice across a busy office, and so on. More important was Barry's experience, the impact it had had and the connections between *Out there* and *In here*. By staying with his experience, listening and empathically sharing her understanding, the therapist met his self need. Later in the session, Barry was able to allow some memories of *Back then* to surface.

Over the next several sessions Barry talked of his past. What became apparent through Barry's recollection of snatches of childhood experiences was that his mother was not only cold and rejecting, but also angrily hostile towards him. She shouted at him for no reason that he could see – except his very existence – threatening him with violence which was sometimes, unpredictably, expressed by physical blows across the head. He recalled hiding under the stairs in physical pain, terrified, bewildered and confused, ignored by his siblings and parents.

The therapist's reformed hypothesis concerning the meaning of the glasses seemed more accurate in the light of his disclosures. Barry shared that compared to his mother's shouting and aggression or her ignoring of him, her fiddling with her glasses in response to his need for attention was some semblance of intimacy with her. Similarly, he was comforted in the knowledge that while she fiddled he was safe from her outbursts.

After the Easter break, Barry had regressed into his withdrawn defensive state which his therapist had come to expect. The sessions seemed ponderous and repetitive. Nothing appeared to be happening, yet the therapist trusted that there was something equally important for Barry, for them both, in these bland periods as in the more observably active times. He was attending without fail. She was listening without expectation. He seemed to trust that she would be there and would listen and understand. Between them they appeared to be creating a 'wanted space' – a place where he wanted to be and a place where he felt his being was wanted, in which he could exist as himself without pressure and without criticism.

Some months later, Barry voluntarily shared his insight into the situation when he described his experience of therapy as 'coming out from under the stairs'. This became the metaphor for their ongoing work together which, by the end of the first year, they agreed would continue, without limitation, as a 'time-expanded' contract (Elton Wilson, 1996).

The Multidimensional Integrative Framework was used by the therapist as a reference point at several stages of their work together. She found it useful in holding in mind the various aspects of Barry's experience and the relation of his experiences to the past, present and future both outside and within the therapy room. Through the framework, she was able theoretically to integrate her knowledge and experience and to formulate hypotheses concerning what Barry brought into the therapy. It also helped her to reflect upon her responses and her strategies of procedure. Their work together has continued for three years and is ongoing. At this point in time, the therapist has summarized their work to date by reference to the framework as follows:

Physiological

Barry has 'softened' in his physical appearance, moves in a more flowing and relaxed way and is less 'held in'. This is reflected in his clothing which is now looser and more colourful. Directed awareness to his breathing has become a useful self-support for Barry. Initially, I introduced Gestalt experiments with breathing based on the Gestalt proposition that with regard to excitement 'the healthy organism responds in simple fashion by increasing the rate and amplitude of breathing' (Perls et al., 1972: 128). Barry did just the opposite, trying to control his breathing, making it shallow and thus constricting his chest. I followed the Gestalt assumption that 'anxiety, the disturbance of breathing, accompanies any disturbance of the self-function; thus the first step in therapy is contacting the breathing' (1972: 401). This focus seems to have assisted Barry gradually to contact some sense of feeling as well as to bring him into relationship with me.

Towards the end of the second year, nearing the summer break, I suggested that Barry might find it beneficial to arrange for some massage sessions. My thinking was that this would both act as a 'holding' over the break as well as provide him with a safe experience of touch. Though he found the first massage 'quite painful', experiencing even the lightest touch as 'burning my skin', by the third session he found the experience pleasurable and relaxing. He continues to have massage on a monthly basis and I believe this has contributed to his general physiological softening.

Behavioural

My first obvious empathic failure in my rushed experimentation with Barry and his glasses proved, over time, to deepen my understanding of Barry's internal world as well as to precipitate him into disclosure of some feeling. There was also a shift in our relationship with Barry's perception of himself as 'the new boy' with me and the specialness this evoked for him despite the accompanying discomfort. This confirmed my understanding that 'these perceptions serve as points of departure for an exploration of the meanings and organizing principles that structure the patient's psychic reality' (Stolorow et al., 1987). Thus my inadvertent error in behavioural focus led to exploration within more affective and cognitive aspects of Barry's experience and his self need of meaning.

In the early stages, I invited Barry to make more eye contact with me as a means of increasing relational contact and communication. Over the past year, such invitations have rarely been necessary, except occasionally, following a break, when Barry still tends to withdraw (though less so) into himself. My introduction of the use of my reading glasses into some sessions gradually had a marked effect on Barry. I would take them off in a deliberate fashion, hold them still while looking at him intently, before replacing them. Barry has incorporated this use of making eye contact instead of lowering his head and fiddling with them. Barry has observed that if he makes eye contact with people at work, not only do they often say 'hello', they are likely to smile at him and engage in conversation. We have looked at this in terms of Stroke Theory in transactional analysis where such 'units of recognition' are seen as vital to our self need of relationship, structure (including the ritual 'hellos' and pastiming), self-esteem and stimulation – indeed, our very experience of existing which is, of course, what Barry has lacked from birth. Such a behavioural shift on his part has led to his feeling more comfortable and secure in his work situation and his performance anxiety has concomitantly decreased. In terms of encouraging Barry to extend his social skills further, he has not been keen to take up my suggestions of joining a personal effectiveness group. However, he has joined an evening group at work which, although computer related, does allow him to pastime more with his colleagues.

One of the most significant behavioural changes in our sessions, with implications for most of the other aspects of his experience, has been his instigation of shaking hands with me before leaving.

Affective

Bearing in mind that this is initially the trap door (Ware, 1983) for working with a person with a schizoid adaptation, and following Johnson's premise that both rage and terror have been chronically 'frozen' from a very early age in a person with this characterological style, I have endeavoured to work slowly and gradually towards helping Barry to access his feelings. Over time, he has come to identify his feelings (and relational contact) as 'the part of me that is missing that other people seem to have'.

From the initial naming of his disappointment at our first break, Barry has gone on to add several other feeling experiences to his repertoire as his ability to translate bodily sensations into feeling words has increased. Mostly, his expression of affect takes the milder forms of annoyance, apprehension and being 'fed up'. However, he has recently talked in angry terms of his mother's treatment of him and, on occasions, spontaneously raised his voice. He has also registered some sadness when exploring his experience of his father and his siblings and their distance from him as a child. As yet, he has not 'melted' enough to express that sadness or to allow the mourning of his early loss and lack to emerge.

We have explored his feeling experiences towards me, particularly around the time of the breaks. My hunch was that he would be angry at my 'abandoning' him at such times much as his mother had abandoned him and his needs as a child. However, while this may be a part of his experience which needs further exploration, what Barry has mostly expressed is his fear in response to my being unavailable. My reformed hypothesis is that his mother's cold fiddling with her glasses, her hostility, even her physical abuse, though painful and frightening was, at least, a form of contact and that what was even more terrifying for Barry was his necessary retreat under the stairs, alone and ignored for hours on end. This hypothesis is supported by Stroke Theory where 'negative strokes are better than no strokes at all. Being insulted may be preferable to 'being sent to Coventry'. Being punished physically may be preferable to the stroke-deprivation of solitary confinement' (Lapworth et al., 1993). Experiencing therapy as 'coming out from under the stairs', it is not surprising that the breaks in our contact may seem like being back in solitary confinement to Barry. His expression of his fear, and my understanding of his experience, seems to be a useful step in 'undoing' his past terror and this is the point we have reached at this time.

Cognition

It was important that I took an interest in Barry's preoccupation with computers and their problems. I needed to meet him in his world before we could 'get behind' it and understand it as a metaphor of his life.

Barry's perception of himself, others and the world has changed mostly through attention at other aspects of the pentagon rather than direct confrontation of his script beliefs. For example, changing his pattern of behaviour in terms of eye contact with me and with others at work has challenged his perception of himself as being automatically rejected, unwanted and having no right to exist or to belong. Others are seen as less threatening and the world is not such a dangerous place – rather there is often a response from others and the world that affirms his existence and confirms his right to belong. These beliefs have, of course, also been addressed within our relationship and the 'wanted' space we have co-created.

In the light of his early experience within his family, Barry's Representations of Interactions that have been Generalized (Stern, 1985) and his later script beliefs are understandable – others were hostile and rejecting, the world was either a dangerous place or, under the stairs, a lonely and frightening place. Discovering the exception of his more positive twinship experience with Fred, his grandfather, provided a starting point for testing out and generalizing the possibility that others may receive him with similar benignity.

In recent months, I have noticed that Barry is self-monitoring and self-correcting the negative thought patterns with which he reinforces his script beliefs. There is markedly less invitation to collusion with his self-discounting remarks. For example, following our discussion of his need to miss a session (for the first time) through attending a course, he was about to complete a throw-away remark about how relieved I would be. He stopped mid-sentence and instead said that he was sorry to be missing the session. I expressed that I too would genuinely miss our session together.

Despite Barry's initial reluctance to 'dig around in the past', over the years we have made several inroads into his childhood experiences. Memories, images and senses of his 'unthought known' (Bollas, 1987) have emerged and enabled us to build up a picture of his early world and his internalization of it. These have included his perception and understanding of himself as 'the new boy', 'the boy under the stairs', the 'frozen' child disconnected from life; of his 'redundancy' in the family, of the impossible demands for him to 'Hurry Up and Grow Up' to 'get on top of things' in a family that hardly acknowledged his existence or, when they did were hostile and abusive towards him, of his longing to be special and of his desire for and avoidance of contact, often expressed through the medium of his unusual form of transitional object (Winnicott, 1965) – his glasses.

Barry's recognition of how his past experiences have shaped his way of being in the world has evolved gradually over the years. The role of his mother, her attitude towards him at conception and her treatment of him from birth, began to emerge more fully towards the end of our first year of working together. Only in the past year has Barry begun to acknowledge the influence of his distant older siblings and, more particularly, the significance and impact of his absent father. We have yet to explore the pairing dynamics within his family that excluded him entirely.

Though these insights are important and helpful, it is only through the attendant focus upon them in relation to other aspects of his self experience – particularly the affective and relational aspects – that Barry is beginning to integrate his past experiences, to satisfy his early unmet needs and to gain a cohesive sense of self.

Spiritual

Unlike some people with a schizoid adaptation, Barry has not 'spiritualized' his experience as a means of finding a realm where he can exist without hate. It seems rather that he has transformed some of his negative experience of being 'the new boy' into a means of achieving a fantasy of specialness: an internal perception that flies in the face of his early external reality. He appears to have withdrawn into himself rather than reach for some higher force to help him survive. And yet he has survived. Perhaps, this is a manifestation of a spiritual aspect in itself though I am also aware that the power of Physis (Berne, 1969/81) can be seen as the natural biological force working at each of the other aspects of the pentagon.

If spirituality is our capacity to stand in awe and wonder at the beauty, power and enormity of the universe, it is not surprising that Barry has no such experience; he is just crawling out from under the stairs. Though he is discovering that the world is not necessarily as threatening a place as it was as a child, he has a long way to go before he will trust it enough to find it a place of wonder. However, I think the very fact that he continues to come to therapy indicates his desire for such enchantment.

Relationship

Out there: Barry is gradually increasing his relational contact with others (see also Behavioural). In the workplace, he is conversationally engaged with some of his colleagues, especially those who also attend the evening group. He has recently gone for a drink with some of the group and reported that he enjoyed his time with them in the pub. The group is all male so he will need to widen his network to increase his social contact with women. Though sexually inexperienced with either sex, he does not think he is gay. At present, his only female relationships are over the internet where he has begun to access chat lines. While this may seem remote from real intimacy, for Barry it has taken enormous courage and I have seen glimmers of excitement when he is describing some of his experiences 'on line'. It may well be a way in for him. He has yet to accept some of the women's offers of meeting. For now, he prefers to 'chat' (some of which he admits to being sexual) over the safe distance of cyberspace.

In here: our therapeutic relationship has slowly developed over the years. Barry has become a real presence in the room and relates to me much more directly. His recent shaking hands with me at the end of the sessions seems to symbolize his growing sense of being 'in touch' with me and with others. I see it also as demonstrating his increasing trust in our relationship which he is generalizing to other areas of his life.

In here/Back then: transferentially, Barry has lessened his projection of his rejecting and critical mother onto me. There have been times, especially in the first year, when my countertransferential feelings of impatience (Hurry Up), and, sometimes, disinterest (especially in his technical discussions), have replicated Barry's experience of his mother. However, one of the most important learnings I have made while working with Barry is that these times of empathic failure, if I honestly and undefensively acknowledge and discuss them, and if I communicate my understanding of his experience of them, not only can be tolerated by Barry but assist him in empathically supporting himself. Kahn, in discussing the theory of 'transmuting internalization'(Kohut, 1971), writes that, if the failure of mirroring does not happen too often, children who are well mirrored most of the time 'can draw on the memory of those [times] and thus discover an ability to get along without the mirror – at least for a brief time, at least once in a while. And when that happens, they discover that at least for a brief time, at least once in a while, they can be their own mirror' (Kahn, 1991: p.85).

I believe that within our co-created relationship we have developed a strong enough working alliance and a good-enough mirroring relationship for Barry to internalize and build up supportive self-structures at times of my empathic failures as well as in his dealings with others out there. In terms of the idealizing transference, I believe that Barry had so little to idealize in his experience of his parents and others that it will be some time before he takes the risk of overtly indicating any idealization of me. Yet I believe the fact that he has been in therapy with me for three years, and that he dedicatedly continues, must reflect the meeting of some of his idealizing needs and the glimmer of hope contained deep within him. I am aware that we have not explored the possible existence or development of an erotic transference within our therapeutic relationship. I am keeping this *in view* as our work together continues.

Perhaps Fred, his grandfather, who provided some twinship needs for Barry, was also a source of idealization but this is not yet as clear as the role he played in answering Barry's later need to be like others. This he is achieving increasingly in his relationship with me, with others and in his general perception of himself in the world.

Context

In the second year of our work together, Barry was offered full-time employment which he readily accepted. This has given him financial security, a sense of purpose and belonging, additional stimulation and greater structure to his life. However, while his work is still extremely important to him, he is not so work orientated as in the past. His evening group, visits to the pub, massage, pastiming with a neighbour in an adjoining flat and, recently, his 'socializing' on the internet have widened his experience of others and the environment in which he lives. He is less 'on the edge' of life.

In view

Barry's earlier hope of where he would be in five years time, namely, that he would again be in full-time employment has been achieved. His less certain vision that 'there will be friends' is just beginning to become more of a reality in the widening of his social network. His aspirations have expanded. He sees himself not only increasing his social network and making good friends who will visit him at his flat and whose homes he will visit, but of being in a one-to-one relationship with a woman. The idea of this being a living together relationship is not one that, at present, appeals to him. Rather, he sees the development and achievement of a close emotional and sexual friendship with a woman as likely to meet enough of his self needs.

Part III
OTHER FRAMEWORKS AND PROCEDURES FOR INTEGRATION

In Part III we have selected five examples of integrative frameworks in order to demonstrate both the commonality and diversity of integrative conceptualizations already in existence. They have been chosen to further illustrate the Framework Strategy and the Procedural Strategy outlined in Chapter 3. Indeed, some encompass both of these levels of integration and it will be evident that many of the examples have informed our own framework.

The reader, having explored the Multidimensional Integrative Framework, has already been exposed to a variety of aspects, categorizations and areas of focus. We are aware that you may feel somewhat bombarded with further frameworks, levels, models and the like in the next part. Inevitably, each framework comes with its own taxonomy and way of deconstructing the therapeutic task. In providing these in addition to our own, we hope you will find it useful to compare and contrast, adopt, adapt or reject according to your own individual views and theoretical perspectives on the way to developing your own personal integrative frameworks.

7
The Therapeutic Relationship

The therapeutic relationship is an essential facet of our Multidimensional Integrative Framework as shown in Part II. It may also be seen as an integrative formulation in its own right. We have, therefore, included it early in this section as an independent integrative framework and also as a more in-depth perspective on the therapeutic relationship already discussed within our multidimensional framework.

Human personality is formed in relationship. From our earliest moments, we are in the process of developing as individuals in a world where we are constantly in relationship with others. Our sense of ourselves, be that strong and robust or fragile and unstable, is dependent, and some may say formed, by that relationship between self and other. It is logical therefore to acknowledge that any change or development in our sense of self also takes place in relationship.

Increasing amounts of research (for example, Bergin and Lambert, 1978; Hill, 1989; Luborsky et al., 1983; O'Malley et al., 1983) have suggested that the most significant factor in therapeutic change is the relationship between the client and the counsellor, psychotherapist or psychiatrist. 'The therapist's interpersonal skills and capacity for forming meaningful therapeutic relationships account for more outcome variants than either theories or methods' (Norcross in Dryden, 1991: 35). Stern (1997) offers a powerful explanation for why this may be so. He refers to the 'intersubjective self' – that sense of ourselves which is capable of connecting with another and knowingly sharing the experience. He suggests that a connection between practitioner and client in this area has a profound impact on what he calls 'relational knowing' – that unconscious, non-verbal, non-symbolic body of knowledge that a person has about self in the world and in relation to another person.

It is important, therefore, to make the establishment and maintenance of the therapeutic relationship a central goal in the process of psychotherapy and counselling. It is also possible to see this relationship as the integrating matrix in which the individual counsellor's philosophical, theoretical and methodological approaches can be viewed.

Many writers have examined the various facets of the therapeutic relationship and its centrality to the therapeutic process (for example, Barr, 1987; Clarkson, 1990; Elton Wilson, 1996; Gelso and Carter, 1985; Greenson, 1965; Horvath and Greenberg, 1994; Hycner, 1985; Hycner and Jacobs, 1995; Kahn, 1991; Rogers, 1951,1957,1967). We believe that such facets provide a type of taxonomy which helps us organize experiences in the therapy and focus on the work.

From the wealth of literature on this topic we describe six aspects: those offered by Gelso and Carter (1985) who delineate three aspects of the therapeutic relationship – the working alliance, the transference and the real relationship; two added by Clarkson (1990), the reparative relationship and the transpersonal, and a sixth from Gilbert (1995), the contextual relationship. We find it useful to group these six aspects into three domains: the professional, the projective and the personal.

1 *The professional relationship* is that area of the relationship defined and imposed by the roles of the participants – the therapist and the client.
2 *The projective relationship* is the area which is created by the (both accurate and inaccurate) assumptions, expectations and constructions of each party.
3 *The personal relationship* is the area in which the partners in the relationship meet as person to person.

The Professional Relationship

The professional relationship refers to that aspect of the counselling or psychotherapeutic relationship concerned with the contract between therapist and client. This contract includes such administrative arrangements as time, place, duration, fees, and so on. It also includes an agreement between the two which defines the focus of the therapy and how it will proceed. In addition to these aspects and, perhaps most importantly, the professional relationship involves the working alliance (Horvath and Greenberg, 1994) which includes an implicit bond between the therapist and the client. This is experienced in terms of a level of trust and respect for each other that can sustain the buffetings which may occur during the course of the therapy.

It is useful to look at Bordin's (1979) model of goals, tasks and bonds which form the working alliance. The goal is the shared articulation of the desired outcome of the therapy. The tasks are the 'specific activities that the partnership will engage in to investigate or facilitate change', while the bond is 'a sense of common commitment and a shared understanding in the activity.'

As part of the integrating framework, this aspect of the whole relationship will be seen by the therapist as a vitally important infrastructure. It is the aspect which provides containment, boundaries and direction. Difficulties in establishing the working alliance will be very relevant to the client's journey and its successful achievement: an essential part of the therapy.

> Jane sought help from a psychotherapist when her relationship of two years with her man friend, John, broke down after a series of verbal fights which often ended in physical violence. The therapist listened attentively in their assessment session. Jane was very distressed and couldn't decide whether she wanted to get her partner back or whether it would be better to resist seeing him again and begin making a new life on her own. She thought that there might be 'something unhealthy' about their relationship but at the same time was afraid of being on her own. The therapist then offered Jane a series of six sessions in which she could receive support while she made up her mind about which path to follow. They agreed to meet for one hour at the same time each week and specified the fee. During the first three sessions, Jane told her story in more detail and began to explore the patterns of overinvolvement which she had developed with John and others before him. Initially, Jane felt a little wary of her therapist. She had never experienced therapy before and was afraid that the therapist might prove critical or undermining. However, during the fourth session she became aware that she trusted and liked her therapist who seemed genuinely interested in her and to want the best for her. She began to relax and look forward to her next session. During that session she stated that she wanted to continue seeing the therapist beyond the sixth session and this was agreed. A revised, open-ended contract was made.

This illustrates how the details in a professional relationship and working alliance are constantly open to review and renegotiation as appropriate.

The Projective Relationship

When the client or the therapist relates to the other in a way which is based on their own constructions rather than on here and now reality, this is normally described as transference and countertransference. Transference and counter-transference are defined in many ways in the psychotherapy literature. For the purposes of this chapter, the transference relationship refers to that aspect of the counselling or psychotherapeutic relationship in which the client brings to the therapeutic space his experiences of important past relationships and acts and feels these as if they were happening now. In other words, in subtle ways he replays his own history (either the one that really happened or the one he hoped for) and transfers past patterns into the present. The therapist's response can be said to be the countertransference. She may find herself feeling and even acting in the way she is being invited to do or, perhaps, from a reaction triggered from her own past.

A more complex version of the transferential process occurs when a client projects onto their therapist their own vulnerable aspects and takes up instead the role of one of the important others who related to that aspect of themselves in their earlier life. The countertransference here occurs when the therapist begins to feel the client's feelings just as they had been projected onto her. Transference and countertransference lead to what Elton Wilson (1996: 33) calls 'stale patterns of interaction'.

Transference occurs in any relationship and more particularly in those relation-ships which involve vulnerability and intimate sharing, such as the relationship between client and therapist. The privacy of the therapy room and the invitation to explore deep feelings and thoughts lead to the therapist becoming a very important figure. All this seems to invite 'earlier selves' and 'unfinished business' into the room. The experience of transferring past material, of staying with the feelings and of understanding them and their connection with the past, can be enormously therapeutic for the client. For the therapist, the experience of staying aware of her response, using it to understand the client and managing the situation in an accepting way can be one of her greatest tools. Transference and countertransference are only harmful and unproductive if they are acted upon without awareness and end up producing a repeat of the client's early damaging experience.

Consideration of transference and countertransference is fundamental to using the relationship as an integrating framework. The therapist needs to decide what significance this aspect has, particularly in relation to methodology – that is, how she will use the transference therapeutically. She will be influenced, of course, by her theoretical trainings and her personal answers to the questions posed in Chapters 3 and 4. She may decide that the transference/countertransference relationship is the essential matrix through which the client will learn about his unconscious feelings and motives; that only by entering fully into this dynamic can stale patterns be resolved. Alternatively, she may decide that what is most therapeutic is the immediate confrontation and unhooking of transference in order to bring the client as fully as possible into a new pattern, broadening options and introducing fresh experiences.

A simple way of understanding this dynamic is found in Menninger's (1958) Triangle of Insight (see Chapter 5). A psychodynamic view is found widely in the literature. Seminal works include Racker (1982) and Klein (1986). Humanistic approaches to transference tend to focus more on its dissolution (Perls et al., 1972; Rogers, 1957), often without referring explicitly to the concept, while transactional analysis straddles both view points (Berne, 1961; Clarkson, 1992; Hargaden and Sills, 1999).

> At times during the first three of her therapy sessions, Jane had transferred her critical and undermining father onto the therapist. However, she was also able to experience the therapist's very real support. Some six months into the therapy, this transference reccurred at a more significant level. Jane discovered that she was feeling reluctant to tell her therapist about decisions she had made to take a course in mystical healing as she was sure that 'she will sneer at me and tell me to stop going'. When she finally mentioned it to the therapist she did it flippantly and as she was leaving the session. The therapist, both from a countertransferential position and because she was 'going off duty' as she escorted the client to the door, made a cursory reply.
>
> The following week Jane arrived late for her appointment and after sitting in silence for several minutes burst out in anger at her therapist for 'never supporting me'. The therapist listened carefully to Jane's tirade and for a moment felt angrily defensive. This was exactly the accusation that her younger sister used to make. She imagined that she could understand how John could have been drawn into shouting at Jane. However, her approach to psychotherapy was sympathetic to the intersubjectivists' view of transference. She believed that it was created both by the Here and Now and the There and Then of Jane's past. She continued to listen empathically to Jane's attack and gently helped her to say how she had felt when she thought her therapist was criticizing her. Later the therapist said, 'Was there anyone in your past who treated you in that critical way?' Jane flinched and cried. When she was calmer she explained to the attentive therapist that her father had seemed always to be on her back about one thing or another.

Another form of projective relationship is the reparative relationship. Here, the therapist in some way repairs or 'makes up for' some deficit in the client's experience. The provision of some response which has hitherto been lacking is felt to be therapeutic and healing by the client (Alexander and French, 1946; Clarkson, 1990; Erskine and Trautmann, 1996; Schiff and Day, 1970; and, arguably, Kohut, 1984). This relationship can be seen to be part of the transferential relationship, as it involves unmet needs from the client's past. However, we believe that it is useful to discuss it separately. In making the separation, we can highlight the importance of differentiating between transference of the relationship which was experienced by the child and transference of the unmet needs which occurred either naturally in the course of the child's development or arose as a result of life events, that is, the need for a relationship that did not occur, as opposed to the transference of one which did occur (or was felt to have occurred).

As early as 1946, Alexander and French described the danger of an analytic relationship recreating the original experience with the parent and repeating the trauma. They talked of the need for a 'corrective emotional experience' in which early feelings would be triggered, but responded to differently so that the analysis would be healing of what transactional analysts nowadays would call the early Child ego state.

There is enormous variety in attitude to the idea that a therapist can in some way offer a reparative experience and give to a client what he or she never had. At one extreme is the process of 'reparenting' (Schiff and Day, 1970) in which severely disturbed young adults, in addition to intensive therapy designed to increase the ego strength of Adult ego state functioning (Berne 1961/80), agree to regress to childhood, often infancy, and be reparented – given a new experience of being nurtured, a new set of values and beliefs to live by and so on. This procedure is carried out in the residential setting of a therapeutic community. Ideally, each resident will have two parents and the staff of the community need to be dedicated and very well supported. Fine and effective work of this nature is carried out in Britain at the Connect Community in Birmingham. From a similar theoretical standpoint, some clinicians practice 're-childing' (Clarkson and Fish, 1988a). Again this aims to provide a new experience of being a child. There is a subtle difference between the two approaches. The focus here, is on the provision of new child experiences rather than new parental input. Rechilding is also normally carried out in a group or residential setting but with less disturbed clients who are managing themselves adequately in the world.

From a completely opposing point of view, some counsellors and therapists believe that it is counterproductive to try to fill in the gaps in a person's childhood. They believe that working in the reparative relationship or 'developmentally needed' relationship (Barr, 1987) fosters dependence or 'transference cure' and that it denies the existential realities of life. If we claim, like the 1960s slogan, that 'It's never too late to have a happy childhood' we may be appearing to say that our clients do not have to come to terms with what happened to them; they do not have to work through the losses or griefs they experienced but can magically make things right again. This could be facile.

We believe that in reality both points of view can be true. Some clients can be immeasurably helped by a reparenting procedure; some are simply infantilized by the same procedure. Somewhere in between the two poles lies the majority of the therapeutic work that is carried out. It involves making a deeply significant and often intense relationship with a client. Very often, it is the quality of this relationship that is in itself reparative. If we, as person-centred therapists, strive to offer the 'core conditions' (Rogers, 1957) to our client we are probably offering those conditions for growth that were lacking in the client's childhood. The same is true, in Gestalt terms, if we offer the 'I–thou dialogue' (Buber, 1984; Jacobs, 1989; Sills et al., 1995) in object relations terms, if we provide a safe 'holding environment' (Winnicott, 1958). At our peril do we deny that this experience is reparative. If we do ignore it, then we fail to understand our clients on the occasions when we 'miss' them, when we accidentally seem to repeat the original hurt rather than repair it. When our clients show their disappointment, it is important that we do not just define their reaction as transference and wonder why they feel so strongly. We must also acknowledge that we have been offering hope to the client at some very deep level; that this time they are being seen, heard, understood. Their ability to tell us when we fail them, for us to understand and to help them manage the experience, is vital to their healing.

Kohut (1984) describes deep, primitive longings or self-object needs that are brought to the therapy by the client. These are the denied longing for mirroring or merger, for an ideal carer, for twinship and for a relationship in which to feel powerful and effective. He believed that these longings, which he called transferences, needed to be met with deep empathy by the therapist in order for them to be re-owned and integrated by the client. He saw self-object needs as a normal part of human functioning. If the early all-consuming longings are empathically addressed, they can be transformed into the appropriate and functional self-object needs in the adult. In this way, it can certainly be seen that psychotherapy performs a reparative function.

Erskine (1996), in describing his integrative approach to psychotherapy (Inquiry, Attunement and Involvement), builds on Kohut's (1984) work in offering an interesting model of what is in fact a reparative relationship. He identifies eight different relational needs – for security, for protection, to be affirmed, to have one's experience confirmed, to define oneself, to have an impact, to have another reach out to one, to express love. He describes them, indicates what the natural human response to each of these needs would be and illustrates by his case examples how important it is for the therapist to respond to the client's relational needs as they emerge in the dialogue between them. Erskine, like Kohut, asserts that these relational needs do not belong solely in childhood but exist throughout life:

> When Jane had found the courage to express her anger to her therapist, she was immeasurably relieved to find that not only was she heard, but it was clear that she had also made an impact on the other woman. The therapist took her very seriously and did not brush aside her account of what had happened. Jane was aware that she had been expecting an impatient dismissal – or at best an impassive reflection of her words ('I hear you are feeling angry'). Instead, the therapist listened carefully to the details of what she had said and done that had made her client feel criticized and acknowledged how she might have seemed to be dismissive. She affirmed Jane's experience and said that, particularly given the relationship she had had with her father but even without that factor, it was understandable that Jane might have felt as she did. At the following session, she told her therapist that she had had a revelation during the intervening week. She had a greater awareness how she transferred her past into the present, but there had been something else. As she had left the previous session, she carried with her an experience that her responses, her feelings and thoughts were important. She realized that when she had had the terrible arguments with John she had always felt as if he did not take her seriously; she felt dismissed and 'put down'. She said, 'I used to get angrier and angrier with him. And in the end I was being so horrible that of course he couldn't take me seriously. Perhaps if I listen to myself and take my own thoughts seriously, I won't be so vulnerable to the way others treat me.'

The Personal Relationship

There are several areas to the personal relationship. The first is that which describes the therapist and client as they meet person to person. It is frequently called the 'real relationship' (Clarkson, 1990; Elton Wilson, 1996; Gelso and Carter, 1985; and others). The 'real relationship' is perhaps a strange expression to use as it implies that the other aspects of the therapeutic encounter (i.e the transferential relationship) have no reality to them whatsoever while some interactions can be completely free of assumptions, fantasies and transferential material. This would be unrealistic. What is meant here is a meeting between two people in the present, unencumbered by transferences (if this is ever completely possible) and unrestricted by the need for contracts. It is perhaps what results when both people are truly congruent in Rogers's (1951) terms or have achieved a moment of what Berne (1964) calls 'autonomy'. The roles of therapist and client are not obscured, neither is the purpose of the meeting as being for the client's benefit. However, this personal aspect of the relationship acknowledges the ordinary actuality of the two beings and their common experience of living. The real relationship encompasses each person's age, gender, sexuality, race, likes and dislikes, and the genuine similarities and differences between them.

Research suggests (Beutler, in Norcross, 1986) that the most effective therapy occurs where the client feels that they have enough in common with their therapist to feel understood and validated, yet experiences enough attitudinal difference to be invited to challenge their frame of reference. It follows, therefore, that the actual relationship is an important part of the healing process and that a therapist need not seek to eradicate the genuine human meeting from the therapy room.

Even those practitioners whose primary focus is on exploring the transference will intend that, during the course of therapy, transference will gradually be dissolved and a real relationship established. Recently some analysts who have previously concentrated on interpretation of the transference as the primary therapeutic factor have identified that the impact of the real encounter can be the other powerful ingredient. Stern (1997) described the 'moment of meeting' in which client and analyst are suddenly precipitated into the here and now contact where neither is in control of the situation and something new emerges. This is an experience which is well understood by Gestaltists (Hycner, 1985; Jacobs, 1989) and by Buber (1984) as well as by person-centred counsellors (Mearns, 1994; Rogers, 1951, 1957, 1967). Some say this is the goal of therapy. Many therapists choose to make the reduction of transference and the establishment of a real relationship the major intention of their interventions.

Whether or not there is emphasis upon the real relationship, it will inevitably exist. Even a practitioner working from 'the blank screen' perspective will be offering clues about himself in the way that he dresses, his accent, where he lives, and so on. The intentional use of the real relationship occurs when a therapist chooses to use some form of self-disclosure as an intervention. This may be to share with the client a feeling she is having at that time or an experience from her own life. The purpose of the self-disclosure might be to confront an assumption the client may be holding, to demonstrate attunement with the client's experience, to normalize a situation the client is describing or to give information. Therapists are often concerned as to when or how much self-disclosure is appropriate. The general 'rule of thumb' is that the practitioner should have a clear reason as to why this self-disclosure would be in the client's best interest. For example, if the therapist is carefully exploring some transferential feelings of the client towards her it might be inappropriate to interrupt and explain how mistaken the client is in their transference. However, later in the therapy, when the client has fully explored and identified the nature of her transference, it might well be beneficial to do just that.

> As a child Jane's impression of what was happening within the family was often discounted by her mother. Her parents used to fight and her mother would become silent and depressed. If Jane asked her what was the matter, her mother would tell her she was just being silly and that everything was fine. Jane was left wondering where her uncomfortable feelings had come from. In one therapy session, Jane thought her therapist seemed withdrawn and unavailable. She felt bad inside and started describing what she felt sure was her own projection and wondered aloud whether she would ever stop 'just being silly'.
>
> The therapist decided that it was important to validate Jane's perception of reality and told her truthfully that she was, in fact, distracted by a toothache which had developed that morning. Jane felt, at first, surprised then relieved to have her experience confirmed.

The personal relationship can also be said to encompass the cultural and socio-political context, although some theoreticians (e.g.Gilbert, 1995) find it useful to treat this aspect as a separate facet of the relationship. It is arguable that no aspect of the relationship should be taken out of context. The environment – sociopolitical, familial, cultural, geographical, historical – as well as the immediate field of the relationship – the gender of the participants, their sexuality, their culture, their class, the setting of the therapy, the current local or world events – all are factors that influence and can be influenced by the therapy itself. They are factors which are particularly relevant to the working alliance and the transferential relationship as well as to the personal relationship. We agree with Gilbert (1995), however, that it is useful to think of the contextual relationship as a separate facet of the therapeutic encounter. This invites the therapist to alter her lens for a while, to allow the thera-peutic dyad to fade into the background of importance and allow the wider field to become the focus.

There are different ways of working with this new focus. One is to take a field theoretical approach based on the work of Lewin (1951). This approach concen-trates on the interconnectedness of people, things, events both current and historical, and looks at how human beings (and their environment) co-create events and relationships constantly. In a sense, the elements in the field create each other and themselves. If we take this to its logical conclusion, it is not so easy to attribute a set of feelings, thoughts and behaviour, let alone a personality, to one individual. What happens between him and another individual is created between them and belongs to both. Further reading about a field theoretical approach to the therapeutic relationship can be found in Wheeler (1991) and McKewn (1997). The perspective of co-creation in the therapeutic relationship is also explored by the intersubjective approach (Stolorow et al., 1994).

Another approach is to look at the impact of various factors of the context on the client, and the therapeutic relationship. This may be to be aware of the social implications and the possibility for psychotherapy and counselling to have an impact upon society as well as vice versa.

> Jane travelled to her session in a bus one morning where the passengers sat in a hushed atmosphere of sadness and shock following the sudden death in a car accident of a member of the royal family. Jane felt similarly affected and when she reached her session, she and her therapist shared their surprise at the impact the event had had on themselves and, seemingly, the whole country and even the people of other nations. Jane then went on to explore the significance of the event in terms of her own life.
>
> On another occasion, Jane described a feeling of hopefulness and a belief in change which she realized was due to the election, the previous day, of a new government which promised social reform for the country. A year later, she and her therapist identified the profound sense of disappointment shared by so many at the apparent failure to manifest of this hoped for change. She and her therapist discussed the coming millennium, the fin-de-siècle lethargy which seemed to abound, some of the amazing technological and spiritual changes which had occurred in the twentieth century as well as hopes and fears for the future.
>
> It was important to Jane to feel part of society, to acknowledge her place in the world and to look both at what she contributed to it and how she was shaped by it.

Clarkson (1990) describes a separate facet of the therapeutic relationship as the transpersonal, although we believe that this is an aspect which occasionally emerges out of the personal relationship. The term 'transpersonal relationship' seeks to name that connection between human beings which reaches a dimension beyond everyday awareness and touches on the surreal, the spiritual, or, in Jungian terms, the collective unconscious. We have described this also in the transpersonal level of Clarkson's seven-level model in Chapter 10. It is also implied in Buber's (1984) I–Thou moment, which is described poignantly by Jacobs (1989). People – not just those involved in counselling, psychotherapy or in the world of religion – frequently describe a connection between individuals that is not explainable in logical terms. Siblings report knowing what is happening to each other; a woman has a dream about her friend which turns out to be true; two people who make contact with openness and goodwill report experiencing a moment of joy and insight.

Using words brings in the analytic and cognitive part of the brain. Words, so useful for naming in some stages of therapy, have the effect of packaging experience into symbols, linked to our civilized world. Defining and naming, therefore, becomes the obstacle to experiencing the ineffable. Hence the Zen saying: 'He who speaks does not know. He who knows does not speak.' The metaphysical philosophers tend to use poetry and imagery to convey a flavour of their experience because they understand that everyday syntax cannot do the job. Being aware of this, we hesitate to try to describe the transpersonal element of the therapeutic relationship. Therapists cannot plan for or use it intentionally in their work. If the transpersonal occurs, it may be through such events as dreams or through synchronicity, that meeting of the intrapsychic and the external event (Jung, 1969). Clarkson (1992) refers to the Jungian notion of the relationship between the unconscious of the therapist and the unconscious of the client and quotes Samuels (1985: 21) who says 'the psychology of the soul turns out to be about people in relationship'. It may be that the transpersonal element of the therapeutic encounter is a vital part of the potential healing.

There is an old Taoist axiom: 'The master points his finger towards the moon but he says, "Don't mistake my finger for the moon."' Suitably warned, we choose not to attempt to give an example here of the transpersonal relationship but again borrow from Clarkson (1992: 309) who quotes Buber as writing: 'Nothing remains to me in the end but an appeal to the testimony of your own mysteries.'

Conclusion

In this chapter we have presented three domains within the therapeutic relationship and indicated how they can be used as a framework for the integration of a therapist's theoretical and procedural approaches. We have also briefly referred to the importance in general of being in relationship with a client. In her article exploring perspectives on the therapeutic relationship, Barr (1987) quotes Kegan (1982) who says:

> It is our *recruitability* as much as our knowledge of what to do once drawn, that makes us of value in our caring for another's development . . . a person's life depends (literally, in the first few years of life and in every other way in all the years that follow) on whether he or she moves someone . . . our survival and development depend on our capacity to recruit the invested attention of others to us. (Kegan, 1982: 17; emphasis added)

Kegan proposes that a psychotherapist or counsellor needs to provide not only a suitable 'holding environment' (Winnicott, 1965), but also an attitude towards the client of 'recruitability'. Polster and Polster (1973) speak of a willingness to be 'captured'. We believe that it is the therapist's chief responsibility to ensure – through the process of her training, her supervision, her own personal therapy and her life experience – that she develops this quality of 'recruitability'; that she be available to be 'captured' by the client in the service of his growth.

8

Multimodal Therapy

We include Lazarus's approach here as an example of the second type of integration we have described in Chapter 3: the Procedural Integration Strategy. Lazarus provides a template for integration (though this is not a word to which he would subcribe) at the level of 'concretely specific working therapeutic operations' rather than at a theoretical level.

Describing his approach as multimodal therapy (Lazarus in Norcross, 1986) Lazarus says, 'although they employ techniques from many sources, multimodal therapists do not necessarily subscribe to any of their underlying theories'. This is not to suggest that practitioners have no theoretical underpinnings to their work (without a theoretical conceptualization, the choice of techniques would be arbitrary and ineffective), but that techniques from other theoretical models may be employed even where the theoretical understanding may differ. Indeed, multimodal therapy using the BASIC ID template is theoretically based in social learning theory (Bandura, 1969, 1977), general system theory (Buckley, 1967; von Bertalanffy, 1974) and group and communications theory (Wazlowick et al., 1974), but is open to the inclusion of other helpful techniques regardless of the theoretical orientation from which they may originate.

Lazarus was the first to coin the term 'behavioural therapy' (Wolpe and Lazarus, 1966) and his earlier work employed a 'pure' behavioural approach. However, research and follow-up studies showed that, although a behavioural approach, even with quite disturbed clients, was beneficial and helped individuals to make some-times speedy gains in recovery, these gains were often short lived. Lazarus could see that additional interventions were necessary to help maintain the progress made by clients. Having noted that the clients who maintained their therapeutic gains were those who had achieved 'a different outlook and philosophy of life and increased self-esteem in addition to an increased range of interpersonal and behavioural skills' (1971: 18), Lazarus added a cognitive aspect to the behavioural approach. Further, he noted that the *Affect*, *Behaviour*, *Cognition* (ABC) approach to interventions employed by most cognitive behaviour therapists and counsellors still remained ineffective, especially at the level of affect, for several clients. Despite these clients being able to apply rational and positive 'self-talk' to their repertoire of coping skills, Lazarus saw that they were still maintaining negative feelings in response to the negative imagery they were wont to hold. Thus, interventions designed to help clients to change the *Imagery* they employed was added to the template of areas for intervention.

Sensory problems too were identified as needing addressing. Such problems as headaches, muscle tension, back pain, were seen often to be interrelated to the other aspects. *Sensation* was as much in need of intervention as the other modalities.

To this increasingly holistic list were added *Interpersonal* relationships and *Drugs/biology*. Looking at the interpersonal relationships in a client's life introduced a systemic dimension which could highlight those areas where a client's interactions could be explored and any patterns of negatively reinforcing aspects of relationships addressed and dealt with, be they at home, work or social situations. By Drugs/biology Lazarus meant not only paying attention to the recreational drugs or the prescribed medications a client may be taking, but a wider perspective including all issues connected with physical well-being like sleep patterns, dietary habits, physical exercise, and so on. Thus, the acronym for the complete 'multimodal spectrum' became the BASIC ID:

Behaviour
Affect
Sensation
Imagery
Cognition
Interpersonal
Drugs/biology

While holding that 'lasting change is at the very least a function of combined *techniques, strategies* and *modalities*', Lazarus emphasized the need for being systematic in the selection of these operational procedures. He advocated experimentation, observation and measurement of outcomes, a constant appraisal and refining of techniques in order to avoid such criticisms voiced by Eysenck (1970) that many practitioners were embracing, 'a mishmash of theories, a hugger-mugger of procedures, a gallimaufry of therapies and a charivaria of activities having no proper rationale, and incapable of being tested or evaluated'.

Before moving on to look at how the BASIC ID can be used both as a diagnostic tool and a treatment planning template, it is worth noting what Lazarus says about one particular aspect of the template, that of 'affect'. He points out that this aspect cannot be directly dealt with, only indirectly through the other modalities. Some practitioners may claim to work directly with affect in that they may invite a client to get in touch with their anger by, for example, shouting and pounding a cushion while saying what they think of the person with whom they are angry. But, as is apparent, it is not affect that is being directly addressed. The client's anger is being encouraged by addressing their *behaviour* (shouting and pounding), their *sensations* while doing this and by generating *imagery* (the image of the person with whom they are angry). The *interpersonal* modality (the relationship with the other person) is also being employed in service of *affect*. Similarly, *cognition* may be used, such as changing the thoughts that reinforce or deny the feelings, or the *drugs/biology* aspect addressed in exploration of how the client's angry feeling may be physically repressed by chemical or dietary intake. With this in mind let us take a look at how the BASIC ID may be used as a diagnostic tool with someone who presents for counselling complaining of anxiety. A brief diagnostic overview may look something like this:

- *Behaviour*: makes little eye contact. Sits rigidly, arms tightly across stomach.
- *Affect*: anxiety (the presenting issue).
- *Sensation*: tension in the stomach. Dizzy feeling in forehead.
- *Imagery*: sees self alone, isolated even in social situations.
- *Cognition*: constantly thinks of himself as different from others, inadequate and uninteresting.
- *Interpersonal*: tries to please others. Unassertive of own needs with others.
- *Drugs/biology*: drinks about eight cups of coffee per day. Takes little exercise.

The practitioner working with this client would now have an overall picture (which can be added to, if necessary, as the work progresses) from which to plan treatment interventions. The type and order of these would depend upon the practitioner's clinical background and skills and upon how receptive the client may be to certain interventions. We will expand upon the ordering of interventions later in this chapter. For now, the interventions may be placed within the BASIC ID template in this instance as follows:

- *Behaviour*: encouragement of eye contact in transactions between therapist and client. Role-play using appropriate eye contact. Experimentation with body posture.
- *Affect*: anxiety addressed via other modalities.
- *Sensation*: relaxation exercises using body tension awareness and focus on diaphragmatic breathing.
- *Imagery*: positive imagery exercises. Images of belonging, being accepted, participating in social situations. Guided fantasy.
- *Cognition*: cognitive restructuring. Replacing negative thoughts with positive ones. Bragging exercises, emphasizing his achievements, interests and intrinsic value as a person. Normalizing interventions.
- *Interpersonal*: assertion techniques. Referral to social skills training group.
- *Drugs/biology*: reduction of coffee intake, at least by half. Encouragement of exercise, preferably recreational and with others (e.g. tennis club).

As can be seen, there are several overlaps here between one modality and another. For instance, it is likely that the behavioural interventions addressing body posture will only be effective when combined with the relaxation and breathing techniques addressed by the interventions at the sensation modality. There is a high correlation too between the imagery and cognitive interventions which may need to go hand in hand with the relaxation techniques in order to be changed constructively and effectively. All of these interconnected modalities would be addressed to bring about the necessary changes in behaviour, sensation, imagery, cognition, inter-personal relationships and biological aspects that would reduce or eliminate the presenting affective problem brought by the client.

It is likely that change in any one of these modalities will bring about some change in another. Often this will be constructive and positive, for example, where changing negative to positive imagery brings about a simultaneous sensation of relaxation and well-being. At other times, the change in one modality may bring about an escalation of negative aspects in another. If, in the above example, the client was encouraged to increase their eye contact with the counsellor, there may be a concomitant increase in anxiety, negative imagery, body tension, and so on. The skilled practitioner may choose not to avoid these changes by addressing another modality at the outset, but to work simultaneously and more intensively within those areas where there is a heightening of the client's experience brought about by this initial choice of modality. It may be that with some clients this approach is useful to bring to the surface more underlying factors that were not apparent in earlier construction of the profile.

Lazarus puts emphasis on the importance of flexibility when using this approach with clients. He is mindful and respectful of individual difference and stresses that the BASIC ID is not a template into which the client is fitted or a rigid treatment plan to be followed unremittingly. He sees the rapport between client and practitioner as central to the effectiveness of this approach and the need to see the client as an individual as paramount. Thus constant assessment and reassessment of the various aspects of the client's life as described by the modalities is integral to this approach – as is the role of the client in this assessment. The client plays a central role in constructing the modality profile and is often asked to complete their own profile independent of the practitioner and then to compare notes with the practitioner. The following instructions (Lazarus in Norcross, 1986: 72) are given to the client to assist them in compiling their profile. You, the reader, might like to complete your own profile following these guidelines:

- *Behaviour*: this refers mainly to overt behaviours – to acts, habits, gestures, responses and reactions that are observable and measurable. Make a list of those acts, habits, etc. that you want to increase and those that you would like to decrease. What would you like to start doing? What would you like to stop doing?
- *Affect*: this refers to emotions, moods and strong feelings. What emotions do you experience most often? Write down your unwanted emotions (e.g. anxiety, guilt, anger, depression, etc.). Note under 'behaviour' what you tend to do when you feel a certain way.
- *Sensation*: touching, tasting, smelling, seeing and hearing are our five basic senses. Make a list of any negative sensations (e.g. tension, dizziness, pain, blushing, butterflies in stomach, etc.) that apply to you. If any of these sensations cause you to act or feel in certain ways, make sure you note them under 'behaviour' or 'affect'.
- *Imagery*: write down any bothersome recurring dreams and vivid memories. Include any negative features about the way you see yourself – your 'self-image'. Make a list of any 'mental pictures' – past, present, or future – that may be troubling you. If any 'auditory images' – tunes or sounds that you keep hearing – constitute a problem, jot them down. If your images arouse any significant actions, feelings or sensations, make sure these items are added to 'behaviour', 'affect' and 'sensation'.
- *Cognition*: what types of attitudes, values, opinions, and ideas get in the way of your happiness? Make a list of negative things you often say to yourself (e.g.

'I am a failure', 'I am stupid', 'others dislike me', or 'I'm no good'). Write down some of your most irrational ideas. Be sure to note down how these ideas and thoughts influence your behaviours, feelings, sensations and images.

- *Interpersonal relationships*: write down any bothersome interactions with other people (relatives, friends, lovers, employers, acquaintances, etc.). Any concerns you have about the way other people treat you should appear here. Check through the items under 'Behaviour', 'Affect', 'Sensation', 'Imagery', and 'Cognition' and try to determine how they influence and are influenced by your interpersonal relationships. (Note that there is some overlap between the modalities, but don't hesitate to list the same problem more then once, for example, under 'Behaviour' and 'Interpersonal relationships'.)
- *Drugs/Biology*: make a list of all drugs you are taking, whether prescribed by a doctor or not. Include any health problems, medical concerns, and illnesses that you have or have had.

Having compiled your own modality profile, you could now construct your own treatment plan. If you were the therapist working with you, what interventions would you make in each modality? What techniques would you employ? Where would your initial focus be? What would be some of the most important factors in your therapist and therapy that would help you to achieve the changes you want to make?

Flexibility and matching are key words in the use of the multimodal approach. The individual proclivities of the client are respected in service of the therapy. Even where two clients appear to be presenting the same problem, the treatment approach is likely to differ according to the individuals concerned. For example, a person whose work and lifestyle places great emphasis on rationality, structure and order is best likely to be met at the cognitive/behavioural level of interventions and techniques where the therapy is highly structured and directive. On the other hand, a person whose fantasies and feelings are their particular way of experiencing and relating to the world is best likely to be met at the affect/imagery level of contact and interventions.

Tracking the client's preferred order of modalities is essential for effective work. Imagine two clients, both about to apply for a job. The first initially thinks of a negative outcome because he believes he is not good enough for the job. He imagines himself at the interview totally lost for words, unable to answer the panel's questions at all. He feels sick in his stomach. He does not send the application form. This client begins in a *cognition* modality, then creates negative *imagery* which brings about a *sensation* of sickness as a result of all of which his *behavioural* outcome is to avoid going for the job at all.

The second client about to fill in the application form, initially experiences anger in response to the questions on the form, she sees the interviewers for the job as 'out to get her', to catch her out by asking such seemingly irrelevant questions, she starts drinking gin rather than fill in the form and picks a row with her partner as soon as he enters the room. The order of modalities presented in this scenario are affect, imagery, behaviour, drugs/biology and interpersonal. Naturally, there is a lot of overlap between the modalities in both of these examples, but broadly speaking (and with experimentation) the treatment is likely to follow the modality order suggested here.

Thus it can be seen that there is no one way to approach a client with a particular problem when using the BASIC ID. Lazarus himself says that if he were to be observed working with different clients, the observer of one particular session with a particular client might conclude that he was a Gestalt therapist because he relies heavily on sensory and imagery techniques. An observer of him with another client might see him as a behaviour therapist because he employs desensitization, behaviour rehearsal and assertiveness training, and classified by yet another observer as a Rogerian because he spends the whole session reflecting back the client's affective reactions. We repeat again, that at this level of integration, what we call the Procedural Integration Strategy, any and all effective techniques may be drawn upon without subscribing to the approaches or theories from which they originated or within which they are often employed.

We conclude this chapter with Table 8.1 which shows the techniques and ingredients of multimodel therapeutic change (Lazarus in Norcross, 1986: 84).

Table 8.1 *Techniques and ingredients of multimodal therapeutic change*

Technique/ingredient	Example
Behaviour	
Positive reinforcement, negative reinforcement, punishment	Contingent praise, time out, aversion therapy.
Counter-conditioning	Graded exposure, desensitization.
Extinction	Flooding, massed practice responsive prevention.
Affect	
Owning and accepting feelings	Bringing affect-laden material into awareness.
Abreaction	Reliving painful emotions in the presence of a trusted ally.
Sensation	
Tension release	Relaxation, physical exercise biofeedback.
Sensory pleasuring	Sensate focus methods for sexual retraining.
Imagery	
Coping images	Picturing self-achievement and self-control.
Changes in self-image	More positive reactions to one's body and to other areas of functioning.
Cognition	
Greater awareness	Less ignorance and naivety. Awareness of past–present linkages. Awareness of how specific 'firing orders' culminate in affective reactions.
Cognitive restructuring	Less self-derogation, overgeneralization, dichotomous reasoning, categorical imperatives, non-sequiturs.

continued

Table 8.1 *continued*

Technique/ingredient	Example
Interpersonal	
Non-judgemental acceptance	When clients are offered desiderata not usually available in social situations.
Modelling	Therapist serving as a role model through selective self-disclosure and using deliberate modelling during role reversal exercises.
Dispersing unhealthy collusions	Treating a family and changing counterproductive alliances.
Drugs/biological	
Exercise and nutrition.	
Substance use cessation.	
Use of psychotropic medication when indicated.	
Complete physical check-ups when warranted.	

Source: Lazarus in Norcross, 1986: 84

9

The Comparative Script System

In this chapter we present an integrative framework described by Sills and Salters (1991) which uses a systemic approach to the development of human personality and provides both a framework and procedural strategy for integration.

Most approaches to counselling and therapy include a belief that we are affected by our past experiences. In other words, although therapists may differ in their understanding of what motivates a human being and how much of personality is innate temperament, they agree that the experiences a person goes through – especially in their early life – have an effect on the sense they make of the world and the assumptions they make about themselves and their relationships to other people. Some psychotherapeutic approaches concentrate on the 'why' of our personality and behaviour. They analyse our pasts to understand our present thoughts and feelings. Some focus almost exclusively on the 'what' and seek to change our behaviour in order to affect the whole. Other therapeutic theories and approaches take a more phenomenological approach and work with the client's current subjective experience. The comparative script system offers a framework for integrating all these angles, both theoretically and in relation to procedure. It makes space for analysing intrapsychic processes and relating them to past experiences. It also shows how these processes are active in the present day and manifested in our communication and our behaviour. It offers to the practitioner a way of understanding how a person's difficulties have been established and how they are maintained moment by moment in everyday life.

Learning Patterns

A systemic way of understanding how children learn to interpret, adapt to and manipulate their world is shown in Figure 9.1. Section A, Original experience and reinforcing events, represents the early developmental experience of the child. This includes the earliest relationships between infant and caretaker and also specific incidents or situations particular to that child's life. For instance, when three-month-old Sam feels hungry he expresses his need, is fed and feels satisfaction.

If the experience at A happens often enough, or with sufficient impact, the child will develop beliefs about himself and his environment. This is the meaning-making process of Section B, Core beliefs and constructed meaning. In Sam's case, although only a baby, his internalized experience of his relationship with the world is one in which his needs are acceptable and appropriate and that the environment will respond to him. An attitude of basic trust in himself and of others begins to be established.

Section C, Internal process, represents the patterns of thinking and feeling based on those beliefs with which the child will respond when a stimulus similar to the one at A is experienced at a later date. As an older child and later as an adult Sam experiences hunger readily, thinks appropriately about what he needs to eat and anticipates eating with pleasure.

Section D, Consequent external experience, represents the individual's behaviour based on the internal beliefs and processes. Sam chooses and prepares a variety of interesting and nutritious food. He thus reproduces, as he eats, a similarly satisfying experience to that of his childhood (return to A). What is also important is that Sam's early experiences of trusting his own feelings and the response of his environment is carried into later life in a variety of other ways as he makes relationships confidently and congruently with people who respond to him appropriately (see Figure 9.1).

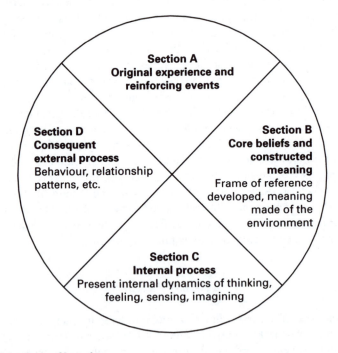

Figure 9.1 **Cycle of learning**

At a slightly more complex level, as a child Sam is taught to read in an exciting way by his father – a man who revels in reading and discovery (A). He therefore 'knows' that learning is stimulating and rewarding (B). When he is faced with a book containing new information he feels excited and expects to understand and feel interested (C); he reads copiously and integrates his reading into his work, trying out theories and techniques (D). He has thus brought about a repetition of his experience at Section A.

Although this system is self-reinforcing by its nature, it is not a closed system. This means that the individual can assimilate new information and, therefore, constantly update his beliefs in the light of new experiences. For example, after several attempts at an engineering manual, Sam decides that not all learning is exciting or pleasurable for him and he chooses to further his study of English literature. This is a model for healthy learning. It is important also to remember the work of Piaget (1954), who showed that children go through significant paradigm shifts in their frames of reference as they develop and respond to the changing demands of life. Thus, beliefs about self, others and the world, found in Section B, are changed or modified, leading to a change in patterns of internal response (C) and new behaviour (D) which creates new experiences at A.

Problematic Patterns of Learning

However, as therapists we may need to focus on the pathological elements of a person's learning and how her or his system of thinking, feeling and behaving becomes a closed one – binding energy and limiting new learning and options. This happens when the responses of the environment are inadequate or inappropriate to the child's needs. Keith was a solitary child who had few friends. His mother did not allow him to play in the street with the other local children and he remembers sitting at his window and watching them play football or tag (Section A). He recalls thinking 'Other people have all the fun – nothing exciting ever happens to me' (Section B). At school when he was invited by the English teacher to audition for the school play he felt depressed and resigned believing he would never have a chance to get a part (Section C). Consequently, he did not attend the auditions (D) and ended up watching the other children enjoy the rehearsals (A) and thinking 'Other people have all the fun' (B). As an adult, Keith spends his leisure hours reading the newspaper and watching the television. He is frequently envious of the people he reads about and sees, and of his friends who seem to have much more exciting lives.

The reader will have noticed that the Script System seems to suggest that meaning making precedes feeling, which may appear to be incompatible with the idea that a bodily experience of sensation and feeling is the primary process. However, we believe that feelings are fully a part of the experience at Section A and that how these are managed is a major part of whether experiences can be healthily integrated into a realistic frame of reference. When the feeling or bodily affective experience is repressed, either because it seems impossible to contain or as a reaction to the response of the environment, there is a higher likelihood of the person developing a closed system.

The concept of script has been taken from transactional analysis where it is used to mean the unconscious life plan formed in childhood and modified at significant stages in a person's life. This script is 'decided' upon as a result of the child's making sense of herself in the world subject to whatever pressures are prevalent at that time. Eric Berne (1966) chose this word to suggest the link between such early childhood 'decisions' and the script of a play in which the actor is assigned a role which they then play out according to the demands of the story line. Berne talked about a client freeing himself from his script and 'putting his own show on the road' (Berne, 1972).

The word 'decisions' has been put in inverted commas because the script starts to be formed from the first days of life (and even before birth) when the infant is, of course, not capable of formal cognitive process and cannot be said to make real decisions about what life is like. However, there is a way in which people form impressions at a somatic or visceral level which they carry forward as a foundation for their frame of reference. Bollas (1987) refers to the 'unthought known' (see also Chapter 4) to name this early scripting process – an expression which encapsulates the sense of the experience. He describes how clients bring their earliest object relationship into the consulting room, inextricably interwoven with, indeed, even *as* their sense of self. This sense of self and other is conveyed to the therapist wordlessly in the transference as an impression or feeling and received countertransferentially again in the form of a feeling, mood or impression. This situation can also be understood within the model.

Keith was the only child of a depressed and unsupported mother. His earliest remembered experience was of endless silent days alone with her in a gloomy room. She would sit silently motionless for hours, only stirring to make something for his supper, then returning again to her chair or to her bed. Keith passed the time staring at the patterns on the fading wallpaper. It is certain that Keith's infant experiences were of the same ilk (Section A). Keith's earliest impression of the environment and of himself was of a heavy, depressed desert (Section B). Although he subsequently achieved academic success and a degree of fame for his pioneering work in electrical engineering and although he married and had two children, his earliest frame of reference was this emotional desert and he brought it with him throughout his life and reproduced it in his relationships. He experienced himself as being quiet, unemotional, slightly bored with life (Section B). His behaviour in the consulting room was somewhat withdrawn with flat affect (Section D) and his therapist felt a strong pull to feel low and flat when she was with him. She also found it hard to be interested in him. There was a danger that the early relationship would be repeated (Section A). In summary, although he later formed many other ways of being, which could be mapped on the Script System, his most fundamental layer was of this unconscious, preverbal experience.

We will now look in more detail at the comparative script system, focusing on theoretical ways of understanding the 'contents' of the four sections and on methods that the therapist may use to address each one.

Many or even most psychotherapists and counsellors give the client the opportunity to 'tell his story' (Section A). This is considered useful for assessment purposes as well as a respectful way of engaging in the identification of the goals which will be made for the therapy (Bordin, 1994). It can also be therapeutic in itself as it gives clients the opportunity to express what has never before been expressed, to raise awareness and perhaps to bring their own life and identity into focus – to be owned more fully as their unique experience (Polster, 1987).

At the same time, the therapist will be thinking theoretically about the story and the client's past experiences. The way she thinks will be informed by her view of human beings (see Figure 9.2). Of course, she will have acquired certain experiences (Section A) which have led to the development of her view of how humans are, how they develop, how distress is caused and so on (Section B). (See also Elton Wilson's questions described in Chapters 3 and 4.) This will lead to her noticing some things more than others, responding in certain ways, thinking and feeling within her theoretical frame (C) and finally making interventions based on these (D). The subsequent result is likely to confirm her theoretical frame of reference. It is commonly observed that research has a tendency to confirm the views of the person who is carrying it out.

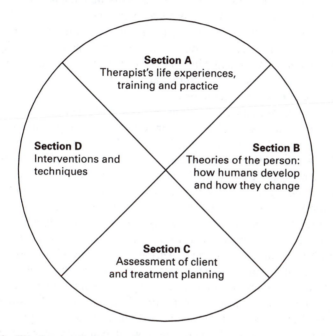

Figure 9.2 **The therapist's approach**

McLeod (1993) identifies three 'images' of the person which correspond to the three major strands of psychotherapy. These are the psychodynamic image of man as an animal with unconscious drives; the cognitive behavioural image of man as a machine such as a computer which is either well or badly programmed and third the humanistic image of man as a plant which, given a healthy environment, grows to its full potential. The Comparative Script System allows for any or all of these images to be applied. Depending on their image of the human being, practitioners will have different ways of listening to the client's story. At Section A they may use object relations theory to understand the crucial early relationships that the client formed with her primary caretaker and others. They may relate such experiences to the theory of psychical determinism (Freud, 1905) or the self-actualizing tendency (Rogers, 1959). They may use such concepts as symbiosis from transactional analysis or the 'precipitating event' from the cognitive behavioural approach. They will listen, and invite their clients to listen to themselves, to identify the meaning they made of their early lives and what beliefs they formed about themselves, other people and the world (Section B). They may invite the client, as she tells her story, to notice whether those early assumptions are still held – and whether they can be changed in the light of the present viewpoint. Frequently, clients have made cognitive or precognitive 'decisions' about how to cope with unhappy experiences – perhaps how to manage them without really facing the pain of some unbearable truth. Which therapist has not met a client who as a small child preferred to think of her or himself as bad and deserving of the punishment they received rather than face the terrifying thought that their mother was mad, unstable or cruel? Therapists may help clients to explore these early scenes, to know what they have avoided knowing, to express the unexpressed pain. Alternatively, they may focus on checking assumptions against reality, telling the story differently (Allen and Allen, 1997) or they may consider the past to be less relevant than the existential truths that clients are currently managing or avoiding by holding their assumptions.

Section C contains all the current thinking, feeling and fantasizing that the client uses in the here and now which is both a product of and a way of maintaining the frame of reference. There are many ways in which the therapist can work with these here-and-now experiences of thought and feeling. For example, they may work using the phenomenological method (described in Sills et al., 1995), paying close attention to exploring the client's experience. When the client is 'in script', feelings are likely to be familiar ones and associated with particular thoughts and memories (state-dependent learning; Baddeley, 1990)). They are also likely to be substitutes for the repressed pain (English, 1971, 1972). The therapist may consider this script feeling in Gestalt terms as an interruption in the natural cycle of experience (Zinker, 1977) and carefully explore with the client when and how this interruption came about in the hope of re-establishing the true expression of the client's feelings. Or the therapist may seek to uncover the fleeting intrusion of a script assumption or introject in order to demonstrate how outmoded beliefs (B) affect the present. Again, the therapist may trace back the feeling or thought to an early scene (A) and seek in that way to unhook the past from the present.

Cognitive behavioural approaches (negative automatic thoughts), neuro linguistic programming (NLP) and transactional analysis (TA) have a rich body of theory for understanding and describing script thinking patterns. TA practitioners use the concept 'redefining' which includes 'discounting' and 'grandiosity' combined with script-based imagination and fantasy (Schiff et al., 1975). Discounting is ignoring or minimizing some aspect of the self, others and the world which can be at the level of the existence of something, its significance or the possibility of its changing. Grandiosity is the necessarily complementary exaggeration of something else. Thus, in the example of Keith, when he thought to himself that there was no chance of his getting a part in the school play, he was redefining the situation. He discounted the existence of any acting talents on his part and the possibility of something good happening to him. This meant that he was being grandiose (exaggerating) about the talents of the other children and about the arbitrariness of fate. He discounted the significance of the fact that the teacher had singled him out to invite him to the audition – which meant that he was either discounting the teacher's capacity for intentional action, or perhaps being grandiose about the teacher's kindness as justification. Discounting and grandiosity were combined with problems of fantasy as Keith imagined how fruitless a trip to the auditions would be.

Therapists may work closely with clients to gently, humorously, or firmly challenge them about the script reinforcing patterns of thinking (and their accompanying feeling). For a useful account of redefining and how to work with it, see Stewart (1989).

The focus in Section D is on the area of client behaviour. All therapists will pay attention to the way a client behaves – in the consulting room and in his or her life, work and relationships. How the individual therapist chooses to work with this material will depend not only upon her integrative theoretical approach and how she conceptualizes the behaviour within her theoretical integrative framework but also, as this is the level of procedural strategy, what she actually says or does with the client will depend upon her experience and accumulation of specific operational procedures. Some therapists may simply aim to raise the client's awareness of how their behaviour might be contributing to their own difficulties; for instance, by inviting an unwanted response from an employer or partner. Therapists who use a systems approach would make behaviour the focus of their intervention. As a procedural strategy, a husband may be instructed to spend half an hour a day with his wife discussing their plans for the children's future. The reason for this intervention would not be explained to the client, but the therapist might have as his intention the restructuring of the alliances in the family system.

A therapist with a more cognitive behavioural background may use a variety of techniques which help a client to change undesirable behaviour; for example, a procedural strategy may be to design a programme of behaviour with the client which the client undertakes to fulfil during the coming week. Some therapists advocate keeping diaries. Some advocate techniques which treat thinking as a behaviour and teach clients to practice thought stopping and the repetition of positive affirmations. Steiner (1971) describes what he calls 'emotional literacy' which involves teaching clients about effective communication – how to express one's thoughts and feelings to another person clearly and non-manipulatively; how to listen and respond to the other person; how to negotiate one's needs and wants assertively but without aggression, and so on. TA's 'game theory' (Berne, 1972; Lapworth et al., 1993; Stewart and Joinnes, 1989) offers an accessible method of analysing and changing repetitive patterns of unhelpful behaviour in relationships. The theory can be used phenomenologically within the therapeutic relationship and can also be taught to clients so that they can be empowered to think about and understand their behaviour as well as develop options for change.

Figure 9.3 shows the Comparative Script System completed with a selection of theoretical concepts from different approaches.

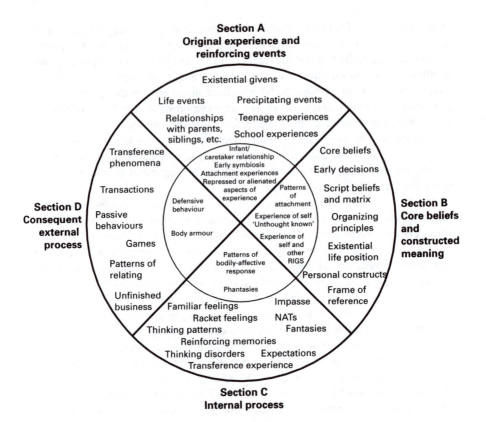

Figure 9.3 **Comparable theoretical concepts (concepts from a variety of different schools of psychotherapy are grouped into clusters)**

Case example

Amanda came to a therapist about her depression. She had been to the doctor complaining of sleeping badly, lack of energy, diminished appetite and tearfulness. The doctor suggested that she see the therapist who was attached to the GP's surgery. The doctor and the therapist agreed that while Amanda was clearly depressed, her state did not warrant the use of antidepressant medication. The therapist started by listening to Amanda's story of her lack of confidence, her anxiety that her husband was not interested in her and her fears of loneliness when her children left home, as they were likely to do in the near future. The research into psychotherapy and counselling depressed people indicates that a successful outcome may be achieved through a cognitive behavioural approach combined with some expression of feeling and some exploration into the person's early life and experiences in order to uncover the influence of modelling and/or early decisions. Consequently, the therapist decided to use a combination of predominantly cognitive techniques with some early script work.

The most evident aspects of Amanda's situation were behavioural ones at Section D – the poor sleep patterns, the inability to be energetic and the frequent weeping and at Section C – the internal experience of self-denigrating thoughts and doom-laden fantasies. The therapist asked Amanda if she would be willing to change the behaviour of staying in bed late thinking about her inadequacies. After some discussion and encouraged by the therapist's interest and support, Amanda remembered a time when she had felt more positive about herself and had been in the habit of going swimming regularly. She agreed to re-establish the practice.

The therapist subsequently concentrated on the patterns of thinking, feeling and fantasizing which dominated the client's life (C). Gradually, Amanda began to be aware of how much she bullied and criticized herself and also of the the feeling of baffled powerlessness with which she met her current life. During the sessions, she was able to link these to her beliefs about herself that she was useless and could do nothing right (B). It seemed that these half-conscious beliefs surfaced whenever she made a mistake or if someone disagreed with her. Using Socratic questioning, the therapist gently confronted Amanda's phenomenological world and invited her to make different statements about herself, about mistakes in general and the meaning of differences of opinion. Gradually, Amanda started to catch herself as she began to have these 'catastrophic' thoughts (Ellis, 1962) and was sometimes even able to tease herself about them. From time to time, when her script experience was very powerful, the therapist would ask her if she had felt like this when she was a child; had anybody ever said those things to her or whom did she know who might have acted like that (A)?

Amanda remembered being a small girl and feeling baffled and panic-stricken when her mother would get angry at something she had done. She remembered not knowing what her mistake was but saying desperately 'I love you mummy' to her mother's unrelenting back. Her mother would often snap back, 'Well I don't love you. No one will ever love you.' As Amanda recalled the scene, she burst into tears and sobbed in a way which was very different from her depressed tearfulness. As she understood how hurt she had been and how much her self-esteem had been affected, she also began to feel outraged at her mother and for the first time expressed her anger about what her mother had said. Returning to the present, she quickly made links with the relationship she had with her husband, and was quite astonished to realize that not only had she been treating him as if he were her unloving mother but that deep down she had also transferred her repressed anger and sense of thwarted entitlement to be unconditionally loved. These archaic expectations were also explored in the sessions, and the therapist helped her to work out an appropriate and self-respecting way of communicating with her husband. Amanda began to report that her life was changing, that she had managed disagreements with her husband and children in a new way and that she was thinking of looking for a job. Shortly afterwards the psychotherapy was ended by mutual agreement and Amanda left, with the understanding that she could return for what she called 'top-up' sessions if she needed them.

The example is, of necessity, altered to preserve confidentiality as well as highly abridged which perhaps gives an impression of unrealistic smooth running of the therapeutic process. However, it serves to offer an example of how a practitioner may use the Script System to integrate theory and procedure and also as a guide to the work. At the start of the work, the therapist used it as a map. It was useful in assessing the situation and noticing where the client was directing her energies. It was also a useful tool for treatment planning as the therapist designed the route he would take in working with his client. He was guided by what he knew about depression as well as his own preferences in working and his theories about human beings – while, of course, remaining responsive to the client, where she was and the material she brought. During the course of the therapy he continued to use the map, monitoring himself and his interventions and ensuring that all sections of the system were addressed.

Figure 9.4 demonstrates how the therapist used the Comparative Script System to assess Amanda and plan a way of working.

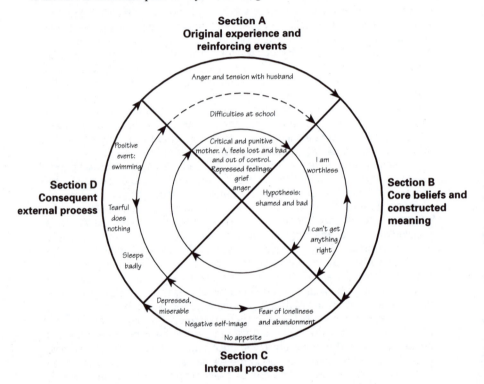

NB The therapist uses the outer ring for the initial assessment – indicating what elements are most accessible. The centre ring is for the earliest protocol. Alternatively, the separate rings can be used to track different developmental or other manifestations of the process.

Life circumstances
Children leaving home

Cultural factors

Contracts
Session 1: To go swimming
Session 3: Affirmations

Figure 9.4 **The assessment form**

The Script System in supervision

Either on his own or with a supervisor, the therapist – perhaps using Figure 9.4, the assessment and intervention template – can collate the information he has about a client, paying attention to where there are gaps and raising questions about possible unexplored avenues. This can be helpful in clarifying assessment and case overview. According to his particular integrative approach he will choose to focus more on some sections than on others, but he is likely to notice that his work naturally takes him from one section to another and back again as he follows the process of his client. If he and his client seem to have 'got stuck' he might use Ware's (1983) 'Doors to Therapy' (as described in Chapter 5) which may help him to identify his client's accessibility in different sections, or he may simply experiment with intervening at the level of behaviour, narrative, assumptions or here and now thinking/feeling in order to discover which is most useful to his client at that point. Using it with several clients, a therapist might discover a previously unidentified area for his own development as he realizes that he has an unnecessary bias towards working in a particular section while neglecting another.

Conclusion

In summary, the Script System is a framework for theoretical integration and procedural strategies for psychotherapists and counsellors. It provides a map for linking early experiences, intrapsychic processes and interpersonal relationships. It shows how a person's difficulties can be approached from a variety of different standpoints. It can be used as a tool for treatment planning and also as a method for supervision.

10
The Seven-level Model

Clarkson's seven-level model provides a framework for three main areas of categorization: it identifies and clarifies various aspects of a person's experience (in this respect it is an holistic view); it provides an integrative overview of therapeutic approaches with their differing, sometimes seemingly contradictory, sometimes overlapping theoretical emphasis; it is also a tool for integration at the level of concrete operations which we have called the 'procedural integration strategy'. Further it may be employed as an aid to diagnosis and treatment planning. Clarkson writes: '[the seven level model] is epistemological for the psychotherapist in the sense that people can sort their experiences into these different categories. Psychotherapeutic areas of knowledge, theories and procedures can also be discriminated by this means, and it can therefore be useful to guide the choice of concretely specific operations' (Clarkson and Lapworth,1992a).

Clarkson first introduced the seven-level model in a paper entitled 'Seven Epistemological Levels' (1975), describing it as a conceptual map or grid. It describes seven different aspects of experience. It is, perhaps, confusing therefore to describe it as a 'model', which implies fixed theoretical structures rather than our preferred description throughout this book of 'framework' into which varying therapeutic approaches, both theoretical and pragmatic, may be integrated. Indeed, Clarkson herself often refers to her model as a framework or a frame of reference.

Though the term 'levels' is employed, Clarkson makes it explicit that there is no hierarchy intended in such a description. Each of these levels co-exists. There is no one preferred or emphasized level at the expense of another. A person's potential as a human being is dependent upon their development at all levels. It is not possible, or desirable, to attend to one level without simultaneously influencing the others. The seven levels are:

- Level 1 – The Physiological.
- Level 2 – The Emotional.
- Level 3 – The Nominative.
- Level 4 – The Normative.
- Level 5 – The Rational.
- Level 6 – The Theoretical.
- Level 7 – The Transpersonal.

Level 1 – The Physiological Level

In terms of human experience, this level concerns bodily experience. It includes all biological, physical, visceral and sensational experience, and bodily processes (movement, sleep, eating, elimination, etc.). Similar to Lazarus's (1981) biological area of experience (see Chapter 8), it would also include consideration of any medication or drug usage and their physiological influence upon the person.

In counselling and psychotherapy, attention at this level may, for example, address physical dysfunction such as back problems, insomnia, the physical symptoms of anxiety, the behavioural aspects of eating disorders, nervous gestures or ticks, illnesses, and so on. Often, clients present for therapy with physical symptoms on which they are more than willing to dwell. Though meeting the client at this level in an accepting and empathic way may initially be vital, it is often the case that movement to the emotional level is indicated, as well as other levels (making connections between body, mind and emotions) in order to make inroads into the presenting physiological symptoms.

Conversely, some clients may need to develop more awareness of their body. They may be too 'mindful' at the expense of their physical being. It may be that depressed clients, with all their understanding and feelings about their depression, may best be helped initially by exploring how physiologically they may be maintaining their mood. Recent research gives strong indications that the physiological act of laughing and taking exercise (particularly through dancing) brings about a chemical change in that part of the brain concerned with our feeling of happiness and that depression may be alleviated by such intervention. Some may argue that this does not address the underlying causes of depression, but to paraphrase Berne (1961/80), if someone comes to you with a splinter in their toe, it's best to take the thorn out first. You can always explore how it got there afterwards and find ways of avoiding its recurrence.

The psychotherapeutic approaches which primarily focus at this level would include bioenergetics and body-oriented approaches inspired by the work of Lowen (1969, 1976), Reich (1972), Keleman (1985) and Wolpe (1961), as would certain aspects of behaviour therapy such as classical conditioning, desensitization, breathing and relaxation techniques.

The therapy may draw upon complementary approaches to health such as homeopathy, acupuncture and osteopathy as well as more orthodox interventions using allopathic medication. Referral of a client for massage, relaxation and breathing techniques and body-posture approaches (such as the Alexander technique) may be useful adjuncts to the therapeutic process. Again, we emphasize (and this applies to all levels) that in this holistic view any work at this physiological level is concomitantly influential at all the other levels. In the treatment of anxiety, for example, attention may be given at this level to the reduction of the physiological symptoms of anxiety through breathing techniques. Simultaneously, the experience of anxiety at the emotional, nominative, normative levels, etc. will be affected and, at some stage in the therapy, require focus. In Gestalt terms, the physiological level, in this instance, may be 'figure' while the other levels remain 'ground'. At a different stage of the therapy, the physiological may join others as the 'ground' against which the 'figure' of another level is clearly silhouetted and focused upon.

In the area of intervention, the psychotherapist may choose from a wide variety ranging from heightening client awareness through to actual 'hands on' manipulation of the body. The choice will, of course, depend upon the theory used and, necessarily therefore, the therapist's view of human beings which defines what is therapeutic.

The necessarily brief example that follows will be continued for each 'level' in the order presented in our list of seven levels. This does not represent the ebb and flow within and between these levels which is inevitably the more natural flow of the therapy, but should give some idea of the use of these levels in terms of describing the client's experience, the therapist's theoretical organization and her procedural interventions.

Jubin, a 45-year-old junior school teacher came to psychotherapy following a period which he described as 'inexplicable exhaustion and depression'. He told his story of the onset of his depression at a time of an inspection at his school and the extra work this had entailed. However, he summarily dismissed any connection between this or other life events and his depressive exhaustion saying that he had always been a 'coper' and there was no reason for him to feel so down. The therapist noted his neatness of dress, his hunched body posture, the stiff and heavy way he moved. She saw him as both carrying some enormous weight while 'holding in' something equally heavy. She took note of his poor sleeping and eating patterns which contributed to this picture of depression and noted too his physical symptoms of stomach tension and chronic constipation. Her hypothesis (her own experience at Level 6) in the early stages of therapy was that Jubin was experiencing an inner conflict between a highly 'driving' introject he was struggling to please and a self which was denied recognition. She saw his denial of his situation, both external and internal, as contributing to his physical (Level 1) and emotional (Level 2) exhaustion.

Having established a working relationship and following her treatment plan based upon her hypothesized diagnosis (see Levels 3 and 6), she suggested Jubin experiment with lying down on the sofa rather than sitting facing him as was her usual way of working with clients. She invited him to become aware of the tensions in his body, the parts that needed more support and the sensational experience of letting go by slowing down his breathing. He reluctantly agreed.

Jubin: This feels strange. It's not something I'd normally let myself do, even at home.

Therapist: Will you let yourself be supported by the sofa? How about your shoulders?

Jubin: It's hard. I feel like the muscles there are stuck.

Therapist: And if you drop your shoulders as you breathe out?

Jubin: It's like putting down a ton weight. I've been carrying it for so long. I feel like I'm floating now. It's very strange. I feel relieved but also scared.

Interventions at this physical level continued throughout the therapy, often leading into work at other levels, particularly in the early stages, at Level 2.

Jubin's fear of 'letting go' was reflected in a pattern of improvement and relapse, a pattern which the therapist recognized as perhaps serving to provoke her impatience, even hostility (the punitive object) towards him.

Level 2 – The Emotional Level

In terms of human experience, this level concerns the affective and emotional life of the client. It includes their experience and expression of the four basic feelings of anger, sadness, fear and joy and the multitude of variants of these, as well as the emotional experience of shame, guilt, despair and anxiety. Clearly, this is a level at which many clients present. The therapist will need to meet the client at such a level with empathy, empathic attunement and resonance. It is the emotional experience of the client which has brought them into therapy and the need will be of acceptance, understanding, support and the 'safe container' of the therapeutic relationship in order to begin to work through these emotions. Whether the emotions are current (for example, recent bereavement), archaic (anxiety rooted in childhood) or in anticipation of a future event, the expression and cathartic release of these feelings may be an important part of the therapeutic work and may involve the expression of emotions towards the envisaged presence of a partner, parent or sibling or directly to the therapist within their therapeutic relationship.

At this level the theoretical considerations may be that of bonding and attachment (Bowlby, 1953; Rutter, 1972; Winnicott, 1958), deconfusion (Lapworth et al., 1993) and early childhood trauma (Miller, 1985). Those approaches which give attention to the experiencing and expression of emotions would include, for example, polarity work in Gestalt, deconfusion and redecision in TA, attention to preverbal experiences in primal therapy, rebirthing and the work of Greenberg and Safran (1987) specifically concerning emotion in psychotherapy. Other approaches which give emphasis to the exploration, experiencing and release of emotions include psychodrama, bioenergetics and rechilding (Clarkson and Fish, 1988a) while visualization and physical release techniques may be used to enhance emotional expression. These latter in particular show the close interconnection between levels 1 and 2.

> Jubin expressed little affect. He complained about his situation and other people in his life in a voice which was flat and heavy. The therapist hypothesized that he was 'depressing' his feelings in order to comply with the internal object driving him to be a 'coper' and that this was also reflected at the physical level and other levels. In particular, in order to work through his depression and lessen his exhaustion, he would need to get in touch with his feelings connected both with his current situation and those repressed from the past, particularly his anger which seeped out in passive-aggressive ways such as 'forgetting' meetings at school or in his complaints about his wife, as well as in relation to his therapist by turning up on occasions either late or far too early for his appointments.
>
> In the early stages, working at the physical level, Jubin would often experience both a sense of relief and a feeling of scare. In inviting Jubin to

express his fear through bodily movements and verbal expression, Jubin made a connection between 'letting go' and 'letting down'. His fear was that he was failing in his duties and that 'people' would be violently angry. The therapist hypothesized that beneath his fear Jubin repressed his anger, even rage, and decided to use heightening and enactment techniques to help him release his feelings.

During one session, when talking about a particular inspector who had sat in on his class at school, Jubin unexpressively described the way the inspector had stood at the back of the room taking notes all the way through.

Jubin: Even when I was reading a story for the children he was scribbling away.
Therapist: What would you have liked to have said to him?
Jubin: Give me a break. I'm just reading a story. Why don't you just listen?
Therapist: I don't think he can hear you. He's at the back of the hall.
Jubin [shouting angrily]:   Leave me alone! Just go away!
Therapist: Who else would you like to have said that to?
Jubin: My father [Jubin cries] He was always looking for something to criticize me for.
Therapist: And when you relax, are you scared you're letting him down?
Jubin: Yes, I'm so scared he'll be really furious with me. I had to do it his way. He was always right! I could never get it right no matter what I did. I just kept on and on trying to get it right. That's what I'm trying to do now at school, even at home with my wife and kids [cries again]. But it's not them, it's him.

Level 3 – The Nominative Level

This level concerns the naming of our human experiences of ourselves, others and the world. It involves awareness, validation and labelling using the skill that distinguishes us from others in the animal realm, that of language. Through language and the ability to name objects, needs and experiences, it is observed that the young child makes great leaps in its development, able now to communicate, make sense of and more usefully manipulate its environment for its own needs (and later, for others). So too in the therapy situation, it is often observed that the ability of the client, through facilitation, sometimes education, by the therapist, to name and categorize their experience brings about a developmental change. The overwhelming emotional and physiological experiences that sometimes bring a client to therapy are made more manageable when named, owned, understood, accepted. There is a shift in the extent of working through these experiences when they are given names. It is almost as if the naming of these experiences gives permission for their existence (and in this respect may be verging on the level of the normative).

In her novel *The Waves*, Virginia Woolf (1931/51) writes, 'Nothing should be named lest by doing so we change it.' Here she is referring to experience valued for its own sake: to enjoy the scent of a flower it is unnecessary to name it; indeed, in the naming, the experience may be altered. The implication here is that the act of naming brings about a change. In therapy, this is exactly what we are often attempting to do by naming when dealing with negative or distressing experiences. It was by naming the 'devils' which 'possessed' people that Christ in the Gospels gained power and control over them; the power to exorcize them and thus transform the 'possessed' person. It seems to us that, as therapists, we are often doing the same thing with our clients. Naming the introject, the abuser, the critical parent, may be an important first step in transformation. Recognizing this effect of naming, the therapist also takes account of the importance of timing; naming something too early can prevent further exploration.

This level might include the naming and labelling of feelings and sensations, and for the practitioner the naming of experience according to their psycho-therapeutic orientation – the naming of ego states, introjects, games, for example, in transactional analysis, of defences and conflicts in psychodynamic approaches, the naming of polarities, top dog/underdog, interruptions in Gestalt, the naming and acceptance of that part of us that may be named 'the shadow' in Jungian conceptualization or various subpersonalities in psychosynthesis. All orientations provide descriptive labels which assist in the understanding, ownership, control and transformation of experience.

In a sense, naming can be seen as diagnosis. This may range from the informal 'What I am feeling is depressed' to more formal diagnosis provided by such categorizations as DSM IV. Some may argue that diagnosis is restrictive, even abusive. We think that diagnosis, used descriptively rather than prescriptively, can be a great asset to the therapeutic process. We do not find useful the fixed labelling of people as 'paranoid', 'passive aggressive' or 'obsessive-compulsive', but it is helpful to name and identify someone's tendency to think paranoid thoughts or behave in certain situations in a passive-aggressive way (including our own tendencies). Used caringly and creatively with the individual, the naming of traits and tendencies can be a valuable asset in treatment planning (for examples, Johnson, 1994; Ware, 1983).

Jubin, through work at the emotional level, had already moved into the nominative level. He had made connections between his current feelings beneath his depression and those belonging to his childhood which had not been allowed expression. He named those feelings as fear, anger and sadness. He felt anger towards his parents and sadness for and within the young Jubin who had been unacknowledged for himself. At this stage, he was able to name his father as the main protagonist, the internal voice that drove him on in the face of almost continuous criticism. This in itself was a big step for Jubin as he recognized that his fear of his father had lead him to repress his other feelings too. The therapist named and acknowledged this silent fear, through which he had 'depressed' his feelings of anger, as a wise 'strategy for survival' (Elton Wilson, 1996). In doing so, she concomitantly named and acknowledged the young Jubin which he himself was then able to acknowledge and to begin to address internally the deficit of his parents' attentions.

It was only later in the therapy that Jubin, till then protective of his mother, began to acknowledge the intrusive and domineering role she played in his early life. By naming her, he contacted early recollections of her constant control of his eating and elimination, remembering her requiring him not to flush the lavatory until he had shown her that he had performed a bowel movement.

In diagnostic terms at this nominative level, the therapist thought in terms of Johnson's (1994) character styles. She found his description of the Defeated Child helpful in conceptualizing Jubin's physiological and psychological style of being in the world and of understanding (see Level 6) the approach to therapy which may be most helpful to Jubin.

Level 4 – The Normative Level

Under this heading are included both statistical and cultural norms: the measurements by which we assess some of the 'oughts' of our belief systems: how to do things, what things mean in our culture, what is the 'usual' and what the 'unusual'. This is not to suggest that therapy should play a normative role in the sense of encouraging conformity or providing further parental 'oughts', but that it looks at norms in terms of their relevance, appropriateness, usefulness and application in specific circumstances. We believe that therapeutic work, with its aims of integration, growth and self-actualization, cannot but challenge and transcend many cultural and societal 'norms'; for example, the 'stiff upper lip' norm of the British male or racist regimes in whatever culture. These are contradictions of health, integration, well-being and growth and fly in the face of what we see as a main tenet of therapy that everyone has worth, value and dignity.

Sometimes clients present for counselling or psychotherapy restricted by the 'norms' they have evolved through their life's experience and the influence of society. In a capitalist society, many people put great expectations upon themselves to reach certain career, relational or financial goals – despite the fact that their enjoyment of life is grossly curtailed by such self-imposed expectations. Others may feel they are 'odd', even ill, if they are not conforming to some cultural norm. For example, many men see themselves as weak or 'over-sensitive' if they express their sadness by openly crying (though many cry alone). Or in the case of women, the media 'norm' in the fashion world of using almost anorexic models, gives rise to many women feeling a sense of failure, even despising themselves and their bodies, if they do not meet this 'norm'. It is to be hoped that therapy may address and challenge these beliefs and expectations by normalizing feelings, body shapes and whatever else may be seen as a problem due to perverse norms rather than 'real' experience and existence.

It is important to add at this point that the therapist must be aware of the powerful influence she will have on the client in terms of the norms she brings (in or out of her awareness) to the therapy situation. Inevitably, she will be bringing her own cultural and societal expectations to the therapy room and 'imposing' them in the field. For this reason, a careful examination of our own norms as well as our clients' is essential.

On a theoretical level the comparison of various approaches in terms of their normative values can give rise to optimism concerning integration. The commonalities, the 'norms', of several approaches are at least enough to reassure us that mutual or complementary beliefs are shared across the three schools and that counselling and psychotherapy integration is therefore possible. For example, the hypothesis that childhood experiences profoundly affect how we interpret and live our later lives seems to be a 'norm' across several approaches. We might also include the 'norms' shared by many approaches that feeling and the expression of feeling is not only normal but important for our holistic health; that our beliefs about ourselves, others and the world can be either restrictive or life enhancing; that being listened to and accepted are, in themselves, therapeutic and that more than any one approach to counselling or psychotherapy it is the therapeutic relationship which holds the most transformative potential.

For Jubin, there were many normative aspects explored within his psychotherapy. In particular, as a British-born Asian, from a Parsee family, there were cultural and religious 'norms' which he had rejected on a conscious level but were still in evidence in the 'oughts' and 'shoulds' of his internal belief system. This was a cause of conflict within him. His driven work ethic came out of both his cultural background and the double minority group in which he found himself as a Parsee in Britain. He experienced a pressure from family and society to conform, to 'prove' himself and, like his father before him, to provide for and maintain his wife and children at a high standard of living – whatever the physical and psychological cost. His mother's conformities for him, apart from his eating and bowel habits, were in his appearance: neat conservative clothes, brushed hair, no ostentation, 'let them know you come from a good family'. The therapist took care to explore the cultural aspects involved here and discovered that for Parsees, with their Zoroastrian beliefs, cleanliness is not just next to godliness – it is godliness.

He explored and reassessed the emotional and behavioural norms he had grown up with, the tendency to belittle emotions in favour of intellect, the disapproval of feelings as 'weakness' and the labelling of relaxation and pleasure as laziness. He referred back to the experiment of lying down in the therapy sessions as 'flying in the face' of all that he had been instructed was the 'right' way of being. 'Letting go' rather than 'taking on' was a challenge to his conditioning.

Jubin: I've been carrying my family's beliefs about so many things.
Therapist: You used to speak of them as if they were set in stone.
Jubin: They seemed that way. And just as heavy!
Therapist: And now?
Jubin: Well, there are probably a few things left but they're more like pebbles that I can pick up or put down more easily.
Therapist: I notice you no longer wear a tie when you come here.
Jubin: That's true. Do you mind?
Therapist: Do you think I mind?
Jubin: No, I don't. You're not my mother.
Therapist: What if I did mind?
Jubin: I'd ask you why it was important to you that I wear a tie!

Level 5 – The Rational Level

In terms of human experience, this level concerns our cognitive function – thinking and making sense of things, looking at cause and effect, learning and appraising factual information and understanding our frames of reference. This is a further development of our experience at the previous levels, moving as it does from physiological, emotional and nominative levels to understanding our experience. At the levels of sensation and emotion we may experience our anxiety and nominatively label it as such, even acknowledge it as normatively acceptable. At this rational level we may begin to explore the origins of our anxiety and find ways of understanding it. Further, this knowledge may provide us with the means to alleviate that anxiety. If we know its 'cause', we are more equipped to discover its remedy. Thus our rational thinking, remembering and consideration may serve in the exploration of solutions to our problems.

Confrontation of irrational thinking plays an important part in therapy. In transactional analysis emphasis is given to the decontamination of the Adult ego state (Lapworth et al., 1993) whereby Parent prejudices and beliefs and Child delusions and magical thinking are separated out to allow clear thinking, reality testing and decision making in the here and now of the Adult ego state. Several approaches (for examples, transactional analysis, cognitive behaviour therapy, neuro linguistic programming) offer precise ways of analysing how clients skew their thinking in order to maintain their frame of reference. Discounting or distortion, problems of over-detailing or generalization, thinking disorders, and so on, are all part of this level. In rational-emotive-behaviour therapy (Ellis, 1962/94; Neenan and Dryden 1996), three stages are provided to assist in disputing irrational beliefs: (1) help the client to distinguish clearly between their rational and irrational beliefs; (2) debate the issue with Socratic questions such as 'Where is the evidence that you must'; (3) use defining to help the client make increasingly accurate definitions in their own language (Dryden, 1987).

Indeed, various approaches to therapy give similar emphasis to this rational level, whether it be termed 'insight' in more psychodynamic models or an 'aha' experience in Gestalt. Both are concerned with the way we think about our experience and the importance of that thinking in finding means of making changes.

Jubin's therapist did not work directly at this level until late on in the therapy realizing that too early interventions at this level would be met with either superficial compliance or passive-aggressive blocking by intellectualization on Jubin's part. The changes in Jubin's thinking came about mostly through working at the physical and emotional levels, being empathically attuned at these levels of Jubin's experience and tolerant of the repeated relapses in response to his challenging his internalized object by behavioural and emotional expression.

Jubin's ceasing to wear a tie on all occasions was an outward sign that he was reassessing his beliefs in the need for conformity and demonstrating his ability rationally to challenge the pervasive and controlling thought that there is only one 'right' way to think, be and behave.

Level 6 – The Theoretical Level

This level concerns our human experience as 'storytellers', the way we make meaning and sense of the world through story, symbol, myth and metaphor. Through our theories we attempt to explain why things are as they are and why people behave as they do. These are not truths in themselves. They are different from the personal 'facts' of the rational level. Rather, they are explorations of truths relative to our experience and understanding at the time.

In the counselling and psychotherapy world, there is a plethora of theories which have been developed in the service of understanding our human condition and which attempt to explain our behaviour and create ways of changing it. Psychoanalysis has one story; behaviour therapy another; humanistic psychotherapy yet another. Between and within these are further stories or metaphors which may be very different or very similar, overlap or interface, but all of which attempt to make sense of our human experience. Integration in counselling and psychotherapy is an attempt to tell other stories inclusive of some of those already told.

In explaining our current behaviour, humanistic approaches have the concept of scripts, behaviour therapy, conditioning, psychoanalysis, the concept of drives, and so on. But whether using TA's script and racket system story, the narrative theories of constructivism, rational-emotive-behaviour therapy's story of the perpetuation of psychological disturbance by negative beliefs in response to negative events, Gestalt's story of 'fixed Gestalts', or behaviourism's conditioning story, they all share an overarching theoretical principle that events in the past influence the way a person thinks, feels and behaves in the present. It's a useful story, a useful relative truth and seems to be supported by current research into the brain. Perhaps, however, one day another story will be told which will drastically alter the face of therapy.

One of the most important tasks at the beginning of therapy is to allow the client to tell his or her 'story'. This will not only involve facts but clients' own perceptions, interpretations and understandings of how their past history has affected their life course. Clarkson (1975) suggests that clients come to therapy with their own theory of life, their working model by which they make sense of events. Very often this model is one which is not efficient for helping the client identify what they want, let alone achieve it. An effective theory is one that is able to deal with a wide range of variables. The therapist comes with his or her own theories of life and own stories, one or more of which will be his or her psycho-therapy model or models. The therapeutic relationship creates a context for the meeting of these stories out of which arises the story of the therapy.

Elton Wilson (1996) describes the client's telling of their story as 'the disclosure stage' and sees the therapist's task as listening with respect as the *history* is told and original strategies for survival are described and validated. She adds useful caution for those therapists who have been trained to facilitate and value emotional expression above all:

> There can be a danger in rushing clients into catharsis, by encouraging and including full demonstration of their deepest feelings. It is better to allow sufficient time for clients

to gain full insight into the roots of the troublesome patterns which they are now experiencing. This will strengthen and inform them when they enter the next catharsis stage of vivid and emotion-laden recall of the original emotional experience. (Elton Wilson, 1996: 39)

In terms of the integration of approaches, we believe it is vital that theories (stories) other than our own are listened to and considered. There is no one true story. There are only stories which hold or do not hold some relevance and usefulness for us. Exploring the similarities and differences between these stories allows for integration – further storytelling in the search for understanding and meaning.

In the course of telling and exploring his story in his therapy, Jubin eventually made connections between his exhaustive depression, current life events at home and at school and his childhood experiences. He recognized the validity of his early decision to hide his anger in the face of both of his controlling, rigid and, sometimes, violent parents. He could understand this survival strategy as being essential to him at the time but could also see how he it had cost him his spontaneous and authentic expression of his true self. He realized he was now acting in the world as if his feelings would be equally squashed by others – his wife, his colleagues, the inspectors, his therapist. He used this realization to allow himself to experiment with 'letting go' of the structures he carried around with him, challenging the beliefs and rules of his controlling internalized object and rethinking the way he wanted to be.

The therapist was respectful of Jubin's story at all times and employed her own psychotherapy story, not as a superimposed grid into which Jubin's story must fit, but as a guide to better understanding his story and helping him make the changes he wanted to make. Using the seven levels as an integrative framework, she brought to the therapy her theoretical understanding gained in her training and experience in psychodynamic, object relations and bioenergetics theory. She was also able to integrate at the procedural level various techniques to aid relaxation, two-chair work to assist in Jubin's emotional expression towards his parents and, in the same vein, bioenergetic body postures to identify and release physical and emotional tension.

Her working hypothesis was based upon Johnson's (1994) description of the Defeated Child: Social Masochism and the Patterns of Self-defeat. She identified the aetiology of Jubin's style of being in the world in the inappropriate, invasive and intrusive parenting of both his parents, their domination, control and eventual subjugation of Jubin's will. She saw his survival strategy as the early shutting down of aggression and natural retaliatory impulses and the development of a personality that was compliant, almost servile, on the surface but internally 'holding on' to anger which, out of his awareness, he allowed expression in passive-aggressive behaviour.

Drawing on the work of Ware (1983) and his 'doors to therapy' for specific personality adaptations, she initially worked with Jubin at his Open Door of behaviour (relaxation techniques, body posture, 'homework' experiments) in order to move through to his Target Door of feelings (working through his fear to his anger and sadness and the expression of each of these) and avoiding the Trap Door of thinking until later stages of their work together.

Throughout the therapy and Jubin's often angry recycling of difficulties, the therapist maintained her ability to offer Jubin a 'real and good' relationship. She knew that this would be constantly tested, but also knew the necessity for her to counter Jubin's inner reality which was interfering with his relationships with others and to offer a different experience. She was supported, especially at those times when she felt provoked into replicating Jubin's parents' response, by her theoretical conviction in his reparative need of a good object. She bore in mind Johnson's quote from Fairbairn: 'the appeal of a good object is an indispensable factor in promoting a dissolution of the cathexis of internalized bad objects, and . . . the significance of the transference situation is partly derived from this fact' (Johnson, 1994: 74).

Level 7 – The Transpersonal Level

Included at this level are those experiences which are beyond theory and rationalization and beyond the individual: dreams, altered states of consciousness, the spiritual, the surreal, the metaphysical, the transcendent, the existentially paradoxical, the mystical, the unpredictable and the inexplicable (Lapworth, 1990). The transpersonal can also be said to include such existential issues as the search for meaning, the embracing of the connectedness between people, the acceptance of responsibility towards the world, and of genuine altruism.

At this level belong Jung's archetypes and the collective unconscious, his dreams and symbols, as well as transpersonal psychotherapies such as psychosynthesis and of some expositions of Gestalt which include a spiritual dimension within their parameters.

In her book *The Inward Arc* (1985) Vaughan writes:

> The spiritual quest is, above all, a search for truth, and in order to be at peace with oneself one must be willing to see truth as it is. Spiritual well-being is characterised by a sense of inner peace, compassion for others, reverence for life, gratitude, and appreciation of both unity and diversity. Healthy spirituality also implies qualities such as humour, wisdom, generosity, and a capacity for non-attachment, self-transcendence, and unconditional love.' She writes further, 'Truth can become a strong force for healing once the commitment is made. In psychotherapy, telling the truth about experience is an essential part of the process, but its relevance to spiritual well-being is rarely recognised. (Vaughan, 1985: 20–1)

In Clarkson's (1990) article, 'A Multiplicity of Therapeutic Relationships', she recognizes this spiritual healing force within the therapeutic relationship itself; a relationship which she calls 'transpersonal'. She writes of each partner in the relationship being deeply enhanced by the presence and impact of the other and, quoting Archambeau (1979), implies that the mutual unconsciousnesses of the partners transform the relationship beyond that of the I–Thou relationship to something greater than the sum of its parts, something that happens in the 'between' of the relationship.

Dreams are often brought by clients to therapy sessions. Fish and Lapworth (1994) argue that dreams are reflections of aspects of the self. As regards the transpersonal self in relation to dreams, they write that some dreams 'concern our search for meaning and purpose in the human condition. Such dreams themselves may seem mystical and hidden within their own symbolism but in some way they are, like the Tarot, the I-Ching or other mystic writings, carrying the essence of a truth within them'. Many clients in the course of their therapy have dreams which bring about a fundamental shift in their understanding of themselves and their lives, containing as they do much transformational symbolism. But they bring not only understanding: often the experience of a person during their dreams is on many other of the seven levels, creating, for example, physiological change (symptom relief) or normative change (acceptance of an aspect of themselves), and so on.

This is a level which some practitioners believe does not belong to the realm of psychotherapy and may deem it preferable for the client to seek guidance from a spiritual leader, healer or guru. What is sometimes viewed as a spiritual dimension may be an avoidance of the reality of experience at other levels. There is a danger that if something is not understood, it is classified as spiritual. In which case, the transpersonal becomes a 'catch-all' for any aspects of the counselling or psychotherapy which do not readily gain explanation or clarity at the other levels. Lapworth has noted that a high proportion of clients who present for therapy with what they call a 'spiritual' problem disclose within a few sessions deep-seated sexual dilemmas or dysfunctions.

> Jubin's therapist was unfamiliar with Parsee beliefs. Though Jubin had declared his total rejection of such beliefs, she nonetheless read up on the basic story of Zoroastrianism and the myths and stories that would likely have been a part of Jubin's childhood.
>
> Jubin brought a dream to therapy in which he had dreamed that he had a twin brother. They were playing by a stream. The twin, who was depicted as spontaneous and happy, fell into the stream while playing at its edge. Jubin ran down to the stream, lay down on his stomach and looked into the water. Seeing his brother looking up at him, he reached into the water to save him. On doing so, he realized that what he had thought was his brother was his own reflection.
>
> In exploring the dream together, Jubin saw clearly that the twin represented the unadapted, spontaneous part of himself. His therapist suggested he talk to his twin.
>
> *Jubin:*   You are how I want to be. You don't have to hide yourself to live. I should be the one to drown in the stream. I am so bad, so very bad.
> *Therapist:*   You seem to be seeing the twins in terms of good and bad.
> *Jubin:*   Maybe good and evil.
> *Therapist:*   Like Ormazd and Ahriman?
> *Jubin:*   Yes, exactly. Ahriman chose untruth and darkness. Ormazd chose truth and light. There is always a battle between them. That's how I feel inside. The struggle is exhausting.
> *Therapist:*   In your dream, you went to rescue your twin . . . there was no battle.

Jubin: No, that's true. He is the lighter part of me but the darker part is not without love. He wants them to be together.

Therapist: What might that lighter part say to you?

Jubin: You have saved me. I am still here. If you had not protected me by hiding me away, I would not have survived at all. We are together. We are one.

11

Change, Time, Place and Community
An Integral Approach to Therapy
Contributed by Keith Tudor

Authors' note

We have chosen this chapter as it provides a somewhat different perspective on integration in its exploration of four contextual domains in counselling and psychotherapy which may be seen as an integrative framework. It seems fitting to conclude this section with Tudor's thoughtful discussion, inviting the reader as it does to take time to consider their own personal and professional development by the provision of questions and suggestions for reflection.

> **Integration**: 1. The making up of a whole by adding together or combining the separate parts or elements. 2. Maths. The operation of finding the integral of a given function or equation. (Onions, 1973: 1088)

Finding the integral in integration

In terms of the two dictionary definitions of integration quoted above, the first, the making up of the whole of therapy by adding together or combining the separate parts or elements, is the one which informs most approaches to integrative therapy. However, it may equally be viewed as a definition of eclecticism. The second (mathematical) definition, of finding the integral of a given function, is a more truly integrating enterprise in that it challenges us to consider:

1 The function of therapy, i.e. the variable quantities or elements of therapeutic practice.
2 Such elements in relation to each other.
3 The integral of this function or activity, i.e. the principle or rationale by which the combining is made.

A truly integral view of therapy then is one which fulfils these definitional requirements. The integrative (integral) framework I elaborate here is one in which:

* the core function of therapy is viewed as that of helping people to change;
* the integral principle of therapy is contextual, and is thus one which acknow-ledges both the culture of therapy and the cultural context of therapeutic practice

(which, historically, is predominantly Western, white and middle-class), viewing personal and social change in the context of *time, a place set aside* and *community*;

- such elements may be viewed in relation to each other.

How to use this framework

The four concepts of this 'core and context' framework – change (*metanoia*), time (*kairos*), a place set aside (*temenos*) and community (*koinonia*) – inspired by their origins in the Greek and illustrated by archetypal symbols delineating helping/healing (change), anywhere (place), across cultures (communities) and time. In the following sections, each concept is briefly introduced and illustrated with reference to the literature, experience and practice. Each concludes with ideas and exercises for developing awareness and application of each concept in the practitioner's personal and professional practice.

Change – metanoia

Based on different and differing philosophical assumptions, each school of therapy has its own views about change. (Some schools and orientations even distinguish between counselling and psycho-therapy on the basis of certain assumptions about the nature and extent of change, e.g. short term, long term.) Concepts of change are often linked to the aims and goals of the particular approach. Thus therapy aims, variously, for consciousness (psychodynamic, Freudian), detachment and identity (psycho-dynamic, Kleinian), individuation (Jungian, analytic psychology), re-education (Adlerian), energy release (Reichian), adjustment to and control of the environment (behaviourism), actualization (humanistic psychology), a fully functioning person (person-centred), holism (Gestalt), cure (transactional analysis), authenticity/self-understanding (existential), etc. One well-known and well-used model of change is Prochaska and DiClemente's (1992) cycle of change which involves: pre-contemplation, contemplation, determination, action, maintenance, relapse, contemplation, and so on. This cycle, which in some respects is similar to the Gestalt cycle of change or formation and destruction, is one which the authors themselves regard as transtheoretical.

Although it may be a commonplace to suggest that change lies at the core of the therapeutic endeavour, it is not uncontentious. It may be argued that such a perspective on change makes therapy itself conditional, that is, conditional on clients agreeing to change and thus antithetical to the notion of the therapist's unconditional positive regard. Aims of 'cure' as, for instance, in transactional analysis (TA) (social control, symptomatic relief, transference cure and 'script' cure), while focusing the mind of both therapist and client and making therapy clearly contractual, carry the disadvantage of an undue focus on therapeutic outcome. Although Berne (1966) was sceptical about 'supportive therapy', integrative practitioners may extend the horizons of therapy beyond narrow definitions of change to include therapy as equally concerned with health and growth promotion (as distinct from illness prevention). However, given that, as organisms, humans are in constant flux or, more accurately, process of flux, from this perspective, we may be viewed as in constant change. Thus change may be seen as an integral part of the human condition rather than as conditional.

From a transtheoretical or integrative perspective, change may be described as a turning point or metanoia which represents both the moment of change as well as a continuing process of change. West (1990: 51), for instance, describes the moment of change and the spiritual quality of metanoia or 'repentance, a change of heart, a new direction'. In the context of the development of learning organisations, Senge (1990: 13) discusses metanoia as 'a shift of mind'. Emphasizing the process or dialectical praxis of therapeutic interaction, Esterson (1970: 240) connotes metanoia with 'dialectical rationality . . . an enterprise of continual and continuing reappraisal and renewal' – a psychological equivalent to the Maoist concept of the 'permanent revolution', the two meeting in the concept of fanshen (Hinton, 1997). Similarly, Clarkson (1989) describes metanoia as a process of transformation and as a unifying (integrating) concept for describing change in life as well as in psychotherapy. Most recently, Keen (1992), in describing the movement from paranoia to metanoia, suggests that metanoia is an ongoing discipline of the spiritual life. Drawing on transdisciplinary sources across ancient and modern literature, Clarkson (1989) identifies various features of metanoia: intensity, despair, surrender (of a previous frame of reference), (experience of the) void, the importance of relationship, (and of) community validation, a sense of mission, and the appearance of archetypal images of transformation – features which I have used to consider how men change in therapy (Tudor, 1999b).

Personal and professional development

The following is a series of suggestions for contacting and developing your own and your clients' capacity to change and for making changes.

1 As organisms, we are in a constant state of change. What are you aware of today that you were not aware of yesterday?
2 Notice the seasons of the year. What do they represent to you?
3 Identify one way in which you have changed today/in the last week/month/ season/year . . . and tell someone about it.
4 Identify a problem. Now view it as a solution.
5 Take some time to meditate. Intensify your awareness.
6 Think about what you say about an enemy. Consider it false. Now think about what they may say about you: try on your enemy's truth (see Keen, 1992). If you do not have an enemy, make one – enemies provide the gift of definition: 'Know a man by his enemies' (old Russian proverb).
7 Welcome and get to know your despair.
8 Have an 'upside down' day: stay in your nightclothes; eat a meal backwards, beginning with dessert, or in a random order.

9   Do something different. Do nothing. You cannot do or be exactly the same –
    you cannot step in the same river twice. Reflect on that.
10 Think about the cycle of change: pre-contemplation, contemplation, deter-
    mination, action, maintenance, relapse, contemplation. In making a change or
    thinking about a change, do you have a familiar place where you stop and/or
    get stuck. How will you overcome that?
11 Identify friends and family who accept you changing.
12 Remember and write down your dreams for a week. During the same week,
    notice images and symbols, particularly if they are repeated.
13 Next time you celebrate an event, a birthday, an anniversary, a festival, a
    holiday, write down what it means to you.

Time – kairos

The Greeks had – and have – two words which translate into English
as time: *chronos*, hence chronological time, and *kairos*, meaning
appropriate time. It is perhaps significant that, of the two, in the West
we have adopted chronological time as a linear measure rather than
the concept of appropriate time. Thus (chronological) time becomes functional: we
spend time, lose time, waste time, serve time and even kill time. Many of us are
concerned about being on time and get irritated when, in other cultures, things do
not appear to run to time within our time frame of reference.

Berne (1966) identifies six modes of time structuring, later recognizing this as
a human need or hunger for structuring time (Berne, 1973). We are not often *in*
time itself, *being* with time, understanding the cyclical aspect of temporality (hence
kairos time is here represented by an ellipse). In our therapeutic work, many work
to a 50-minute hour, unaware that we do so because Freud did and that he did, in
turn, because he was used to 50-minute lectures. Feltham (1997) reviews attitudes
to time in counselling and psychotherapy and different models of short-term/time-
limited counselling. Encouraging a different frame of reference about this, Elton
Wilson (1996) discusses time-*conscious* therapy.

Reflecting on this, both the process and the structure of time in therapy become
matters for analysis, discussion and negotiation. If we view time as cyclical, then
we will be more accepting both of our clients and of ourselves returning to and
recycling previous issues, themes or decisions, for example, through regression. If
we view time as kairos time, then we will be more flexible and creative about
appropriate time in therapy. Thus, in response to a client's needs, and subject to
contracting, we may agree to see them twice a week for a half session or twice a
day for a short period or even when they want to see us: by negotiation rather than
the imposition of a regular set time – although, for some, this may be kairos time.
Some clients with whom I have worked have found this a therapeutic way of ending
their psychotherapy, returning from time to time or sending me an occasional
postcard or letter. The logic of kairos time may lead us to a Lacanian position
about deciding the appropriate length of individual sessions: we may agree to meet
at a certain time to work together on an issue rather than for a set, limited period

of time. Obviously all this has practical, resource and financial implications. Nevertheless, I have found thinking about and experimenting with appropriate time therapeutic rather than administrative, person-centred and present-centred rather than structure-centred.

Moments of psychic time

Although he referred himself, Al presented as very angry about 'having to come for therapy'. He wanted to come when he wanted, 'in my own time'. After some assessment and consideration, his therapist agreed to this. After a couple of months of coming intermittently, Al decided he wanted to come regularly.

Bea had been severely abused by her parents. After a couple of years in therapy she began to remember specific incidents of abuse. When she did so, at first she re-experienced her terror as if she was in that previous (historical) time. When she 'came back' to the present she expressed surprise about the actual time, saying that she thought she had been talking about her abuse for longer than she had.

Gemma was ending her therapy. Given her issues of trust and reliability, she and her therapist agreed that it would be most therapeutic to have a process of ending whereby Gemma could 'check in' with her therapist from time to time. This involved some meetings spaced out over months, some telephone contact and Gemma writing postcards from her holidays. Having tested her therapist's reliability over time, Gemma was able to end and leave therapy.

Personal and professional development

1 Analyse your day/week/month in terms of Berne's time structuring: the time you spent in *withdrawal*, e.g. being alone, taking 'time out'; in *rituals* e.g. washing your hands, picking up the post, saying 'Hello'; *pastiming*, i.e. passing the time of day with someone (beyond 'Hello'); in *activity*, e.g. work and social activities; playing *psychological games* (where you end up feeling 'bad'); and in *intimacy*, i.e. being intimate with yourself or others.
2 Draw a time line – or, in the spirit of kairos time, a time spiral – noting significant events in your life, for instance, in relation to seeking personal and/or professional help.
3 Take your watch off, stop the clocks.
4 Eat when you want to eat rather than at set 'mealtimes'.
5 Observe your sabbath (seventh day/'holy day'/holidays), keep it holy, take a sabbatical ('sabbath time').
6 Follow different time cycles:

  • The cycle of the day – with no artificial light. A number of religious traditions have specific times in the day when the faithful are called to observe, for example, the Christian offices and the Moslem call to prayer.

- The lunar cycle of the (28-day) month, associated with the female menstrual cycle.
- The cycle of the seasons/year for example, the Celtic Sun and Moon festivals.

7 Consider kairos/appropriate time as regards work in terms of:

- The length/duration of the therapy session – e.g. longer sessions.
- The regularity of sessions – weekly, fortnightly, intermittently.
- The counselling relationship – consider the therapeutic value of taking breaks, e.g. half-term breaks; i.e. time for both client and counsellor to integrate the work.

A space set aside – temenos

Temenos is both the space set aside and the boundary which marks the space. Jung (1944/53) comments on the 'establishing [of] a protected *temenos*, a taboo area where [the client] will be able to meet the unconscious' (p.53), the crucible in which the therapeutic alchemical reaction takes place. Adler (1979) discusses temenos as a vas or container inside which transmutation (change) takes place. Embleton Tudor and Tudor (1999) elaborate the concept of temenos in terms of creating and developing therapeutic space in discussing the history and philosophy of the creation and work of a centre 'Temenos' in Sheffield (Embleton Tudor and Tudor, 1999; Tudor and Embleton Tudor, 1999).

The concept of temenos is important both in practical terms of providing the suitable space (room) for the therapeutic encounter and, in psychological terms, of providing a boundaried, confidential, safe space set aside for therapy which is both containing and enabling (represented here by the symbol of a square). These requirements are easily translated into the therapeutic context in terms of the location, a place to meet, and the confidential nature of this space. Practitioners in the public and voluntary/independent sectors often have to work with the space they are given which may not be suitable: two chairs in a prison visiting area, a room in a GPs surgery consulting room, an office with a desk, even a walk-in store cupboard in a hospital ward are all places in which I have counselled clients.

Practitioners in private practice often work in a room in their own home which may be specially 'set aside' for this purpose or which, more commonly, may be a room they use themselves such as their living room. In all and any of these cases it is important to recognize the spatial and material context in which we work with clients and the likely impact this has either at a perceived or a 'subceived' level (Rogers, 1957/90). I once counselled someone as a 'one off' in a room in an institute labelled 'Freud'; subsequently, the client was very angry that (unusually) I had 'interpreted' her feelings. Given the importance of confidentially to and in the therapeutic relationship, the confidentially of the temenos as a reflection of this is also important. If, while waiting, a client can hear the therapist's neighbours, then the subceived message is that what is said in psychotherapy sessions is not confidential. Thus, a 'safe space' may involve something as material (and as expensive) as soundproofing. In many cultures it is expected that you take off your outdoor footwear before entering a temenos and I ask clients to remove their shoes before coming into my consulting room. Most clients accept this; some actively appreciate it; several regard it as symbolic of entering a sacred space in which they are undertaking a psychological/spiritual journey. Only one person has expressed any discomfort with this 'house rule'.

The significance of space

> Del used to arrive early and before his therapist, take his shoes off, pause for a moment and incline his head before entering the therapist's room. One day his therapist came in a little early and Del asked him to give him some more time on his own. More often than not Del spent some time in the room after the end of the session. He later explained that he regarded the room as sacred space, and that he had created his own rituals for before and after entering and for before leaving this room which he imbued with spiritual significance.

Personal and professional development

1 Create your own personal temenos. You may do this through a meditation or self-guided fantasy.
2 What is your counselling temenos?
3 What are its boundaries?
4 Does it contain a special place, a focal point, a shrine?
5 In what way/s is it containing and enabling?
6 What do your clients and colleagues say about it?
7 Before meeting, take time to sit in your consulting room and reflect on the client you are about to see.
8 After a counselling meeting, open the window, light a candle, wash your hands and face, take time and space between clients (in addition to writing or reading any notes).
9 If you work in someone else's space, create a ritual to make it yours for the time you are there; include time and space before and after meetings with clients.

Community – koinonia

What life have you if you have not life together?
There is no life that is not in community.
(T.S. Eliot, 1934, Choruses from *The Rock*)

Paraphrasing Eliot, there is no psychotherapy or counselling relationship that is not located in community or koinonia (represented here by the encompassing circle).

Every society in every age has understood the need for some form of *therapia* or healing and has designated some person – healer, shaman, wise woman/man, witch/doctor – to fulfil this role, thereby giving community validation for metanoia (Clarkson, 1989). Based on its origins in a particular culture and class, psycho-therapy and counselling are (too) often viewed as an individual activity and an individualizing process. Individual therapy is assumed to be the therapy of choice, rather than, say, group therapy – for a critique of which see Tudor (1999a). Nevertheless, over the past one hundred years, theories of counselling and psychotherapy have also been applied to analyses of group/s, community and society, and there are a number of (largely forgotten or ignored) traditions of radical, social therapy (see Tudor, 1997). Castel et al., (1982) summarize the logic of such approaches and the role of the counsellor/activist:

> This kind of therapeutic method demands not only that therapists be well versed in the use of sophisticated techniques but also that they be immersed in the same milieu as their clients. If therapists and clients truly form an endogamous community, then the boundaries between personal problems and social problems vanish; the personal and social become merely polar points on a spectrum, and therapy can deal with the whole spectrum by working to transform the individual and his surroundings at the same time. (Castel et al., 1982: 160–1)

Our particular communities are the context for therapeutic practice, and the provision of therapy is part of the social contract we have as members of society – expressed through legislation, the organization of counselling and psychotherapy, membership of professional associations or networks and our subscription to codes of ethics and professional practice (see Tudor, 1997). The precise nature of our contractual relationship with society and with each other, and how we organize and recognize each other as therapists, is the subject of much debate around issues of statutory registration, accreditation and validation (see House and Totton, 1994).

Of the several Greek words which mean community, koinonia most reflects a sense of spiritual and human communion, of transformation and of participation. Dramatically, the Greek chorus represents this koinonia feeling and witness. Significantly, the concept of koinonia has been taken up by psychotherapists in the group-analytic tradition (de Marè et al., 1991) and Sturdevant (1995) compares this with the large person-centred community group. Fundamentally, the community is the context for the therapeutic relationship, particularly the person-to-person, 'I–You' relationship which expresses a 'communal disposition' (Macmurray, 1957).

The importance of community

After some time working in individual therapy, Ephraim joined a therapy group in which he resolved issues of belonging. He made friends with two or three members of the group and began to suggest and organize some events for the group outside the regular meetings. Issues which arose and which were unresolved on such occasions were brought back to the group meeting with the therapist.

Personal and professional development

1 Define your community. Now reflect on your definition. Do you define community by function, geography, subjectivity, critique, culture, class, ethnicity, sexuality or profession? Hillery (1955) identifies 94 different sociological definitions of community. Is your definition reportive, stipulative or mythogenic?
2 Are you known as a counsellor/psychotherapist in your local community, for instance, by local shopkeepers?
3 Do you live in the same area in which your clients live? (One survey showed that most GPs lived on the opposite side of the city from where most of the clients lived.)
4 Are you known as a counsellor/psychotherapist by the local GPs, health and social services departments, mental health services, voluntary agencies?
5 Do you do any voluntary work in your local community? Do you have a public profile as a community activist, school governor, local councillor. If not, would you take on such a role?
6 What is your attitude to dual relationships – a common phenomenon when living and working in a local community?
7 Do you discuss social/political issues with your clients (see Samuels, 1993)?

Conclusion

 Implicit in any counselling or psychotherapy relationship is a concept of change, and implicit to any context in which therapy takes place are notions of time, place and community. Furthermore, each of these concepts impacts on and requires the others:

- Metanoia (change) without kairos (time) encourages a compulsive approach to constant change.
- Metanoia without temenos (space set aside) tends towards chaos.
- Metanoia without koinonia (community) remains individualized and individualizing.
- Kairos without metanoia is repetition.
- Kairos without temenos is mania.
- Kairos without koinonia is an abstraction.
- Temenos without metanoia becomes an edifice and an institution.
- Temenos without kairos leads to stagnation.
- Temenos without koinonia is unaccountable and encourages self-satisfied and incestuous relationships.
- Koinonia without metanoia becomes totalitarian.
- Koinonia without kairos is hypothetical.
- Koinonia without temenos leads to authoritarianism.

Therapy for personal and/or social change requires all four: change at the right (appropriate) time in the right place in context. Change or metanoia is a transformation, in kairos time, which requires a temenos to provide the boundary within which the relationship is defined and a koinonia in which the relationship is acknowledged. Integral therapists working at a serious level of integration across different schools of therapy may find such concepts useful in grounding and developing their creative practice.

The core and context integral framework of therapy described in this chapter does not preclude other integrative models or frameworks. Frameworks which focus on the development of the individual or on the therapeutic relationship enhance our understanding of the core function of therapy. There is a current and increasing interest in time-focused therapy which, at best, focuses the practitioner's attention on the issue of time in therapy. Frameworks which emphasize the client in their social context enhance our understanding both of place (set aside) and of community and the context of therapy. This integral framework is presented not as the definite, defined article, rather as one which encourages practitioners to think about and act upon both the core of what we offer as well as the context in which we offer it.

Acknowledgement

I am grateful to John Hillman for his comments on an earlier draft of this chapter.

Part IV
INTEGRATIVE TRAINING

12

The Integrative Practitioner's Training and Development

There seem to be two distinct approaches to the training of the integrative practitioner. Some training centres provide the student, much as we have done in this book, with a framework or frameworks for integration. Within these frameworks, a personal, integrative approach or model can be developed. The second type of training tends to present the student with an already integrated approach or model. An example of this is the Cognitive Analytic Therapy (CAT) model as described briefly in the first chapter. We will refer to the former as a framework training and the latter a single model training.

The advantages of a framework training are that a wide range of theories and techniques may be integrated, providing the therapist with a broad choice in their development of a personal approach. The therapist can draw upon her knowledge, strengths and skills and incorporate any previous training and experience which is compatible within the framework. For example, someone trained in bioenergetics, using most of the frameworks presented in this book, would find it possible to incorporate their bodywork approach.

In a framework training, the students will be weaving together many different approaches which allows for an extensive and rich cross-pollination of the different bodies of theory, experience and techniques. This may develop and encourage divergent and lateral thinking and experimentation with the emphasis on an integrating process rather than a prescribed content.

This approach also fosters communication and co-operation within the field of therapy. For example, at a conference the practitioner can, using mutual understanding of a shared framework, hold discourse and share ideas and experience with others even though the approaches each person has integrated may be dissimilar.

The disadvantages of a framework training are that students may feel overwhelmed by the diversity and complexity involved in the choice of approaches that they can integrate within their training frameworks where much of the responsibility for selection of what is to be integrated is placed upon each individual trainee. Emphasis on the trainees building their individual constellation could also result in a sense of loss with regard to peer identity. Further, if the training offers no fundamental counselling or psychotherapy skills teaching (and we hold that there ought to be), students might find that they have no shared language or understanding of what therapy is basically about. It is like learning several languages simultaneously without having first learnt what speaking means. It is likely that, through the encouragement of divergent thinking, particularly in the early stages, students may feel unheld or uncontained and have their convergent and linear thinking less stimulated.

With regard to the integrative literature available to trainees, this may be limited (though it is increasing) and there could be no texts specific to the individual's personally tailored integrative approach. Similarly, finding a supervisor experienced or knowledgeable in a particular constellation of integration may prove difficult. Often the trainee will need to educate their supervisor in certain areas of their work. Also the monitoring of a student's progress may be difficult if the trainers are not experienced in the approaches which the student is integrating.

The main advantage of a single integrative model training is that trainees are provided with a tried and tested model of integration for which the training modules and prescribed reading will be restricted for the most part to those approaches already integrated into the model. Literature on the theories and practice incorporated into that model and the integrative model itself will be easily available.

Another advantage is an inherent clarity in a single model training which allows for unambiguous communication between all members of the course – trainers, students and supervisors – because of the shared language. Equally, the criteria for monitoring a student's progress is clear and structured. This clarity can be achieved by the trainees early on in a training where the integration has already been devised or selected by the course.

The disadvantages of a single integrative model training are that the contents of the course may be restrictive and not allow for previous trainings and experience of the students to be integrated. Furthermore, the model may quickly become simply another 'brand-name' approach with all the attendant dangers of a blinkered frame of reference which fits the client to the theory rather than vice versa and fosters an exclusivity which may discourage the exploration of other approaches and mitigate against a wider integration. In believing that this model is integrative psychotherapy rather than one of many possibilities for integrative psychotherapy it could become elitist as well as misrepresentative.

Integrative Training

The content of an integrative course will naturally depend upon the integration or the framework for integration being developed or employed. In Appendix I we use the Multidimensional Integrative Framework as an example of a foundation for an integrative training and provide a general reading list for such a course in Appendix II. The course would necessarily include those theories and procedures relevant to our headings as well as the wider implications of integrative psycho-therapy training. It would be structured so that each module provides time for group processing, theoretical input, group discussion of personal integration, fish-bowl supervision and practice triads.

We believe that a part-time training is most effective for practitioner learning and development, allowing time between modules for 'integration' and reflection, for practise of the material with clients, for supervision, reading, personal develop-ment, and so on. For example, the course described in Appendix I would comprise 30 modules (10 per year) of 14 hours per module, leading to an examination which would consist of a dissertation and an oral presentation.

Possible requirements during training

Some of the following may seem like stating the obvious. However, in our experience of being trainers and supervisors, many trainees balk on discovering that they are usually required to undertake personal therapy, attend regular training sessions, read, integrate and write essays, keep personal journals or projects around training content, give presentations about their work and find an appropriate psychiatric placement in which to learn about severe pathology. At some stage they are normally expected to start seeing clients and obtain supervision to monitor their work, attend periodic tutorials, participate in peer and tutor assessment. Finally, there will be some form of overall assessment such as the requirement to write a case study/dissertation about one of their clients and, in some cases, undergo an oral examination during which some of their work is seen or heard and questions about it answered.

The requirements of any integrative training will vary according to the content and rules pertaining to each course. However, these courses often require of participants that they undergo their own *personal counselling or psychotherapy*. This is so that prospective integrative practitioners have, to a large extent, 'cleared their own backyard' before attempting to assist clients to clear theirs. This is not to say that therapists need to be perfect (no one is) but to suggest that awareness of the major unresolved issues in our lives will lessen the possibility of using clients for our own therapeutic ends. Furthermore, in addition to personal therapy, if the student's intention is to work as a group or couples therapist, experience of these specific types of therapy is advisable.

Different integrative training courses have different *attendance* requirements. Some require one weekend a month attendance and others weekly weekday attendance. As far as we know, no integrative courses are held in the evening so prospective integrative trainees need to realize the implications of this for their current employment and time structuring.

Because of the breadth of material to be covered in any integrative training course, participants are expected to undertake extensive *reading*. Trainees are usually required to present a set number of *essays, projects* or *journals* relating to their reading, therapy and course work experience. These are prescribed in order to assist the monitoring of the student's progress and to help the trainee integrate the new material by asking them to conceptualize and articulate their thinking and learning.

In many integrative courses, trainees are requested to give *presentations* to the training group during which they would show some aspect of their work and their integrative conceptualization.

Integrative psychotherapy students are usually required to undertake a *psychiatric placement* in order to become familiar with and have first-hand experience of the thinking and clinical methods practised within the mainstream psychiatric profession. It is suggested that ideally the placement will involve attendance at case conferences, ward rounds and initial assessment interviews and, if possible, active participation (e.g. co-leading) in psychotherapy or other groups. The intended outcomes of the psychiatric placement are to gain familiarity with psychiatric assessment and treatment practices and with specific categories of disorders, for example, schizophrenia, major affective disorders, eating disorders and organic brain syndromes. The placement also fosters an awareness of how a psychiatric diagnostic system, such as the ICD10 or DSMIV, is used, with special reference to evidence of psychosis and of how differential diagnoses are made, for example, differentiating between a diagnosis of manic depressive psychosis, temporal lobe epilepsy, or possible brain tumour. Knowledge of professional etiquette, administrative procedures of referral and procedures with regard to hospital admissions may also be gained, as well as the valuable experiences of immersion in the institutional psychiatric milieu, holding dialogues with other professionals who may speak a different clinical language and working within a wide variety of contexts and client groups.

During the course of an integrative training, trainees will be expected to be *working with clients*. The number of these clients will depend on the trainee's previous experience before entering the training. For absolute beginners, BAC advises starting practice within an already established voluntary organization as this could not only provide the trainee with a client(s), but in addition could give them a sense of containment and collegial support.

Once a student is working with a client or clients it is essential that their work is supervised by an appropriate supervisor. *Supervision* in the early stages is likely to be on a weekly basis. It offers the student the necessary support, encouragement, attention to basic skills and consideration of professional practice and ethical issues. Furthermore, it highlights transferential and countertransferential aspects of the work which might be interfering with the course of the therapy and need attention in the trainee's personal therapy or which may be used constructively in the work with the client.

All integrative trainings will have methods of requiring the trainee to demonstrate their learning, practice, progress and development. Though these will vary from course to course, they may include:

1 Occasional *tutorials* where the integrative trainee and the trainer meet together to review the trainee's progress on the course. Time in tutorials also provides an opportunity for reviewing the student's arrangement for their own therapy, clients and supervision and will continue the monitoring of their suitability to see clients.

2 *Peer assessment* provides the trainer and trainees time during which to give informal assessments of the progress of all the members of the course.

Near the end of an integrative training course the students will usually be expected to undertake some form of final assessment, for example, the submission of a *case study/dissertation*. This document will demonstrate, with examples – a description of how the trainee sees himself as a practising, integrative counsellor or psychotherapist; a discussion of the influences that have contributed to the trainee's development as an integrative practitioner; a professional self-portrayal; and a case study representing the trainee's integrative practice at this stage. (Some aspects of these are more relevant to the framework system than to that of the single model.)

Part of the final assessment of an integrative student may be a *viva examination*. Through presentation of pieces of the candidate's practical client work and collegial discussion, the candidate may demonstrate their competence as an integrative practitioner. The viva examination, as devised by the staff of an integrative course well known to the authors, provides assessment in the following areas:

- capacity to make and work in an effective therapeutic relationship;
- understanding of the theory of integration;
- capacity to compare and contrast theoretical approaches and treatment options;
- capacity for flexibility and range in their work;
- ethical understanding and sensitivity;
- capacity to understand and use their own personal process in service of the clinical work;
- capacity to make hypotheses, differential assessment and treatment options without losing sight of the personhood of the client and their unique situation.

Continuing development for the qualified integrative psychotherapist or counsellor

It is important that any therapist has a *life outside counselling*. By this we mean that therapy is about life and living and it is impossible to attend to another's life experience without participating in life oneself. Furthermore, by attending to one's own personal needs we are taking sensible precautions against the risk of burn-out. The areas defined in our integrative framework (Chapter 5) are not simply applications for therapy but describe life's experience and areas of need. There is understandably a stage in training and sometimes beyond training where the practitioner may feel immersed in all aspects of the therapy world. However, if this continues as an all-encompassing preoccupation, the resources and contributions a therapist brings to the therapeutic relationship will become increasingly impoverished.

Many experienced counsellors and psychotherapists come to understand that people benefit from several 'bouts' of counselling or therapy, at different times in their lives. Therefore it is important for the qualified therapist to recognize that it is not only their clients who may need to return to therapy at various future stages in their lives, but that they too may need to do the same.

There seem to be different depths and types of therapy. We see three stages in the personal therapy of a trainee. The first is the place where he explores his own structural and intrapsychic issues in order to achieve a more solid sense of self. As mentioned earlier in this chapter, we believe that personal counselling and/or therapy prepares the prospective therapist far more for his/her future role than does the actual training. The second stage is in finding a therapist whose work models, to a large extent, the type of therapy in which the student is training. The third is the place of exploring and experiencing other approaches for the support, challenge, enrichment and expansion of the integrative practitioner he has become.

Following a basic training in integrative therapy it may be that in the course of working with a variety of clients and in different situations the therapist discovers a particular penchant for a specific area of therapy. They may discover that they have an affinity for working with couples, with children or families, or that their preference is for short-term counselling or counselling in the work situation, and so on. Apart from their interest and experience with clients this will probably necessitate *focused further training* tailored to their interest.

The integrative practitioner, particularly if trained in the framework approach, is likely to be interested in learning other approaches to the ones already integrated within their framework. They may come to identify the weak points in their work that may be better addressed by expanding their skills and understanding by training in a different approach or approaches. Often this need may be met by supervision, interdisciplinary discussion and a willingness to read and study across a range of approaches and to keep abreast of current thinking and research in the field.

All practitioners require *continuing supervision.* To remain ethical and professional, our work with clients needs monitoring. This is stated as a requirement of registration with many organizations and accrediting bodies such as the British Association for Counselling (BAC). Without supervision, the therapist would be working in isolation and their work would remain unmonitored. There could be the danger that the therapist is working within a blind spot and missing important therapeutic clues. Audio or video tapes, transcripts and discussion allow the experience of the consulting room to be brought to the attention of an experienced other who can assess, advise, support and educate the therapist in her development no matter what level of qualification or experience she has achieved. Because of the individual nature of integrative approaches, it may be difficult to find a supervisor who matches one's own particular approach. However, as long as the framework for integration shares enough of the supervisor's own philosophy and theory of human beings and the change process, most supervisors are able to adapt to the preferred approach by acknowledging the frame of reference and becoming engaged with the process of the work. The integrative therapist, besides having a regular supervisor who can monitor his development and countertransferential issues over time, may benefit by receiving supervision from differently schooled supervisors.

Concluding Remarks

Integrative counselling and psychotherapy are exciting and continuously evolving approaches to working with people. As we have stressed throughout this book, there is not one integrative approach but many. The ongoing process of assessing, discarding and integrating theories and procedures from the wealth of ideas and expertise in the field towards the betterment of our practice with clients is, for us, both stimulating and demanding. It is this excitement and challenge in the integrative process which we hope will be reflected in the trainings offered by the various institutes and universities you may attend.

We have tried to capture the excitement and challenge of the integrative process in this book. Yet how do you capture a process? Words and theories cannot really do it. We agree with the sentiments of Virginia Woolf when she writes: 'All is experiment and adventure' (1931/51). We hope your own experiment and adventure with integration, developing your own personal approach, is exciting, challenging and fruitful.

Appendix I

Content of an Integrative Training Course Using the Multidimensional Integrative Framework

In the first year, many of the topics would be at an introductory level and would be expanded upon over later years. The following topics would be covered in the first year:

1 Definitions of integration; comparison and contrast with eclecticism, pluralism, etc.
2 The history of integration.
3 Research into counselling and psychotherapy: outcome studies, generic elements across the schools.
4 The philosophy and aims of this integrative training. Definitions of psychological health.
5 Strategies for integration: the framework strategy for theoretical integration and the procedural strategy at the technical level.
6 Developing a theory of human beings, their needs and aspects of experience.
7 The Multidimensional Integrative Framework introduced in its entirety as a holistic template for description, diagnosis, treatment direction, theoretical and procedural integration.
8 Consideration and focus on individual aspects of experience as described on the pentagon of the Multidimensional Integrative Framework in relation to each other and to the relational, contextual and time-frame dimensions. For example, child developmental stages, transferential consideration, etc.
9 Continuous examination of views of the therapeutic process, relationship, communication and listening skills.
10 Context and culture.
11 Setting up and maintaining a professional practice.
12 Ethics.

In the second and third years, besides expansion on the above topics, the following subjects would be introduced:

1 Current psychiatric diagnostic categories (DSMIV and ICD10), treatment issues and medical considerations.
2 Descriptions and comparisons of various other frameworks and models of integration.
3 Developing a personal approach to integration.
4 Time-focused, time-extended and time-expanded psychotherapy.

5 Differences in the approaches to individual, group, couple, family, child, adolescent and adult psychotherapy.
6 Context and culture.
7 Different work settings (for example, private practice, GP practice, NHS, employee assistance programmes).
8 Expansion on transference and countertransferential aspects of the therapeutic relationship.

In Appendix II we provide a reading list relevant to this suggested integrative course.

Appendix II

Further Reading

The following is a broad reading list relevant to various aspects of psychotherapy in general and integrative psychotherapy in particular organized under the module topics as described in Chapter 12. These are works with which we ourselves are familiar or which have been recommended by colleagues. We by no means intend this to be a definitive or compulsory list, but rather to act as a guide. We would encourage students to draw upon their own past readings and compile their own bibliography according to their particular style and content of integration using the Multidimensional Integrative Framework or others.

History

Arkowitz (1984, 1991a, 1991b); Dryden (1991, 1992a), Freedheim (1992); McLeod (1993); Norcross (1986); Norcross and Goldfried (1992).

Research

Bergin and Lambert (1978); Bordin (1994); Gurman and Razin (1982); Lambert et al. (1986); Luborsky et al. (1975, 1983); Mahrer (1988, 1989); Norcross (1986); Reason and Rowan (1981).

Strategies for integration

Mahrer (1989); this book.

Multidimensional Integrative Framework

This book.

Multidimensional Integrative Framework components

This book in conjunction with the following titles.

Self

Clarkson and Lapworth (1992b); Freud (1937); Guntrip (1971); Jung (1971); Kohut (1971, 1977); Laing (1965); McKewn (1997); Maslow (1968); Masterson (1985); Ryce-Menuhin (1988); Stern (1985); Stolorow et al. (1987); Winnicott (1965).

Self needs

Berne (1973); Frankl (1964); Lapworth et al. (1993); Maslow (1976); Perls et al. (1972); Rogers (1967); Winnicott (1965); Yalom (1980).

Physiological

Dychtwald (1986); Greenberg (1975); Johnson (1994); Keleman (1985); Lowen (1969, 1976); Reich (1972); Schore (1994).

Behavioural

Bandura (1969); Berne (1964); Beutler et al. (1986); Eysenck and Rachman (1965); Lazarus (1971); Leboyer (1975); Pavlov (1928); Skinner (1953); Wolpe (1961).

Affective

Averill (1980); Berne (1966); Breuer and Freud (1895); Darwin (1873); English (1971, 1972); Greenberg and Safran (1987); Izard and Beuchler (1979); Jung (1968); Lapworth et al. (1993); Schore (1994); Thompkins (1962, 1963, 1981).

Cognitive

Beck et al. (1979); Berne (1972); Ellis (1962/94); Erskine and Zalcman (1979); Moorey (1990); Piaget (1954); Stern (1985); Weiss and Sampson (1986).

Spiritual

Assagioli (1975); Brazier (1995); Ferrucci (1982); Fromm (1969); Hillman (1979); Jung (1984); Maslow (1964/70); Moore (1992); Peck (1978); Rowan (1993); Vaughan (1985); Wilber (1980).

Relationship

Beaumont (1993); Bergin and Lambert (1978); Berne (1972); Bordin (1979); Bowlby (1969, 1973, 1980); Clarkson (1995); Combs (1986); Erskine and Trautman (1996); Freud (1905); Gelso and Carter (1985); Hycner and Jacobs (1995); Kohut (1971, 1977); Perls et al. (1972); Rogers (1957/90); Rowe and Mac Isaac (1989); Stolorow et al. (1994); Ware (1983); Winnicott (1965).

Context

Adams (1996); Bell and Weinberg (1978); Chaplin (1999); Clarkson and Pokorny (1994); Davies and Neal (1996, 2000); De Ardenne and Mahtani (1989); Feltham (2000); Fernando (1988); Golding (1997); Gonsoriek (1982); Hart (1984); Kareem and Littlewood (1992); Lewin (1951); Littlewood and Lipsedge (1993); Locke

(1998) Marcus and Rosenberg (1989); O'Connor and Ryan (1993); Perls et al. (1972); Ponterotto et al. (1995); Samuels (1993); Sills et al. (1995); Sketchley (1989); Sue and Sue (1990); Tannen (1991).

Time frame

Bordin (1994); Bowlby (1969, 1973, 1980); Clarkson (1995); Crits-Christophe and Barber (1991); De Shazer (1985); Elton Wilson (1996); Erickson (1950/63); Fairbairn (1954); Freud (1912/58); Garfield (1989); Holmes (1993); Jacobs (1986); Kernberg (1980); Kohut (1971); Levin (1974, 1988); Mahler et al. (1975); Malan (1976, 1979); Mann (1997); Marteau (1986); Menninger (1958); Miller (1986); Parkes et al. (1991); Person et al. (1993); Pine (1981, 1985); Rutter (1972); Ryce-Menuhin (1988); Stern (1985); Vaughan (1985); Winnicott (1958); Worden (1983); Zinker (1977).

Therapeutic process

Clarkson (1995); Egan (1990); McLeod (1993); Prochaska and DiClemente (1992); Rogers (1951); Yalom (1980); Yontef (1993).

Ethics

Bond (1993); Corey et al. (1988); Dryden (1992b); Jenkins (1997); Masson (1988); Miller and Thelen (1987); Rutter (1989); Van Hoose and Kottler (1985).

Diagnosis and treatment direction

APA (1995); Benjamin (1966); Berne (1961/80, 1969/81, 1972); Bion (1970); Clarkson (1992); Goulding and Goulding (1978); ICD10 (1992); Johnson (1994); Kahn (1991); Kohut (1971); Mearns and Thorne (1988); Norcross and Goldfried (1992); Rogers (1951); Ryle (1990); Storr (1979); Ware (1983).

Comparative frameworks and models

This book; Clarkson (1992, 1995); Dryden (1992a); Erskine and Moursund (1988); *Journal of Psychotherapy Integration*; Mahrer (1989); Norcross (1986); Norcross and Goldfried (1992); Ryle (1990).

Other types of constellation of therapies

Groups

Ashbach and Schermer (1987); Berne (1966); Bion (1961); Boyd (1991); Dryden and Aveline (1988); Durkin (1981); Foulkes (1948, 1964); Long (1988); MacKenzie (1992); Moreno (1972); Yalom (1975).

Couples

Crowe and Ridley (1990); Dryden (1985, 1992a); Gilbert and Shmukler (1996); Gurman (1985); Hawton (1985).

Family Therapy

Bentovim et al. (1987); Hinde and Stevenson-Hinde (1989); Hoffman (1981); Jones (1993); Minuchin (1974); Minuchin et al. (1978); Parkes et al. (1991); Satir (1972).

Child Therapy

Alvarez (1992); Axline (1947, 1964); Bowlby (1969, 1973, 1980); Cameron (1995); Campos (1986); Clarkson and Fish (1988a, 1988b); Crowe (1983); Freed (1971, 1976); Ginott (1961); Jewitt (1997); Klein (1932); Moustakas (1953, 1967); Pine (1985); Smith (1997); Stern (1985); Sunderland (1993); Wickes (1978); Winnicott (1957/81, 1971/91).

Adolescent

Bazalgette (1971); Erikson (1968); Rutter and Hersov (1985); Steinberg (1983, 1986); Winnicott (1958); York et al. (1982).

References

Adams, M.V. (1996) *The Multicultural Imagination*. London: Routledge.

Adler, A. (1979) *Dynamics of the Self*. London: Couventure. (First published 1951.)

Ainsworth, M.D. (1979) 'Attachment as related to mother–infant interaction', in J.B.Rosenblatt, R.A. Hinde, C. Beere and M. Bushel (eds), *Advances in the Study of Behavior*. New York: Academic Press. pp.1–51.

Alexander, F. and French, T. (1946) *Psychoanalytic Psychotherapy*. New York: Ronald Press.

Allen, J.R. and Allen, B.A. (1997) 'A new type of transactional analysis and one version of script work with a constructionist sensibility', *Transactional Analysis Journal*, 27(2): 89.

Alvarez, A. (1992) *Live Company – Psychoanalytic Psychotherapy with Autistic, Borderline, Deprived and Abused Children*. London: Routledge.

American Psychiatric Association (1995) *Diagnostic and Statistical Manual of Mental Disorders (DSMIV)*, 4th edn. Washington, DC: American Psychiatric Association.

Archambeau, E. (1979) 'Beyond countertransference: the psychotherapist's experience of healing in the therapeutic relationship'. Doctoral dissertation, San Diego, California School of Professional Psychology.

Arkowitz, H. (1984) 'Historical perspective on the integration of psychoanalytic therapy and behaviour therapy', in H. Arkowitz and S.B. Messer (eds), *Psychoanalytic Therapy and Behaviour Therapy: Is Integration Possible?* New York: Plenum Press. pp. 1–30.

Arkowitz, H. (1991a) 'Introductory statement: psychotherapy integration comes of age', *Journal of Psychotherapy Integration*, 1:1–3.

Arkowitz, H. (1991b) 'Psychotherapy integration: bringing psychotherapy back to psychology'. Invited address presented at the American Psychological Association, August, San Francisco.

Ashbach, C. and Schermer, B.L. (1987) *Object Relations, the Self, and the Group: A Conceptual Paradigm*. London: Routledge and Kegan Paul.

Assagioli, R. (1975) *Psychosynthesis*. London: Turnstone Books.

Atwood, G. and Stolorow, R. (1984) *Structures of Subjectivity: Explorations in Psychoanalytic Phenomenology*. Hillsdale, NJ: Analytic Press.

Averill, J.R. (1980) 'A constructivist view of emotion', in R. Plutchick and H. Kellerman (eds) *Emotion: Theory, Research and Experience (vol. 1: Theories of Emotion)*. New York: Academic.

Axline, V. (1947) *Play Therapy*. New York: Ballantine.

Axline, V. (1964) *Dibs: In Search of Self*. London: Gollancz.

Baddeley, A. (1990) *Human Memory: Theory and Practice*. Hove: Lawrence Erlbaum.

Bandura, A. (1969) *Principles of Behavior Modification*. New York: Holt, Rinehart and Winston.

Bandura, A. (1977) *Social Learning Theory*. Englewood Cliffs, NJ: Prentice Hall.

Barr, J. (1987) 'The therapeutic relationship model: perspectives on the core of the healing process', *Transactional Analysis Journal*, 17 (4): 134–40.

Bazalgette, J. (1971) *Freedom, Authority and the Young Adult*. London: Pitman.

Beaumont, H. (1993) 'Martin Buber's I–Thou and fragile self organization: contributions to a Gestalt couples therapy', *British Gestalt Journal* 2 (2): 85–95.

Beck, A.T. and Greenberg, R.L. (1974) *Coping with Depression*. New York: Institute for Rational Living.

Beck, A.T., Rush, A.J., Shaw, B.E. and Emery, G. (1979) *The Cognitive Therapy of Depression*. New York: Guilford Press.

Bell, A. and Weinberg, M. (1978) *Homosexualities: A Study of Diversity Among Men and Women.* New York: Simon and Schuster.

Benjamin, L.S. (1966) *Interpersonal Diagnosis and Treatment of Personality Disorders.* New York: Guilford Press.

Bentovim, A., Gorell Barnes, G. and Cooklin, A. (eds) (1987) *Family Therapy: Complementary Frameworks of Theory and Practice.* London: Academic Press.

Bergin, A.E. and Lambert, M.J. (1978) 'The evaluation of therapeutic outcomes', in S.L. Garfield and A.E. Bergin (eds), *Handbook of Psychotherapy and Behaviour Change*, 3rd edn. New York: Wiley.

Berne, E. (1961/80) *Transactional Analysis in Psychotherapy.* London: Souvenir Press.

Berne, E. (1964) *Games People Play.* New York: Grove Press.

Berne, E. (1966) *Principles of Group Treatment.* New York: Grove Press.

Berne, E. (1969/81) *A Layman's Guide to Psychiatry and Psychoanalysis.* Harmondsworth: Penguin.

Berne, E. (1972) *What Do You Say After You Say Hello?* New York: Bantam.

Berne, E. (1973) *Sex in Human Loving.* Harmondsworth: Penguin.

Beutler, L.E. (1986) 'Systematic eclectic psychotherapy', in J.C. Norcross (ed.), *Handbook of Eclectic Psychotherapy.* New York: Brunner/Mazel. pp. 94–131.

Beutler, L.E., Crago, M. and Arizmendi, T.G. (1986) 'Therapist variables in psychotherapy process and outcome', in S.L. Garfield and A.E. Bergin (eds), *Handbook of Psychotherapy and Behaviour Change*, 3rd edn. New York: Wiley.

Binswanger, L. (1946) 'The existential analysis school of thought', in R. May, E. Angel and H.F. Ellenberger (eds), *Existence.* New York: Basic Books.

Bion, W.R. (1959) *Experiences in Groups.* New York: Basic Books.

Bion, W.R. (1961) *Experience in Groups and Other Papers.* London: Tavistock.

Bion, W.R. (1970) *Attention and Interpretation.* London: Karnac.

Blackburn, I.M. and Twaddle, V. (1996) *Cognitive Therapy in Action: A Practitioner's Casebook.* London: Souvenir Press.

Bollas, C. (1987) *The Shadow of the Object.* New York: Columbia University Press.

Bond T. (1993) *Standards and Ethics for Counselling in Action.* London: Sage.

Bordin, E.S. (1979) 'The generalizability of the psychoanalytic concept of the working alliance', *Psychotherapy Research and Practice*, 16: 252–60.

Bordin, E.S. (1994) 'Theory and research in the therapeutic alliance', in O. Horvath and S. Greenberg (eds), *The Working Alliance: Theory, Research and Practice.* New York: Wiley.

Boss, M. (1963) *Psychoanalysis and Daseinsanalysis*, trans. I.B. Lefebre. New York: Basic Books.

Bowlby, J. (1953) 'Some pathological processes set in motion by early mother–child separation', *Journal of Mental Science*, 99: 265.

Bowlby, J. (1969) *Attachment and Loss. Vol.1: Attachment.* New York: Basic Books.

Bowlby, J. (1973) *Attachment and Loss. Vol. 2: Separation: Anxiety and Anger.* New York: Basic Books.

Bowlby, J. (1980) *Attachment and Loss. Vol. 3, Loss: Sadness and Depression.* New York: Basic Books.

Boyd, R.D. (1991) *Personal Transformation in Small Groups: A Jungian Perspective.* London: Tavistock/Routledge.

Brazier, D. (1995) *Zen Therapy.* London: Constable.

Breuer, J. and Freud, S. (1895) 'Studies on hysteria', in *The Standard Edition of the Complete Psychological Works of Sigmund Freud*, vol. 2. London: Hogarth Press and the Institute of Psychoanalysis.

Buber, M. (1984) *I and Thou*, 2nd edn. Edinburgh: T. and T. Clark. (First published 1958.)

Buckley, N. (1967) *Modern Systems Research for the Behavioural Scientist.* Chicago: Aldine.

Butler, S.F. and Strupp, H.H. (1986) 'Specific and nonspecific factors in psychotherapy: a problematic paradigm for psychotherapy research', *Psychotherapy*, 23: 30–40.

Cameron, S.K. (1995) *Balancing the Request to be Good: A Visit to the Outskirts of Child Psychotherapy.* London: Free Association Books.

Campos, L.P. (1986) 'Empowering children: primary prevention of script formation', *Transactional Analysis Journal*, 16 (1): 18–23.

Castel, R., Castel, L. and Lovell, A. (1982) *The Psychiatric Society*. New York: Columbia University Press.

Chaplin, J. (1999) *Feminist Counselling in Action*, 2nd edn. London: Sage.

Clarkson, P. (1975) 'Seven epistemological levels'. Invitational paper, University of Pretoria, SA.

Clarkson, P. (1989) 'Metanoia: a process of transformation', *Transactional Analysis Journal*, 19: 224–34.

Clarkson, P. (1990) 'A multiplicity of therapeutic relationships', *British Journal of Psychotherapy*, 7 (2): 148–63.

Clarkson, P. (1992) *Transactional Analysis Psychotherapy: An Integrated Approach*. London: Routledge.

Clarkson, P. (1995) *The Therapeutic Relationship in Psychoanalysis, Counselling Psychology and Psychotherapy*. London: Whurr.

Clarkson, P. and Fish, S. (1988a) 'Rechilding: creating a new past in the present as a support for the future', *Transactional Analysis Journal*, 18 (1): 51–9.

Clarkson, P. and Fish, S. (1988b) 'Systemic assessment and treatment considerations in TA child psychotherapy', *Transactional Analysis Journal*, 18 (2):123–32.

Clarkson, P. and Lapworth, P. (1992a) 'Systemic integrative psychotherapy', in W. Dryden (ed.), *Integrative and Eclectic Therapy*. Buckingham: Open University Press.

Clarkson, P. and Lapworth, P. (1992b) 'The psychology of the self in transactional analysis', in P. Clarkson, *Transactional Analysis Psychotherapy: An Integrative Approach*. London: Routledge.

Clarkson, P. and Pokorny, M. (eds) (1994) *The Handbook of Psychotherapy*. London: Routledge.

Cohn, H.W. (1997) *Existential Thought and Therapeutic Practice*. London: Sage.

Combs, A.W. (1986) 'What makes a good helper?', *Person-Centred Review*, 1: 51–61.

Coopersmith, S. (1967) *The Antecedents of Self-esteem*. San Francisco: Freeman.

Corey, G., Corey, M.S. and Callanan, P. (1988) *Issues and Ethics in the Helping Professions*, 3rd edn. Pacific Grove, CA: Wadsworth.

Critchley, W.G. (1997) 'The gestalt approach to organisational consulting', in J.E. Neumann, K. Kellner and A. Dawson-Sheperd (eds), *Developing Organisational Consultancy*. London: Routledge.

Crits-Christophe, P. and Barber, J. (eds) (1991) *Handbook of Short-term Dynamic Therapies*. New York: Basic Books.

Crowe, B. (1983) *Play is a Feeling*. London: Allen and Unwin.

Crowe, M.J. and Ridley, J. (1990) *Therapy with Couples: A Behavioural-Systems Approach to Marital and Sexual Problems*. Oxford: Blackwell.

Darwin, C. (1873) *The Expression of the Emotions in Man and Animals*. London: John Murray.

Davies, D. and Neal, C. (1996) *Pink Therapy*. Buckingham: Open University Press.

Davies, D. and Neal, C. (eds) (2000) *Pink Therapy Two: Therapeutic Perspectives on Working with Lesbian, Gay and Bisexual Clients*, Buckingham: Open University Press.

De Ardenne, P. and Mahtani, A. (1989) *Transcultural Counselling in Action*. London: Sage.

Deurzen-Smith, E. (1988) *Existential Counselling in Practice*. London: Sage.

De Shazer, S. (1985) *Keys to Solutions in Brief Therapy*. New York and London: Norton.

de Marè, P., P'.,er, R. and Thompson, S. (1991) *Koinonia: From Hate, through Dialogue, to Culture in the Large Group*. New York: Brunner/Mazel.

Dryden, W. (ed.) (1985) *Marital Therapy in Britain*. London: Harper and Row.

Dryden, W. (1987) *Counselling Individuals: The Rational Emotive Approach*. London: Taylor and Francis.

Dryden, W. (ed.) (1990) *Individual Therapy: A Handbook*. Milton Keynes: Open University Press.

Dryden, W. (1991) *A Dialogue with John Norcross*. Buckingham: Open University Press.

Dryden, W. (ed.) (1992a) *Integrative and Eclectic Therapy: A Handbook.* Buckingham: Open University Press.

Dryden, W. (1992b) *Hard-earned Lessons from Counselling in Action.* London: Sage.

Dryden, W. and Aveline, M. (eds) (1988) *Group Therapy in Britain.* Milton Keynes: Open University Press.

Durkin, J.E. (ed.) (1981) *Living Groups: Group Psychotherapy and General Systems Theory.* New York: Brunner/Mazel.

Dychtwald, K. (1986) *Bodymind.* New York: G.P. Putnam's Sons.

Egan, G. (1990) *The Skilled Helper: A Systematic Approach to Effective Helping,* 4th edn. Belmont, CA: Brooks/Cole.

Ellis, A. (1962/94) *Reason and Emotion in Psychotherapy,* 2nd edn. New York: Carol Publishing.

Elton Wilson, J. (1993) 'Towards a personal model of counselling', in W. Dryden (ed.), *Questions and Answers in Counselling in Action.* London: Sage.

Elton Wilson, J. (1996) *Time-conscious Psychological Therapy.* London: Routledge.

Elton Wilson, J. (1999) 'Integration and eclecticism in brief/time-focused therapy', in S. Palmer and R. Woolfe (eds), *Integrative and Eclectic Counselling and Psychotherapy.* London: Sage.

Embleton Tudor, L. and Tudor, K. (1999) 'The history of temenos', *Self and Society,* 27 (2): 28–31.

English, F. (1971) 'The substitution factor: rackets and real feelings, part I', *Transactional Analysis Journal,* 1 (4): 225–30.

English, F. (1972) Rackets and Real Feelings, Part II. *Transactional Analysis Journal,* 2 (1): 23–5.

Erikson, E. (1950/63) *Childhood and Society.* New York: Norton.

Erikson, E.H. (1968) *Identity, Youth and Crisis.* New York: Norton.

Erskine, R.G. (1975) 'The ABC's of effective psychotherapy', *Transactional Analysis Journal,* 5 (2): 163–5.

Erskine, R.G. and Moursund, J.P. (1988) *Integrative Psychotherapy In Action.* Newbury Park, CA: Sage.

Erskine, R. and Trautmann, R. (1996) 'Methods of an integrative psychotherapy', *Transactional Analysis Journal,* 26 (4): 316–28.

Erskine, R. and Zalcman, M. (1979) 'The racket system', *Transactional Analysis Journal,* 9 (1): 51–9.

Esterson, A. (1970) *Leaves of Spring.* Harmondsworth: Penguin.

Eysenck, H.J. (1970) 'A mish-mash of theories', *International Journal of Psychiatry,* 9: 140–6.

Eysenck, H.J. and Rachman, S. (1965) *Causes and Cures of Neuroses.* London: Routledge and Kegan Paul.

Fairbairn, W.R.D. (1952/74) *Psychoanalytic Studies of the Personality.* New York: Routledge, Chapman and Hall.

Fairbairn, W.R.D. (1954) *An Object Relations Theory of the Personality.* New York: Basic Books.

Feltham, C. (1997) *Time-limited Counselling.* London: Sage.

Feltham, C. (1999) *Understanding the Counselling Relationship.* London: Sage.

Feltham, C. (ed.) (2000) *Handbook of Counselling and Psychotherapy.* London: Sage.

Fernando, W. (1988) *Race and Culture in Psychiatry.* London: Croom Helm.

Ferrucci, P. (1982) *What We May Be: The Visions and Techniques of Psychosynthesis.* Wellingborough: Turnstone Press.

Fish, S. and Lapworth, P. (1994) *Understand and Use Your Dreams.* Bath: Dormouse Press.

Foulkes, S.H. (1948) *Introduction to Group-Analytic Psychotherapy.* London: Heinemann.

Foulkes, S.H. (1964) *Therapeutic Group Analysis.* London: Allen and Unwin.

Frankl, V. (1964) *Man's Search for Meaning: An Introduction to Logotherapy.* London: Hodder and Stoughton. (First published 1959.)

Freed, A.M. (1971) *TA for Kids.* Sacramento: Jalmar Press.

Freed, A.M. (1976) *TA for Teens and other Important People.* Sacramento: Jalmar Press.

Freedheim, D.K. (ed.) (1992) *History of Psychotherapy: A Century of Change*. Washington, DC: American Psychological Association.

Freud, S. (1905) 'On psychotherapy', in *The Complete Psychological Works of Sigmund Freud*. (1955–74), ed. and trans. J.Strachey. London: Hogarth Press and the Institute for Psychoanalysis.

Freud, S. (1912/58) *The Dynamics of the Transference*. London: Hogarth Press. (Standard edn 12, pp. 97–108.)

Freud, S. (1937) *The Ego and the Mechanisms of Defence*. London: Hogarth Press.

Fromm, E. (1969) *The Heart of Man: Its Genius for Good and Evil*. New York: Harper and Row.

Garfield, S. L. (1986) 'An eclectic psychotherapy', in J.C. Norcross (ed.), *Handbook of Eclectic Psychotherapy*. New York: Brunner/Mazel.

Garfield, S.L. (1989) *The Practice of Brief Psychotherapy*. New York: Pergamon Press.

Garfield, S.L. (1992) 'Eclectic psychotherapy: a common factors approach', in J. C. Norcross and M. R. Goldfried (eds), *Handbook of Psychotherapy Integration*. New York: Basic Books.

Gelso, C.J. and Carter, J.A. (1985) 'The relationship in counselling and psychotherapy: components, consequences and theoretical antecedents', *Counseling Psychologist*, 13 (2): 155–243.

Gilbert, M. (1995) *Integrative Psychotherapy Handbook*. London: Metanoia Institute.

Gilbert, M. and Shmukler, D. (1996) *Brief Therapy with Couples: An Integrative Approach*. Chichester: Wiley.

Ginott, H.G. (1961) *Group Psychotherapy with Children*. New York: McGraw-Hill.

Golding, J. (1997) *Without Prejudice: Mind Lesbian, Gay and Bisexual Mental Health Awareness Research*. London: MIND.

Golfried, M.R. and Newman, C. (1986) 'Psychotherapy integration: an historical perspective', in J.C. Norcross (ed.), *Handbook of Eclectic Psychotherapy*. New York: Brunner/Mazel.

Gonsoriek, J.C. (ed.) (1982) *A Guide to Psychotherapy with Gay and Lesbian Clients*. New York/London: Harrington Park.

Goulding, M.M. and Goulding, R.L. (1978) *The Power is in the Patient*. San Francisco: TA Press.

Goulding, M.M. and Goulding, R.L. (1979) *Changing Lives Through Redecision Therapy*. New York: Grove Press Inc.

Greenberg, I.A. (ed.) (1975) *Psychodrama: Theory and Therapy*. London: Souvenir Press. (First published 1974.)

Greenberg, L.S. and Safran, J.D. (1987) *Emotion in Psychotherapy: The Process of Therapeutic Change*. New York: Guilford Press.

Greenson, R.R. (1965) 'The working alliance and the transference neuroses', *Psychoanalytic Quarterly*, 34:155–81.

Guntrip, J.S. (1971) *Psychoanalytic Theory, Therapy and the Self*. New York: Basic Books.

Gurman, A.S. (ed.) (1985) *Casebook of Marital Therapy*. New York: Guilford Press.

Gurman, A.S. and Razin, A.M. (1982) *Effective Psychotherapy: A Handbook of Research*. New York: Pergamon Press.

Hargaden, H. and Sills, C. (1999) 'Deconfusion of the Child Ego State', *ITA News*, February; 20–24 and April: 19–23.

Hart, J. (1984) *So You Think You're Attracted to the Same Sex?* Harmondsworth: Penguin.

Hawton, K. (1985) *Sex Therapy: A Practical Guide*. Oxford: Oxford Medical Pubs.

Hill, C.E. (1989) *Therapist Techniques and Client Outcomes*. Newbury Park, CA: Sage.

Hillery, G.A. (1955) 'Definitions of community: areas of agreement', *Rural Sociology*, 20: 111–23.

Hillman, J. (1979) *The Dream and the Underworld*. New York: Harper Colophon.

Hinde, R.A. and Stevenson-Hinde, J. (eds) (1989) *Relationships within Families: Mutual Influence*. Oxford: Oxford Scientific Pubs.

Hinton, W. (1997) *Fanshen: A Documentary of Revolution in a Chinese Village*. Santa Monica, CA: University of California Press. (First published 1970.)

Hoffman, L. (1981) *Foundations of Family Therapy*. New York: Basic Books.

Holmes, J. (1993) *John Bowlby and Attachment Theory*. London: Routledge.

Horvath, A.O. and Greenberg, L. (1994) *The Working Alliance: Theory, Research and Practice*. Chichester: Wiley.

House, R. and Totton, N. (1994) *Implausible Professions: Arguments for Pluralism and Autonomy in Psychotherapy and Counselling*. Llangarron: PCCS Books.

Hycner, R.H. (1985) 'Dialogical Gestalt therapy: an initial proposal', *Gestalt Journal*, viii (1): 23–49.

Hycner, R.H. and Jacobs, L. (1995) *The Healing Relationship in Gestalt Psychotherapy*. New York: Gestalt Journal Press.

ICD10 (1992) *The Classification of Mental and Behavioural Disorders: Clinical Description and Diagnostic Guidelines*. US Dept of Health and Human Services: World Health Authority.

Isen, A. et al. (1991) 'The influence of positive affect on clinical problem solving', *Medical Decision Making*, July–September:

Izard, C.E. (ed.) (1979) *Emotion in Personality and Psychopathology*. New York: Plenum Press.

Izard, C.E. and Buechler, S. (1979) 'Emotion expression and personality integration in infancy', in C.E. Izard (ed.), *Emotion in Personality and Psychopathology*. New York: Plenum Press.

Jacobs, L. (1989) 'The dialogue in theory and therapy', *Gestalt Journal*, xii (1) 25–67.

Jacobs, M. (1986) *The Presenting Past*. Buckingham: Open University Press.

Jenkins, P. (1997) *Counselling, Psychotherapy and the Law*. London: Sage.

Jewitt, C. (1997) *Helping Children Cope with Separation and Loss*. London: Free Association Books.

Johnson, S. (1994) *Character Styles*. New York and London: Norton.

Journal of Psychotherapy Integration, New York: Plenum Press.

Jones, E. (1993) *Family Systems Therapy: Developments in the Milan Systemic Therapies*. Chichester: Wiley.

Jung, C.G. (1944/53) *The Collected Works of C.G. Jung. Vol. 12 Psychology and Alchemy*. H. Read, M. Fordham and G. Adler (eds) and R.F.C. Hull (trans.). London: Routledge and Kegan Paul.

Jung, C.G. (1958/70) *The Collected Works of C.G. Jung. Vol. 5 Psychology and Religion: West and East*. H. Read, M. Fordham and G. Adler (eds) and R.F.C. Hull (trans.). London: Routledge and Kegan Paul.

Jung, C.G. (1968) *Analytical Psychology. Its Theory and Practice*. London: Routledge and Kegan Paul.

Jung, C. G. (1969) 'Synchronicity: an acausal connecting phenomenon', in *The Structure and Dynamics of the Psyche. Collected Works. Vol. 8*, 2nd edn. Princeton and London: Routledge and Kegan Paul.

Jung, C.G. (1971) *Psychological Types, Collected Works Vol. 6*. London: Routledge and Kegan Paul.

Kahn, M.D. (1991) *Between Therapist and Client*. New York: Freeman.

Kareem, J. and Littlewood, R. (1992) *Intercultural Therapy*. London: Blackwell.

Karpman, S. (1968) 'Fairy tales and script drama analysis', *Transactional Analysis Bulletin*, 7: 26.

Keen, S. (1992) *Fire in the Belly: On Being a Man*. London: Piatkus.

Kegan, R. (1982) *The Evolving Self: Problem and Process in Human Development*. Cambridge, MA: Harvard University Press.

Keleman, S. (1985) *Emotional Anatomy: The Structure of Experience*. Berkeley, CA: Center Press.

Kernberg, O.F. (1980) *Internal World and External Reality: Object Relations Theory Applied*. New York: Jason Aronson.

Kierkegaard, S. (1980) *The Concept of Anxiety*. Trans. R. Thomte. Princeton, NJ: Princeton University Press.

Klein, M. (1932) *The Psychoanalysis of Childhood*. London: Hogarth Press.

Klein, M. (1986) *The Selected Melanie Klein*, ed. J. Mitchell. London: Peregrine.

Kohut, H. (1971) *The Analysis of the Self*. New York: International Universities Press.

Kohut, H. (1977) *The Restoration of the Self*. New York: International Universities Press.

Kohut, H. (1984) *How Does Analysis Cure?* Chicago: University of Chicago Press.

Laing, R.D. (1965) *The Divided Self*. Harmondsworth: Penguin.

Lambert, M.J., Shapiro, D.A. and Bergin, A.E. (1986) 'The effectiveness of psychotherapy', in S.L. Garfield and A.E. Bergin (eds), *Handbook of Psychotherapy and Behaviour Change*, 3rd edn. New York: Wiley.

Lapworth, P. (1990) 'The seven level model of experience as a guide to integrative psychotherapy'. Paper presented at the Society for the Exploration of Psychotherapy Integration Conference, London.

Lapworth, P. (1994) 'Social systems and TA', editorial foreword in *The Maastricht Papers* from the EATA Conference, July.

Lapworth, P., Sills, C. and Fish, S. (1993) *Transactional Analysis Counselling*. Bicester: Winslow Press.

Lazarus, A.A. (1971) *Behavior Therapy and Beyond*. New York: McGraw-Hill.

Lazarus, A.A. (1973) 'Multimodal behavior therapy: treating the BASIC ID', *Journal of Nervous and Mental Disease*, 156: 404–11.

Lazarus, A.A. (1981) *The Practice of Multimodal Therapy*. New York: McGraw-Hill.

Lazarus, A.A. (1986) 'Multimodal therapy', in J.C. Norcross (ed.), *Handbook of Eclectic Psychotherapy*. New York: Brunner/Mazel.

Lazarus, A.A. (1992) 'Multimodal therapy', in J.C. Norcross and M.R. Goldfried (eds), *Handbook of Psychotherapy Integration*. New York: Basic Books.

Leboyer, F. (1975) *Birth without Violence*. New York: Knopf.

Levin, P. (1974) *Becoming the Way We Are*. Berkeley, CA: Pamela Levin.

Levin, P. (1988) *Cycles of Power*. Hollywood: Health Communications.

Lewin, K. (1951) *Field Theory in Social Science*. New York: Harper and Brothers.

Littlewood, R. and Lipsedge, M. (1993) *Aliens and Alienists. Ethnic Minorities and Psychiatry*. London: Routledge.

Locke, D.C. (1998) *Increasing Multicultural Understanding*, London: Sage.

Long, S. (ed.) (1988) *Six Group Therapies*. New York: Plenum Press.

Lowen, A. (1969) *The Betrayal of the Body*. New York: Collier-Macmillan.

Lowen, A. (1976) *Bioenergetics*. Harmondsworth: Penguin.

Luborsky, L., Crits-Cristophe, R., Alexander, L., Margolis, M. and Cohen, M. (1983) 'Two helping alliance methods of predicting outcomes of psychotherapy', *Journal of Nervous and Mental Disease*, 171: 480–91.

Luborsky, L., Singer, B. and Luborsky, L. (1975) 'Comparative studies of psychotherapies: is it true that "everybody has won and all must have prizes"?', *Archives of General Psychiatry*, 32: 995–1008.

MacKenzie, K.R. (ed.) (1992) *Classics in Group Psychotherapy*. New York: Guilford Press.

McKewn, J. (1997) *Developing Gestalt Counselling*. London: Sage.

McLeod, J. (1993) *An Introduction to Counselling*. Buckingham: Open University Press.

McLeod, J. (1999) *Practitioner Research in Counselling*. London: Sage.

Macmurray, J. (1957). *Persons in Relation*. London: Faber and Faber.

Mahler, M.S., Pine, F. and Bergman, A. (1975) *The Psychological Birth of the Human Infant*. New York: International Universities Press.

Mahrer, A. R. (1988) 'Research and clinical applications of "good moments" in psychotherapy', *Journal of Integrative and Eclectic Psychotherapy*, 7: 1.

Mahrer, A. R. (1989) *The Integration of Psychotherapies*. New York: Human Sciences Press.

Malan, D.H. (1976) *The Frontiers of Brief Psychotherapy*. New York: Plenum Press.

Malan, D.H. (1979) *Individual Psychotherapy and the Science of Psychodynamics*. London: Butterworths.

Mann, D. (1997) *Psychotherapy: An Erotic Relationship Transference and Countertransference Passions*. London: Routledge.

Marcus, P. and Rosenberg, A. (eds) (1989) *Healing their Wounds: Psychotherapy with Holocaust Survivors and their Families*. London and New York: Praeger.

Marmar, C.R., Gaston, L., Gallagher, D. and Thompson, L.W. (1989) 'Alliance and outcome in late-life depression', *Journal of Nervous and Mental Disease*, 177: 464–72.

Marmor, J. (1982) 'Change in psychoanalytic treatment', in S. Slipp (ed.), *Curative Factors in Dynamic Psychotherapy*. New York: McGraw-Hill.

Marteau, L. (1986) *Existential Short Term Therapy*. London: Dympna Centre.

Maslow, A.H. (1964/70) *Religions, Values and Peak Experiences*. New York: Viking.

Maslow, A.H. (1968) *Toward a Psychology of Being*, 2nd edn. New York: Van Nostrand.

Maslow, A.H. (1976) *The Farther Reaches of Human Nature*. Harmondsworth: Penguin.

Massey, R. F. and Dunn, A. B. (1999) 'Viewing the transactional dimensions of spirituality through family prisms', *Transactional Analysis Journal*, 29 (2): 115–29.

Masson, J. (1988) *Against Therapy: Emotional Tyranny and the Myth of Psychological Healing*. Glasgow: Collins.

Masterson, J.F. (1985) *The Real Self: A Developmental, Self, and Object Relations Approach*. New York: Brunner/Mazel.

May, R. (1950) *The Meaning of Anxiety*. New York: Norton.

Mearns, D. (1994) *Developing Person Centred Counselling*. London: Sage.

Mearns, D. and Thorne, B. (1988) *Person-centred Counselling in Action*. London: Sage.

Menninger, K. (1958) *The Theory of Psychoanalytic Technique*. New York: Basic Books.

Miller, A. (1985) *Thou Shalt Not Be Aware*. London: Pluto Books.

Miller, A. (1986) *The Drama of Being a Child*. London: Virago Press.

Miller, D.J. and Thelen, M.H. (1987) 'Confidentiality in psychotherapy: history, issues and research', *Psychotherapy*, 24: 704–11.

Mintz, E.E. (1972) *Marathon Groups: Reality and Symbol*. New York: Avon.

Mintz, E.E. (1983) *The Psychic Thread: Paranormal and Transpersonal Aspects of Psychotherapy*. New York: Human Sciences Press.

Minuchin, S. (1974) *Families and Family Therapy*. Cambridge, MA: Harvard University Press.

Minuchin, S., Rosman, B. and Baker, L. (1978) *Psychosomatic Families*. Cambridge, MA: Harvard University Press.

Moore, T. (1992) *Care of the Soul*. New York: Walker.

Moorey, S. (1990) 'Cognitive therapy', in W. Dryden (ed.), *Individual Therapy: A Handbook*. Milton Keynes: Open University Press. pp. 226–51.

Moreno, J.L. (1972) *Psychodrama*. New York: Boston House.

Moustakas, C. (1953) *Children in Play Therapy*. New York: Ballantine.

Moustakas, C. (1967) *Creativity and Conformity*. New York: Van Nostrand.

Neenan, M. and Dryden, W. (1996) 'Rational emotive behaviour therapy: an overview', *Counselling*, 7 (4): 317–21.

Norcross, J. C. (ed.) (1986) *Handbook of Eclectic Psychotherapy*. New York: Brunner/Mazel.

Norcross, J. C. and Goldfried, M. R. (eds) (1992) *Handbook of Psychotherapy Integration*. New York: Basic Books.

O'Connor, N. and Ryan, J. (1993) *Wild Desires and Mistaken Identities*. London: Virago.

O'Malley, S.S., Suh., C.S. and Strupp, H.H. (1983) 'The Vanderbilt psychotherapy process scale: a report on the scale development and a process outcome study', *Journal of Consulting and Clinical Psychology*, 51: 581–6.

Onions, C.T. (ed.) (1973) *The Shorter Oxford English Dictionary*. Oxford: Clarendon Press.

Palmer, I. (1995) *Counselling and Psychotherapy Resources Directory 1996*. Rugby: British Association for Counselling.

Palmer, S. and Woolfe, R. (eds) (1999) *Integrative and Eclectic Counselling and Psychotherapy*. London: Sage.

Panksepp, J. (1988) *Affectove Neuroscience - The Foundations of Human and Animal Emotions*. Oxford: Oxford University Press.

Parkes, C.M., Stevenson-Hinde, J. and Marris, P. (eds) (1991) *Attachment across the Life Cycle*. London: Routledge.

Pavlov, I.P. (1928) *Lectures on Conditioned Reflexes*. New York: International Publishers.

Peck, M.S. (1978) *The Road Less Travelled: A New Psychology of Love, Traditional Values and Spiritual Growth*. New York: Simon and Schuster.

Perls, F., Hefferline, R.F. and Goodman, P. (1972) *Gestalt Therapy: Excitement and Growth in the Human Personality*. London: Souvenir Press. (First published in USA 1951.)

Person, E.P., Hageline, A. and Fonaghy, P. (eds) (1993) *On Freud's 'Observations on Transference-Love'*. Cambridge, MA: Yale University Press.

Piaget, J. (1954) *The Construction of Reality in the Child*. New York. Basic Books.

Pine, F. (1981) 'In the beginning: contributions to a psychoanalytic developmental psychology', *International Review of Psychoanalysis*, 8: 15–33.

Pine, F. (1985) *Developmental Theory and Clinical Process*. London: Yale University Press.

Polster, E. (1987) *Every Person's Life is Worth a Novel*. New York: Norton.

Polster, E. and Polster, M. (1973) *Gestalt Therapy Integrated*. New York: Random House.

Ponterotto, J.G., Casas, J.M., Suzuki, L.A. and Alexander, C.M. (eds) (1995) *Handbook of Multicultural Counselling*, London: Sage.

Prochaska, J.O. and DiClemente, C.C. (1992) *The Transtheoretical Approach: Crossing the Traditional Boundaries of Therapy*. Homewood, IL: Dow Jones-Irwin.

Racker, H. (1982) *Transference and Countertransference*. London: Maresfield. (First published 1968.)

Rapoport, D. (1976) 'Leboyer follow-up', *New Age Journal*, January: 14–15.

Reason, P. and Rowan, J. (eds) (1981) *Human Inquiry: A Sourcebook of New Paradigm Research*. Chichester: Wiley.

Reich, W. (1972) *Character Analysis*, 3rd edn. New York: Simon and Schuster.

Rice, L.N. and Greenberg, L.S. (eds) (1984) *Patterns of Change*. New York: Guilford Press.

Rogers, C. (1951) *Client Centred Therapy*. London. Constable.

Rogers, C. (1957/90) 'The necessary and sufficient conditions of therapeutic personality change', *Journal of Consulting Psychology*, 21 (2): 95–103.

Rogers, C. (1959) 'A theory of therapy, personality, and interpersonal relationships as developed in the client centered framework', in S. Koch (ed.), *Psychology: A Study of a Science, Vol 3: Formulations of the Person and the Social Context*. New York: McGraw-Hill.

Rogers, C. (1967) *On Becoming a Person: A Therapist's View of Psychotherapy*. London: Constable.

Rowan, J. (1992) 'Integrative encounter', in W. Dryden (ed.), *Integrative and Eclectic Psychotherapy: A Handbook*, Buckingham: Open University Press.

Rowan, J. (1993) *The Transpersonal in Psychotherapy and Counselling*. London: Routledge.

Rowe, C.E. and Mac Isaac, D.S. (1989) *Empathic Attunement: The Technique of Psychoanalytic Self Psychology*. Northvale, NJ: Jason Aronson.

Rutter, M. (1972) *Maternal Deprivation Reassessed*. Harmondsworth: Penguin.

Rutter, M. and Hersov, L. (eds) (1985) *Child and Adolescent Psychiatry: Modern Approaches*. Oxford: Blackwell.

Rutter, P. (1989) *Sex in the Forbidden Zone*. London: Mandala.

Ryce-Menuhin, J. (1988) *The Self in Early Childhood*. London: Free Association Books.

Ryle, A. (1990) *Cognitive-Analytic Therapy: Active Participation in Change: A New Integration in Brief Psychotherapy*. Chichester: Wiley.

Safran, J.D. and Greenberg, L.S. (eds) (1991) *Emotion, Psychotherapy and Change*. New York: Guilford Press.

Samuels, A. (1985) *Jung and the Post-Jungians*. London: Routledge and Kegan Paul.

Samuels, A. (1993) *The Political Psyche*. London: Routledge.

Satir, V. (1972) *Peoplemaking*. Palo Alto, CA: Science and Behavior Books.

Schiff, J.L. and Day, B. (1970) *All My Children*. New York: Pyramid.

Schiff, J. et al (1975) *The Cathexis Reader*. New York: Harper and Row.

Schore, A. (1994) *Affect Regulation and the Origin of the Self (The Neurobiology of Emotional Development)*. New Jersey: Lawrence Erlbaum.

Schore, A. (2000) 'Minds in the making'. Paper presented at the Seventh Annual John Bowlby Memorial Conference (CAAP), London.

Schutz, W. (1973) *Elements of Encounter*. Big Sur: Joy Press.

Schutz, W. (1989) *Joy: 20 Years Later*. Berkeley, CA: Ten Speed Press.

Senge, P.M. (1990) *The Fifth Discipline*. London: Century.

Shapiro, D.A. and Firth, J. (1987) 'Prescriptive v. exploratory psychotherapy: outcomes of the Sheffield psychotherapy project', *British Journal of Psychiatry*, 151: 790–9.

Shmukler, D. (1999) 'Conference presentation on psychotherapy research'. ITA Conference, Edinburgh.

Sills, C. and Salters, D. (1991) 'The comparative script system', *ITA News*, 31: 1–15.

Sills, C., Fish, S. and Lapworth, P. (1995) *Gestalt Counselling*. Bicester: Winslow Press.

Sketchley, J. (1989) 'Counselling and sexual orientation', in W.Dryden, D. Charles-Edwards and R. Woolfe (eds), *Handbook of Counselling in Britain*, London: Tavistock-Routledge. pp. 237–51.

Skinner, B.F. (1953) *Science and Human Behaviour*. New York: Macmillan.

Smail, D.J. (1978) *Psychotherapy: A Personal Approach*. London: Dent.

Smith, H. (1997) *Unhappy Children: Reasons and Remedies*. London: Free Association Books.

Smith, M.L. and Glass, G.V. (1977) 'Meta-analysis of psychotherapy outcome studies', *American Psychologist*, 32, 752–60.

Steinberg, D. (1983) *TU*. New York: Wiley.

Steinberg, D. (ed.) (1986) *TU*. New York: Wiley.

Steiner, C. (1971) 'The stroke economy', *Transactional Analysis Journal*, 1 (3): 9–15.

Stern, D. N. (1985) *The Interpersonal World of the Infant*. New York: Basic Books.

Stern, D. N. (1997) 'The fourth annual John Bowlby memorial lecture'. Centre for Attachment-based Psychoanalytic Psychotherapy, London.

Stewart, I. (1989) *Transactional Analysis Counselling in Action*. London: Sage.

Stewart, I. and Joinnes, V. (1989) *TA Today*. Nottingham: Lifespace.

Stiles, W.B., Shapiro, D.A. and Elliot, R. (1986) 'Are all psychotherapies equivalent?', *American Psychologist*, 41: 165–80.

Stolorow, R. D., Atwood, G. E. and Brandchaft, B. (1987). *Psychoanalytic Treatment*. Hillsdale, NJ: Analytic Press.

Stolorow, R. D., Atwood, G. E. and Brandchaft, B. (eds) (1994) *The Intersubjective Perspective*. New Jersey and London: Jason Aronson.

Storr, A. (1979) *The Art of Psychotherapy*. London: Secker and Warburg.

Strupp, H.H. and Hadley, S.W. (1979) 'Specific vs. non-specific factors in psychotherapy: a controlled study of outcome', *Archives of General Psychiatry*, 36: 1125–36.

Sturdevant, K. (1995) 'Classical Greek "koinonia", the psychoanalytic median group, and the large person-centered community group: dialogue in three democratic contexts', *Person-Centered Journal*, 2 (2): 64–71.

Sue, D.W. and Sue, D. (1990) *Counselling the Culturally Different*. New York: Wiley.

Sunderland, M. (1993) *Draw on Your Emotions*. Oxford: Winslow Press.

Szasz, T.S. (1974) *The Ethics of Psychoanalysis: The Theory and Method of Autonomous Psychotherapy*. London: Routledge and Kegan Paul.

Talley, P.F., Strupp, H.H. and Butler, S.F. (1994) *Psychotherapy Research and Practice: Bridging the Gap*. New York: Basic Books.

Tannen, D. (1991) *You Just Don't Understand: Women and Men in Conversation*. London: Virago.

Thompkins, S.S. (1962), *Affect, Imagery and Consciousness: Vol. 1. The Positive Affects*. New York: Springer.

Thompkins, S.S. (1963) *Affect, Imagery and Consciousness: Vol II. The Negative Affects*. New York: Springer.

Thompkins, S.S. (1981) 'The quest for primary motives: biography and autobiography of an idea,' *Journal of Personal Social Psychology*, 41: 306–29.

Tudor, K. (1997) 'Social contracts: contracting for social change', in C. Sills (ed.), *Contracts in Counselling*, London: Sage. pp. 207–15.

Tudor, K. (1999a) *Group Counselling*. London: Sage.

Tudor, K. (1999b) 'Men in therapy: opportunity and change', in J. Wild (ed.) *Working with Men for Change*. London: UCL Press. pp. 73–97.

Tudor, K. and Embleton Tudor, L. (1999) 'The philosophy of temenos', *Self and Society*, 27 (2): 32–7.

United Kingdom Council for Psychotherapy (UKCP) (1999) *National Register of Psychotherapists*. London: Routledge.

Van der Kolk, B.A., Macfarlane, A.C. and Veisaeth, L. (eds) (1999) *Traumatic Stress: The Effects of Overwhelming Experience on Mind and Body*. New York: Guilford Press.

Van Hoose, W.H. and Kottler, J.A. (1985) *Ethical and Legal Issues in Counseling and Psychotherapy*, 2nd edn. San Francisco: Jossey-Bass.

Vaughan, F. (1985) *The Inward Arc*. Boston, MA: New Science Library.

von Bertalanffy, L. (1974) 'General system theory and psychiatry', in S. Sarieti (ed.), *American Handbook of Psychiatry*, vol. 1. New York: Basic Books.

Wachtel, P.L. (1987) *Action and Insight*. New York: Guilford Press.

Wachtel, P.L. and McKinney M.K. (1992) 'Cyclical psychodynamics and integrative psychodynamic therapy', in J.C. Norcross and M.R. Goldfried (eds), *Handbook of Psychotherapy Integration*. New York: Basic Books.

Wachtel, E.F. and Wachtel, P.L. (1986) *Family Dynamics in Individual Psychotherapy: A Guide to Clinical Strategies*. New York: Guilford Press.

Ware, P. (1983) 'Personality adaptations', *Transactional Analysis Journal*, 3, 1: 11–19.

Wazlowick, P., Weakland, J. and Fisch, R. (1974) *Change: Principles of Problem Formation and Problem Resolution*. New York: Norton.

Weiss, J. and Sampson, H. (1986) *The Psychoanalytic Process: Theory, Clinical Observation and Empirical Research*. New York: Guilford Press.

Wertsch, J.V. (1985) *Vyotsky and the Social Formation of Mind*. Cambridge, MA: Harvard University Press.

West, M. (1990). *Lazarus*. London: Methuen.

Wheeler, G. (1991) *Gestalt Reconsidered*. New York: Gardner Press.

Wickes, F. (1978) *The Inner World of Childhood*. Boston, MA: Sigo Press.

Wilber, K. (1980) *The Atman Project: A Transpersonal View of Human Development*. Wheaton: Theosophical Publishing House.

Winnicott, D.W. (1957/81) *The Child, the Family and the Outside World*. Harmondsworth: Pelican.

Winnicott, D.W. (1958) *The Collected Papers*. London: Tavistock.

Winnicott, D.W. (1965) *The Maturational Process and the Facilitating Environment*. London: Hogarth Press.

Winnicott, D.W. (1971) *Therapeutic Consultations in Child Psychiatry*. London: Hogarth Press and Institute of Psychoanalysis.

Wolfe, B.E. and Goldfried, M.R. (1988) 'Research on psychotherapy integration: recommendations and conclusions from an NIMH workshop', *Journal of Consulting and Clinical Psychology*, 56: 448–51.

Wolpe, J. (1961) 'The systematic desensitisation treatment of neuroses', *Journal of Nervous and Mental Disease*, 132: 189–203.

Wolpe, J. and Lazarus, A. (1966) *Behavior Therapy Techniques*. New York: Pergamon.

Woolf, V. (1931/51) *The Waves*. Harmondsworth: Penguin.

Worden, J.W. (1983) *Grief Counselling and Grief Therapy*. London and New York: Tavistock.

Yalom, I. (1975) *The Theory and Practice of Group Psychotherapy*, 2nd edn. New York: Basic Books.

Yalom, I. (1980) *Existential Psychotherapy*. New York: Basic Books.

Yontef, G.M. (1993) *Awareness, Dialogue and Process*. Gestalt Journal Press.

York, P., York, D. and Wachtel, P.F. (1982) *Tough Love*. New York: Bantam/Doubleday.

Zinker, J. (1977) *Creative Process in Gestalt Therapy*. New York: Brunner/Mazel.

Index